MODEL
OR ALLY?

MODEL OR ALLY?

THE COMMUNIST POWERS AND THE DEVELOPING COUNTRIES

Richard Lowenthal

New York
Oxford University Press
1977

Copyright © 1977 by Oxford University Press, Inc.
Library of Congress Catalogue Card Number: 76-9273
Printed in the United States of America

Acknowledgments

Over the long period during which the following essays were written, I have profited more than the notes indicate from the two excellent Western publications that specialized in the regular reporting of Soviet discussions concerning the developing countries. The first is the *Mizan News Letter*, published until a few years ago by the Central Asian Research Centre in London under David Morison; the other is the *Vierteljahrshefte und Monatsberichte* of the Forschungsinstitut der Friedrich Ebert-Stiftung in Bonn, edited respectively by Kurt Müller and Henrik Bischof. The work of following the numerous Soviet publications in this field has been greatly facilitated by the many useful pointers to relevant books and articles appearing in those periodicals. In addition, I have benefited much from personal discussions with Kurt Müller and Henrik Bischof.

The updating of my earlier work for the present book has naturally required considerable time, which I was able to find by using for it part of two research grants: as a Visiting

Fellow of All Souls College, Oxford, in 1972–73, and as a Fellow of the Research Institute on International Change of Columbia University, New York, in 1975–76. I am grateful to both institutions not only for supporting my work, but for leaving me full freedom to divide my time between several tasks, and last but not least for the stimulating environment provided by discussions with scholars in many fields and from many nations.

R. L.
New York, N.Y.
Nov. 1976

Bibliographical Note

All the chapters in this book have been published before. But apart from updating corrections, Chapters 2, 3, 4, and 8 have been substantially expanded for this edition, and Postscripts have also been added to Chapters 5, 6, and 7.

Here are the details. Chapter 1 was first published in English in Henry W. Ehrmann (ed.), *Democracy in a Changing Society* (New York: Praeger, 1964), under the title "Government in the Developing Countries. Its Function and Its Form." Reprinted by permission of Praeger Publishers, Inc.

Chapter 2 was first published in the Chatham House volume *The Impact of the Russian Revolution, 1917–1967* (London, 1967), under the title "The Model of the Totalitarian State." For the present version, a section on "the doubtful case of Mexico" has been added, and the sections on African and Arab One-Party States rewritten and expanded, as well as the conclusion. Reprinted by permission of Oxford University Press, Inc.

The part of Chapter 3 dealing with the strategy of national democracy was first published in *Survey,* London, No. 47, Apr. 1963, under the title "On National Democracy: Its Function in Communist Policy." The general background of previous Soviet strategy has been added here. Reprinted by permission of *Survey.*

Chapter 4 was first published in *Survey,* London, No. 58, Jan. 1966, under the title "Russia, the One-Party System, and the Third World." Apart from minor expansions, a long Postscript dealing with developments since 1965 has been added. Reprinted by permission of *Survey.*

Chapter 5 first appeared in R. Lowenthal (ed.), *Issues in the Future of Asia* (New York: Praeger, 1969), under the title "Development vs. Anti-Westernism: Russia, China and the Dilemma of the New States." A Postscript on China after 1965 has been added. Reprinted by permission of Praeger Publishers, Inc.

Chapter 6 first appeared in Donald Treadgold (ed.), *Soviet and Chinese Communism: Similarities and Differences* (Seattle: University of Washington Press, 1967). Again there is a short Postscript on China. Reprinted by permission of University of Washington Press.

Chapter 7 first appeared in *Encounter,* London, Nov. 1969. Reprinted by permission of *Encounter.* A substantial Postscript has been added.

The Epilogue, in a slightly abridged form, first appeared in *Problems of Communism,* Dec. 1976.

I am grateful to all the publishers and periodicals concerned for permitting the use of my texts for the present volume.

R. L.
New York, N.Y.,
Nov. 1976

Contents

x   Contents

MODEL OR ALLY?

Introduction:
The Contradictions
of a Dual Relationship

In the last analysis, the outcome of the struggle will be determined by the fact that Russia, India, China, etc., account for the overwhelming majority of the population of the globe. And during the past few years it is this majority that has been drawn into the struggle for emancipation with extraordinary rapidity, so that in this respect there cannot be the slightest doubt what the final outcome of the world struggle will be. In this sense the complete victory of socialism is fully and absolutely assured.

Lenin, "Better Fewer But Better," March 1923[1]

Lenin wrote that prediction in his last published article, two years after Russia's transition to the New Economic Policy and less than one year before his death. By then, his early hopes for a rapid advance of the proletarian revolution in industrial Europe had faded. Correspondingly, the importance of the national revolutions of the colonies and semi-colonies, which in 1920, at the Second Congress of the Communist International, he had still seen only as a major

auxiliary of the imminent revolutions of the Western industrial proletariat, had grown in his mind until the numeri-
cal strength of the auxiliary appeared to him as the principal
guarantee for the ultimate victory of his cause. There seems
to be no proof that Lenin ever said that the revolution
would "reach London and Paris via Calcutta"—a formula
corresponding rather to the strategic views of the later Mao
Tse-tung; but the sentences quoted above come closer to
that view than anything he had written before.

Yet Lenin's concept of the relations between the Soviet
power and the colonial revolutions contained a hidden am-
biguity. In the first stage, as he had pointed out in his
theses for the Second Congress of Comintern, they would
be in their nature "bourgeois-democratic" revolutions, and
the Soviet Union would be linked to them as their *ally*
against imperialism, the common enemy. In the second
stage, they were expected to grow over into socialist revolutions, and the Soviet Union would become a *model* for
their development along a non-capitalist road. Yet, the two
relationships that were envisaged as successive stages in
Lenin's original concept might easily turn into strategic
alternatives if events did not evolve in accordance with his
vision.

As we know, this is what actually happened. On one side,
there has not been a single proletarian revolution in any
industrial country in the course of fifty years. On the other,
decolonization has been successful everywhere, but it has
proceded peacefully in many cases, and even the real anti-
colonial revolutions have only exceptionally come under
Communist leadership, as in China and Vietnam. The result
was a world divided in three parts: a Soviet bloc to which
China was closely tied for a decade, a group of industrially
advanced democracies in North America, Western Europe,
and Japan, and a "Third World" consisting of states that
had emerged from colonial or semi-colonial dependence
in one form or another without falling under Communist

rule—states that have achieved full political independence from the Western powers without becoming committed to "socialism" as defined in Moscow or Peking.

That situation has posed a strategic dilemma for the Communist powers. Their Marxist-Leninist view of the world tells them that the Third World countries can only solve their problems of development by choosing the non-capitalist road, and that the laws of history ensure their transformation in a "socialist" direction. But their practical foreign policy needs demand that they should seek to draw the present, in their view mostly non-socialist, governments of those countries to their side by offering them support against the imperialists and development aid on favorable terms independent of their internal system. On ideological grounds, they ought to try and transform these countries in their own image—to insist on being their model. On grounds of *Realpolitik,* they are interested in winning or keeping them as allies, even if they persist in rejecting that model.

From the time of the decisive breakthrough of decolonization after the Second World War, the phases of Soviet and Chinese Communist policy toward the new Third World can therefore be analyzed in terms of varying responses to that fundamental dilemma. Thus Stalin in his last years was convinced that the non-revolutionary origin of the majority of the new states precluded their real independence from imperialism—that they could not be viewed as potential allies unless their governments were first overthrown by a Communist insurrection according to the Soviet model. By contrast, Khrushchev realized from the outset that these states, being in fact independent from imperialism, could at least be "neutralized," that is, kept out of the Western system of alliances, and at best be turned into political allies of the Communist powers on many issues under their existing "bourgeois" governments, without having followed the Soviet model. Again, beginning in 1958–59, the Soviets were impressed by the evidence of new economic conflicts

between a number of these countries and some of the imperialist powers, and of a post-colonial revolutionary potential in them due to both internal and external barriers to
their development; they responded in 1960 by seeking to
promote the rise of "national-democratic" governments,
based on a coalition of "national-revolutionary" and Communist forces in which the Communists should strive eventually to win the leadership—an attempt at a synthesis
which would strengthen the guarantees for their external
pro-Soviet orientation by assuring their internal development in the direction of a Soviet-type system. When that
strategy showed little success because of the reluctance of
the revolutionary nationalists, many of whom had imitated
the Soviet model selectively by setting up single-party
regimes of their own, to accept the Communists as independent partners in a coalition, the Soviet leaders in 1963
gave the concept a new twist by ordering the Communists
in "progressive" nationalist one-party states—now described
as "revolutionary democracies"—to join the ruling parties
and renounce their separate organization; and this turn
went with a marked optimism that the right way had at last
been found not only for winning more and more developing
countries as allies, but for leading them along the non-
capitalist road of development to follow the Soviet model.

Meanwhile the Chinese, who in the early post-Stalin years
had shared in the Soviet courting of "bourgeois" Third
World governments and even been its pioneers, did not go
along with the new Soviet hopes for a development of the
national-revolutionary regimes in a socialist direction. From
1958 onward they began, on the basis of their analysis of
the sharpening of the worldwide struggle against imperialism, harshly to attack all neutralist governments again, but
at the same time offered active support to all countries and
movements who would engage in militant conflict with the
West regardless of their regime and ideology. They thus
stuck strictly to the primacy of the search for allies, for

whom they set up demanding standards of militancy, over the wish to play the role of a model; indeed, their optimism for the anti-imperialist struggle went with skeptical indifference to the chances of early socialist developments anywhere.

By 1966, both the Soviets and the Chinese had suffered a number of disappointments in their respective strategies. The Chinese found that anti-Western guerrilla uprisings had not spread in the expected way; that their most important Third World ally, Sukarno's regime in Indonesia, had collapsed; that they had been unable to support Pakistan effectively against India and to prevent the Soviets from arbitrating between them at Tashkent; and that their plan for a "Second Bandung" conference at Algiers that would rally Third World opinion against both the USA and USSR had fizzled out. The Soviets were far more successful in the general strengthening of their influence, but had suffered sobering setbacks in their reliance on the evolution of "revolutionary-democratic" regimes along the non-capitalist road: the overthrow of Ben Bella by Boumedienne in Algeria was followed by an anti-Communist purge; the fall of Kwame Nkrumah in Ghana showed the hollowness of his single-party regime; and the massacre of the Indonesian Communists after the abortive coup in which their leaders had been involved was a further shock even though this once powerful party had been in the Chinese camp. In Russia, there followed some years of political and economic reappraisal, during which sanguine hopes for rapid successes of non-capitalist development according to the Soviet model were corrected while the granting of new development aid was seriously slowed down. In China, there followed the years of the Cultural Revolution, during which relations with the Third World suffered along with all other international contacts of a regime preoccupied with its internal convulsions.

When the two great Communist powers emerged from this

pause, both pursued less ideological policies than before. The Chinese, eager after 1969 to resume normal relations with a maximum number of countries and soon also to take their seat in the Security Council of the United Nations, no longer looked for a small band of militant allies against imperialism but for the broadest possible range of diplomatic support without more far-reaching commitments; correspondingly, their policy toward the developping countries became somewhat similar to what it had been between 1954 and 1958. The Soviets, when they once again stepped up their grants of development aid in the early 1970s, concentrated them increasingly on the geographic regions to their south, from the Mediterranean to the Indian Ocean, regardless of whether the countries concerned followed a capitalist or a non-capitalist road. But while they were less interested in presenting themselves as a model, they no longer were content to offer themselves as a mere ally of the countries in these regions: increasingly, they now relied on the political and economic pull of a neighboring Great Power—a potential hegemonial power.

In thus moving from their traditional anti-imperialism to what I have here called counter-imperialism—the creation of privileged political and economic ties with neighboring countries by a Great Power—the Soviets have in part been motivated by the long-term economic needs of their country and their bloc, above all in the field of raw materials and fuel. In part they follow the strategic imperative to secure their southern flank, and in particular to neutralize the Western alliance with the CENTO countries as far as possible. But in part they are also consciously exploiting the potential of conflict between the producers of fuel and raw materials and the advanced industrial countries of the West, which they have recognized in good time. In that sense, the present phase of Soviet policy toward the developing countries, which has to some extent transcended the earlier dilemma between "model or ally," has rather better chances of success than its predecessors.

The inner unity of the essays collected in this volume is constituted by the recurrent attempt to interpret Soviet and Chinese policy toward the developing countries from the two angles sketched out in the preceding pages—the efforts to win imitation for their system as a model, and the efforts to win support for their overall international policies from existing governments. Of course, as the essays were not originally written with the present book in mind, some of them contain also more general reflections transcending its subject, particularly in the theoretical opening section. There, I have allowed such passages to stand because they indicate the broader context of ideas in which my views on the problem under discussion have arisen.

The opening section unfolds the implications of the "Model" concept in two different ways. The first essay, "The Nature of 'Underdevelopment' and the Role of the State," discusses the reasons why non-Western countries have fallen behind in the Western-initiated process of "modernization," and why they cannot solve their problems of development in the way once followed by the West, but only with the state and political movements playing a far more active role; and it attempts to list some of the respective advantages and handicaps of different political systems, including the Communist system, in undertaking that task. The second essay, "The Soviet Model of One-Party Rule and its Impact," discusses in greater detail the rise of the single-party system in Russia and its connection with the long-term tasks of a "dictatorship of development," and it offers a survey of the principal attempts at "selective imitation" by countries that have adopted some form of economic planning for development under single-party rule, but have rjected the Communist ideology and its specific consequences.

The central section then deals with the history of the strategic problems resulting from the dualism of goals of Soviet policy toward the developing countries. Chapter 3 gives the background of the evolution of Soviet ideas from Lenin's vision of the colonial revolution through the Chinese experience of the 1920s to Stalin's dogmatic hostility toward the ex-colonial states and its revision by Khrushchev, and analyzes in greater detail the rise of the concept of "national democracy" as a slogan for the post-colonial revolution. Chapter 4 gives the history of the strategy of "licensed infiltration" of non-Communist single-party systems adopted by Khrushchev in 1963 and attempts a balance-sheet of its results. Chapter 5, "Development vs. Anti-Westernism," contrasts the rise of the Maoist fixation on a total rejection of Western—and Soviet—methods of industrialization, based on the appeal to the material interests of "economic man," with the increasing economic rationality in Soviet discussion of the problems of the developing countries, which tends toward a convergence of means, though not of ends, with the West. The latest strategic mutation, the Soviet strategy of counter-imperialism, is only treated in the Epilogue.

Before that, the third section of the book unites two essays concerned with the ideological repercussions of the development problem on the Communist powers and the international Communist movement, Chapter 6, "Soviet and Chinese Communist World Views," seeks to show to what extent the originality of "Maosim" is based on the identification of the Chinese Communists as leaders of an ex-colonial nation, who cannot adopt Western Marxism without transforming it in important respects. Chapter 7, "Unreason and Revolution," discusses this transformation of Marxism in its migration from Marx via Lenin and Stalin to Mao and finally to Castro, and its effects on Communist and para-Communist movements in the West.

I
THE USES
AND LIMITS
OF THE
"COMMUNIST MODEL"

1
The Nature
of "Underdevelopment"
and the Role of the State

Though most of the "developing countries" have emerged from decolonization with Western-style democratic constitutions, few of them have remained democracies, in the sense given to the term in the advanced industrial countries of the West. Today it is widely agreed that this fact is connected with the specific nature of the problems of development faced by these countries, in the solution of which a liberal, pluralistic democracy of the Western type appears to be at a disadvantage compared to various kinds of dictatorship now usually described as "mobilization regimes," but that the chances of Western-type democracy in such countries may improve with the progess of development.

The following essay, based on a lecture delivered in Berlin in 1962 and published in English in 1964, was an early attempt to analyze the specific functions of the state in developing countries and to discuss the effectiveness of different modern forms of government—notably Western democracy, Communist party rule, and nationalist "dictatorships of development"—in discharging those functions.

In approaching the subject of the interconnection between the progress of economic and social modernization and the forms of government, we must first of all beware of the comfortable simplification that would treat the growth of democracy as exclusively determined by the stage of social development—as if a definable degree of social "maturity" would guarantee the emergence of political democracy. The memory of the totalitarian outbreak in highly industrialized Germany that caused a world conflagration in our lifetime should by itself be sufficient to immunize us against such one-way determinism. More generally, the present state of our historical knowledge precludes a type of approach that would insist on treating the political system of any country as a mere expression of its level of social development—as the necessary "superstructure" to its socio-economic "basis"—regardless of the historical and cultural context.

We know today that the relation between state and society may assume a radically different character in different civilizations, and even in different phases of the history of a given civilization. To mention only two examples: Our conceptual distinction between a "social" and a "political" sphere is of doubtful value for dealing with the European Middle Ages, when the landowning upper class of feudal society was at the same time the holder of whatever public power existed; it is hardly accidental that our term for the "state" derives from the Italian Renaissance—just as does the rise of a relatively autonomous political sphere in Western history. Again, it seems that in the great empires created by Oriental despotism, cooperation between the largely autarchic village communities and clans that formed the basic social units was assured chiefly by the public power; there, one can hardly speak of an interlocal network of social relations apart from the state, so that the concept of society as a collective existing independent of its political organization has little meaning above the local level.

If our political science is to avoid rash ideological generalizations on the value of different forms of government, it must above all bear in mind that those forms of government are not simply different answers to one and the same need, but that they represent attempts to meet a great variety of needs, to fulfill quite different functions according to the historical context, the cultural characteristics and the stage of development of the society in which we find them. As soon as the political analyst ventures beyond the confines of his native culture and period—as he cannot help doing when dealing with developing countries—he must therefore begin by asking *which are the specific tasks whose solution constitutes the yardstick for the effectiveness of political institutions in those countries.*

THE CONCEPT OF UNDERDEVELOPMENT
AND THE UNIQUENESS OF THE WEST

In order to answer this question, we must first of all clarify what we mean by "developing countries," and how far it is possible at all to make useful generalizations about them.

In contemporary language, the term "developing countries" (or, more frankly, "underdeveloped countries") covers a wide and varied range of social and political entities: countries in Asia, Africa, and Latin America; seats of ancient civilization like China, India, and the historic centers of Islam along with regions still struggling to emerge from the chaos of tribal warfare like the Congo, and with Latin American societies hiding their specific cultural attitudes and problems under a deceptively European surface. At first glance, the differences of history, culture, and social structure seem to defy any meaningful general statement about these areas.

Of course, a common formula can easily be found once we limit ourselves to economic and social indicators capable of being measured statistically. It is fairly simple to define an underdeveloped country as one where the income per head, or the per-capita consumption of certain goods, or the percentage of urbanization or of literacy is below a certain minimum level. The advantage of such a statistical definition is that it shows at a glance the existence of common problems in these otherwise heterogeneous societies; its danger is that it may easily lead to a purely quantitative view of the problem of development itself—as if all these countries were inevitably developing along the same road once taken by the old industrial countries of the West, and had only so far remained one or more stages behind those models.

If we read, for instance, W. W. Rostow's stimulating study *The Stages of Economic Growth,* the total impression conveyed by his graphs and tables is—despite all the cautious reservations the author makes as a learned historian—that the process of development has everywhere been the same, whatever the differences of cultural background and forms of government. Rostow even attempts to prove statistically that the same stage in the process of industrialization takes approximately the same time in countries showing a wide variety of political and cultural conditions.

Such an approach inevitably raises the question why, if the process is really the same everywhere, so many countries are lagging behind—why they have been such late starters; and to that question, only mythical answers are possible. On one side, there is the racial myth that some peoples are naturally unfit for continuous effort, for industrial development, for all the requirements of a modern state owing to some defect in their hereditary, biological substance, and that they have failed to make the necessary effort for this reason. As the racial myth has not only become unfashionable, but has been repeatedly refuted by the successful "catching up" of a series of laggard countries, the Leninists have gained ground with their equally mythical claim that the countries in question have been prevented from developing "normally" merely by the stunting intervention of the Western imperialists—by colonialism, capitalist exploitation, and slave trade.

I am, of course, far from denying that biological differences may exist, and I am fully aware that colonial oppression and exploitation once played a great role and still exist to some extent. But the idea of using the damage done by colonialism as a universal explanation for the problem of underdevelopment, in spite of the obvious fact that the countries in question could only be colonized because they were materially inferior to the West *at the time* and had not then brought forth a Western type of industrial development, clearly belongs into the realm of mythology and not of social science.

There is a simple reason why we can get only mythical answers to the question of why these countries started so much later on our road: The question is wrong—it asks for an explanation of something that did not happen. It is not true that the underdeveloped countries ever set out on the same road, from the same starting point, as the old industrial countries, yet inexplicably lagged behind them. The truth is that they set out from utterly different starting points—that the traditional, premodern, preindustrial social structures of these countries were utterly different from the premodern social order from which modern Europe and its overseas settlements have emerged.

In other words: *We are not confronted, in the developing countries of our time, with earlier stages in our own process of development, but with a process of development that is different in kind because it starts from a different basis.* Neither the traditional societies of the despotic Asian empires nor the traditional societies of Africa have tended to generate that dynamism of development which created the first modern industrial countries in the West.[1] The different levels of development we observe in present day societies can be explained neither by colonial exploitation nor by differences in biological substance, but only by the differences in the structure and culture of the premodern, traditional societies from which they have sprung—in the historical starting point.

Turning now to ask what specific historical conditions may account for the presence of a self-generated dynamism of social development in a particular civilization and period and its absence in others, one is struck by the fact that this question is not new to the social science of our century: It was first raised and answered in a comprehensive manner in the writings of Max Weber. It is characteristic of the true classics of social and political thought that in their work each new generation may find tools for tackling the new problems it is facing. In Max Weber's introduction to his *Essays on the Sociology of Religion,* the very first sentence states: "In dealing with problems of universal history, the native of contemporary European civilization will inevitably and rightly ask the question: What peculiar combination of circumstances has caused the emergence in the West, and only in the West, of certain cultural phenomena which nevertheless represented—as we at least are fond to imagine—a trend of *universal* significance and validity?"

I believe it is no overstatement to say that this search for the conditions in which the unique development of Western society became possible was at the very core of Max Weber's life work. Yet our present search for the characteristics that distinguish the traditional social structures of the developing countries from those of the premodern West is merely the obverse of the same question. The answers Max Weber found in looking for the conditions of Western uniqueness are therefore directly relevant to our inquiry for the distinctive historic background of the developing countries. Of course, historical research has not stood still since Max Weber's time, and some of his theses have become the subject of detailed controversies on which, for lack of the necessary historical learning, I should not presume to express an opinion. Yet the general outline resulting from Max Weber's analysis seems to me so illuminating when applied to the problems of the developing countries that I make no apologies for using it as a guide map.

Some of the preconditions for the unique dynamism of the West, as analyzed in a number of widely dispersed passages in Max Weber's work,[2] belong to the realm of culture, particularly of religion; others concern the structure of society and the character of the political order. Six of them must be mentioned here.

The first is the early *liberation of thought from magic,* which in the West has taken place both *within* religion owing to the prophetic element in Judaism and Christianity, and *outside* religion thanks to the legacy of Greek enlightenment. The prophetic effort to cleanse the monotheistic faith from magic remnants on one side, and the Hellenic discovery of the autonomy of reason on the other, have converged in the West to make possible not only scientific thought as an elite occupation, but the penetration of rational standards into the general modes of thinking and living, and this long before their modern secularization.

The second is the comparatively early and thorough *emancipation of the community of religious faith from the community of blood ties,* starting with the Judaic step from a tribal god to the only God and completed by the rejection of all tribal limitations in Pauline Christianity, which created the basis for giving religious sanction to communities that radically transcend all ties of blood. Here is the germ for the growth of an active sense of community in large units up to the level of the modern nation-state, and for the ultimate subordination to these larger units of the more restricted communities based on blood ties—the clans and tribes, but also the castes and hereditary sects—that to this day divide the social fabric of many developing countries by their feuds.

The third is the *moral value placed on labor in this world,* including physical labor, by Western Christianity, beginning with the rules that distinguished the earliest Western monastic orders from the hermits of the desert as well as from Eastern monasteries. This has become the cultural foundation not only for the transforming activism of the West, but also for the later compatibility of upper-class social prestige with productive activity in the West, as well as for the growth of collective pride and sustained egalitarian claims among classes engaged in physical work, beginning with the medieval guilds. The importance of this factor is shown both by the strength of the cultural resistance most non-Western upper classes have opposed to any engagement in production and by the prolonged passivity and submissiveness of some (though by no means all) non-Western lower classes except for sporadic outbursts.

The fourth is the crucial fact that only the West has produced the social stratum that has become the specific initiator of modern dynamic development—the *urban middle class* in its Western form as a "bourgeoisie" consisting of self-confident invididuals whose individual independence has developed on the background of an *urban commune organized for defending its collective independence.* As a sworn union of individuals of heterogeneous origin, the urban commune is an outstanding example of the historic significance of the Western ability to form communities not based on ties of blood; it is at the same time a natural center for the development of rational thought and it is a community of self-respecting producers. But above all, this independent Western bourgeoisie was to become, in the course of the following centuries, the direct initiator of the growth of a capitalist economy.

Fifth, such a growth could unfold only in the framework assured by a *modern state* of the Western type—a state equipped with a rationally organized bureaucracy of trained officials and with a ssytem of legal rules that, building on the Roman legal tradition, served not only to protect the public order and the purposes of the state, but to give security to the citizen by being known and calculable in its effects. Such a state presupposes not only a capacity to organize rationally for collective needs, but also the concept of law as an autonomous network of relations among individuals, i.e., of a social fabric that is not merely created by state power.

Finally, the sixth and last indispensable element for the process of Western modernization—that process with which the developing countries are seeking to catch up—was the victory of a *rational outlook in economic life:* the increasing subordination of other values to the value of economic effort, manifested by the capitalist entrepreneur as willingness to invest in production and by the worker as discipline and continuity of labor. The drive for profit, the capitalism of the pirate, the usurer, and the trader have existed in all civilizations. But the rationalization of the profit instinct and the rationalization of conduct in general under its rule, the discipline of the reinvestment of profits, of the continuity of production and labor, are specific results of Western development since the age of the Reformation and Counter-Reformation.

If I interpret the views of Max Weber correctly, he held that the six factors enumerated here were chiefly responsible for the unique dynamism of Western society, hence for the rise of the modern world from Western roots. It seems evident that some of these are also among the preconditions of our modern Western democracy—that our democratic order based on the rule of law and our type of civic sense largely derive from the same factors we have mentioned as preconditions of the Western dynamism of development.

It is time to face the obvious objection that so far our analysis has yielded only a kind of negative insight regarding the developing countries—the statement that some or all of the factors enumerated here were missing in their traditional social structures. That is indeed true: The enumeration of the conditions of Western uniqueness amounts to a negative definition of the common characteristics of the developing countries. But the absence of these conditions is fundamental not only for understanding their historical "lag," but also for defining the tasks of the process of development that is now being undertaken to assure their "catching up." I therefore have no hesitation in offering such a negative as a criterion for a historical and sociological concept of our subject: *A "developing country" is a country with a nondynamic traditional social order in which dynamic aspirations have been aroused by its clash with the outside world.*

The above statement implies that the societies in which some or all of the conditions of a self-generating dynamism are absent would have continued in their traditional way of life but for their clash with a dynamic outside world. Not that the non-Western civilizations had undergone no internal changes: In the course of their thousands of years of history, the empires of ancient China or of ancient Egypt have lived through major transformations. But none of them has known the characteristic chain reaction of development which we mean when talking of "dynamism"—the constellation in which one change necessarily leads on to another, and which seems so "natural" to our modern sense of history. Hence the present wish for "development" and "modernization" has not been an indigenous product of the history of those countries but has been aroused by the impact of the developed world from outside—by the intrusion of Western "imperialism," and more recently also by the impact of the Communist states that have already been "infected" with Western dynamism.

WESTERN INTRUSION AND THE ROLE OF THE INTELLIGENTSIA

The first result of this Western impact has generally been the disruption and decay of the traditional, nondynamic social order of those countries. This process of disruption is an essential aspect of the phenomena usually described as

"colonialism" or "economic penetration." It arises whenever foreign political or economic organizations, equipped
with superior technology and therefore superior power,
enter a country—not with the intention of replacing its traditional social order by a new one, but completely unaware
of this problem and merely seeking to use some particular
resources of the weaker country for their own economic
or power-political needs.

Looking first at the strictly economic effects of the Western intrusion on these societies, we find that Western capital has tended to promote the lopsided development of
those branches of industry and agriculture that could directly serve its needs—the mining of metals and oil and the
large-scale culture of industrial plants and tropical fruits for
export to the advanced countries. In those branches, a completely new type of production for the market was thus
suddenly introduced, often combined with new forms of
labor organization ranging from outright slavery through
unfree, long-term "contract labor" to "free labor" of the
capitalist type. At a second stage, the Western intrusion into
the economic life of those countries typically led to the
general spreading of monetary exchanges and market production; the combination of subsistence agriculture and
cottage crafts, which had been prevalent in the traditional
economic system, was gradually undermined as the import
of cheap goods produced by Western industry and the need
to acquire cash for the payment of taxes and the purchase
of those goods caused more and more peasants to turn to
the market. As a result, the traditional economic security of
the village was profoundly shaken; the rural population began to appear as an overpopulation in the new conditions,
and the newly "superfluous people" started to migrate to
the towns. On the lowest level, in tropical Africa, this tear-
ing of people from their rural economic roots, hence from
their familiar social and cultural moorings, appears as "de-
tribalization," on more developed levels merely as urbanization and proletarization; but the underlying economic

process is the same, and it produces similar social and cultural effects on both levels.

Modern accounts of this process of disruption of traditional societies, whether written by Western critics, by Communists, or by the spokesmen of the people concerned, mostly convey the impression that the typical effect of the coming of the West had been a general increase in economic and even physical misery. This is true for some but by no means for all cases. The influx of Western capital quite often brought a rise in the standard of living for substantial groups of people employed in the new capitalist branches; and most of the areas under direct colonial administration soon showed an improvement in health standards and a lengthened expectation of life. Nevertheless, the subjective impression of having become more miserable is not confined to individual critics but is genuinely typical for the peoples concerned—due to the loss of their traditional security of existence, to the dissolution of the familiar subsistence economy, to the new dependence on the ups and downs of the labor market and indeed of the world market.

But as these peoples lose their traditional sheltered economic existence, their whole concept of the world order, their ideas about the meaning of life are being shaken. A way of life that used to be lived within and for a given community as a matter of course now comes to be questioned.[3] For not only has the traditional economic and social order been disrupted, but the traditional political order, too, has lost face: After all, the native political rulers of these—normally autocratic—countries have proved unable to resist the foreign intruder and have inevitably lost much of their former authority in the process. Yet where the traditional social order and the inherited political authority had their ultimate sanction in a religious conception of the world, the crisis of the social and political order inevitably leads people to doubt the truth of the whole conception built around it. *The social and political crisis turns into a crisis of ultimate beliefs about life and the world, and a sense of meaninglessness appears as the basic values of the inherited civilization are called into question.* At the same time, this doubting of traditional beliefs is not part of a self-generated intellectual development toward the emancipation of reason and of the critical individual, but is a by-product of the disruption of the traditional order from without; the new doubts plague people who still hunger for authority, for their psychic structure is socially conditioned to require it. Thus we have both a crisis of authority and a continued need for it—hence typically the search for a new authority to take the place of the discredited one.

As this crisis of the traditional world view develops while the achievements of Western science and technology and the "miracles" of a Western standard of living come to be perceived by a minority of the "underdeveloped" nation, as Western power and its technical and organizational instruments come to exert a fascination mixed of admiration and envy, a cultural schism arises in those countries. Initially, it is only the urban upper strata and above all the educated classes that gradually make contact with the alien structure of thought underlying the Western achievements and have to come to terms with it, while the bulk of the rural population is still willy-nilly continuing in the decaying old framework and knows of little else. A process of mutual alienation thus takes place between the Western-educated elements of the urban upper classes and the intelligentsia on one side, and the rural—or freshly proletarianized ex-rural—masses on the other; and this alienation is reflected as a problem in the mind of the intelligentsia, as a schism in its soul—a soul torn between admiration for the new ideas and the will to preserve the values of the native tradition, between eagerness to learn from the West and a sense of obligation toward their own people.

To this situation, the intelligentsia of the developing coun-

*tries can only react with a violently ambivalent attitude
toward the West—with the deisre to equal its skill in producing wealth and acquiring military and political power, yet
to protect the independence and distinctiveness of their
own culture against its alien influence.*

This phenomenon is the more marked the less a country's
original culture has in common with the West's; but it is
not entirely new, for prototypes of the same ambivalence
have appeared as one country followed the other in the
course of modern Western development. After all, almost
every Western country was "underdeveloped" at one time
or another, though in a more relative and less structural
sense than the term is used here. As late as the seventeenth
century, the English felt underdeveloped in relation to the
Dutch, and the British economist William Petty had to explain to his compatriots that they could succeed in trade
and industry without such "angelical wits" as the Dutch
were supposed to have. In eighteenth-century France, a
wave of intellectual Anglophobia arose for the same reason—because the British were ahead in economic development and many Frenchmen wished to emulate their
achievements without adopting their "grocers' outlook."[4]
But it was in Germany that this typical "Cinderella complex" of the intellectuals of the laggard country was first
turned into an ideological system: Toward the end of the
eighteenth century, the resentment of the German petty-
bourgeois intelligentsia against the "frenchified" style of the
princely courts was for the first time expressed in the ideological antithesis between *"deutscher Kultur"*—supposedly
inward and genuine—and *"welscher Zivilisation"*—supposedly purely external and mendacious. That antithesis, which
has since played an enormous role in the German romantic
movement, in German official propaganda during World
War I and down to the Nazi era, is essentially just one more
version of the same ambivalent attitude toward countries
that had been ahead of one's own in the development of

technology and general civilization—of the desire to catch up with them while remaining different in the soul.

Finally, this ambivalence of an alienated intelligentsia was to be given its classical form in nineteenth-century Russia—in the debate between "Slavophiles" and "Westernizers" and in the victory of the ideological synthesis of the Narodniki, who aimed at the revolutionary modernization of their country but were looking for a specifically Russian, non-capitalist road of development based on national traditions that would avoid the horrors which the materialist pursuit of private gain had brought about in the West.[5]

As Russian society, whose prolonged stagnation was overcome thanks only to external impulses from the West, was an early example of a "developing country" within Europe, it is not surprising that the ideas of the Russian populist intelligentsia should have become a direct model for the mixture of socialist and nationalist, modernistic and traditionalist, ideas that characterizes the intelligentsia of the developing countries today.[6] *It is in the minds of this intelligentsia that the contrast between the developed West and the condition of their own countries first becomes conscious, and it is this stratum that first reacts with the "will to development"—with the typical determination to catch up with the West yet preserve the individuality of their own culture.*[7]

DEVELOPMENT BY STATE ACTION: THE TASKS

But how is this goal to be reached? In a society that has failed to generate by itself a dynamism of development comparable to that of the West, that has merely passively suffered the Western impact until this conscious awakening of the intelligentsia took place, there is only one road for satisfying the dynamic aspirations of this conscious minority: the road of political action. *The nationalist intelligentsia conceives the task of creating a new "political superstructure" as an instrument for transforming the non-dynamic "social basis." * In other words: *They assign to political action and to state power a creative, revolutionary function that differs fundamentally from the role played by these factors in the development of the dynamic societies of the West.*

Of course, the state has played a certain role in Western development, too: The absolute monarchies of Europe did in their time attempt to foster the growth of trade and industry by the policies of mercantilism. But the importance of those measures for the over-all process of Western development was comparatively marginal; one needs only to recall the brevity of the mercantilist period in some of the decisive Western countries, or the fact that even some of the greatest colonial enterprises were originally started by private companies. By contrast, it is literally true for the developing countries that "politics is destiny": here, the success or failure of modernization really depends on political decisions, on the creation of a new type of state power.

This becomes evident as soon as one envisages in detail the tasks which in those countries, in contrast to the West, have to be accomplished with primarily political means. What is at stake is nothing less than the attempt to replace some of the missing social conditions for Western-type dynamism by corresponding political institutions, and to develop others in the forcing-house of political pressure. Thus the missing economic initiative of an independent middle class must largely be replaced by state initiative; the educational and disciplining function, which in the West was objectively fulfilled by religious movements animated by motives of a quite different order, must be replaced by the conscious re-educating activity of political movements. Only with the help of those forms of state and political action will it then be possible to build up on one side the missing material skeleton of a modern country—its industrial and military equipment, its transport and communications machinery—and on the other to develop the corresponding rational habits of thought and attitudes to economic effort.

1.) *The first place among the tasks of government in the developing countries is thus held by the speedy and direct procurement of the necessary capital funds for material development,* which in the West took place in the course of a long period of private capital accumulation, though often with some initial aid from state power. Where there is no broad stratum of native entrepreneurs, those funds either must be squeezed out of the people concerned— chiefly the peasant masses—by government pressure, or must be obtained from abroad as development aid by government diplomacy. The lower the level of productivity and income per head at the beginning of the process of development, the more intense the pressure of an increasing population and the smaller the foreign aid available, the more brutally a regime of development will have to exploit its own people.

2.) *Further, the government must also be responsible for distributing the funds thus procured among various uses in accordance with the goal of development—for investing them under an overall plan.* We had noted that spontaneous capitalist development in these areas has been lopsided, tending to be restricted to the production of raw materials and tropical fruits for the needs of the old industrial countries. If this lopsidedness is to be overcome—if power stations and heavy industrial plants are to be built, but also if the productivity of agriculture for domestic needs is to be raised and local industries are to produce consumer goods, and above all if the country is to be opened up by road building and other transport development, if hospitals and canalization, schools and universities, are to help in creating the kind of infrastructure of modern society that yields direct profit to none but indirect benefits to all—then the state must assign the necessary funds.[8] *It is not realistic to expect the developing countries to catch up with Western economic development by following the classical Western road of a liberal market economy:* If a liberal market economy could do the job in countries with this type of social structure, they would not have remained under-developed in the first place.

3.) Moreover, the radical re-education of the people for rational thought and a rational attitude to work and economic activity in general, which have been the outcome of centuries of intellectual and cultrual evolution in the West, also becomes a political task in the developing countries. The Soviet Communists, who were the first consciously to face this task, have rightly described it as a *"cultural revolution."* This comprises first the struggle against superstition and magical beliefs, which the Communists conduct with the blunt instrument of general antireligious propaganda, but which must be carried out in some form in all developing countries if a modern outlook on science, technology, and economics is to spread and resistance against any change in traditional methods of production is to be broken. It comprises further the struggle against illiteracy, which means not only the effort to make schools and teachers available in the numbers needed for universal elementary education (including in not a few cases the original creation of a written language with a suitable alphabet and the translation of basic texts in all teaching subjects into it), but also the effort to arouse the will to learn and to overcome, in this field as well, the traditional resistance of the old generation (and of the priesthood of certain religions). It also includes the struggle against forms of family life that are incompatible with the rational organization of production, such as the seclusion of women and the lack of individual mobility involved in living together in the large family or clan or in the rigid subordination of adult members of the younger generation to the patriarchal authority of their elders. And it comprises finally the struggle for discipline, care and continuity in industrial work, for punctuality and neatness at the job, for responsibility toward the machine and the work team, and for the willingness to work not just until one has earned enough to afford a little free time, but to subordinate one's entire personal life to the rhythm of work—a sad, basic fact of life in the old industrial countries, but a difficult innovation in the developing ones. In short, *the cultural revolution aims to achieve in a single generation what Reformation and Counter Reformation, enlightenment and universal school education, have contributed toward the formation of modern man in the course of centuries; and in all the developing countries, this becomes a political task in the sense that it must be tackled in part by government compulsion and in part by politically motivated educational movements.*

4.) But—and here we encounter the central political problem of the developing countries—*the very political factors that are to accomplish these gigantic tasks, the state and the political movement that are to become the promotors and driving forces of development, will usually first have to be created themselves.* In countries under colonial rule, the assumption of this role by government presupposes the achievement of national independence and the founding of a new, sovereign state; in underdeveloped countries that, though legally sovereign, have lone been economically dependent on foreign capitalist concerns and their protecting powers, it presupposes the rise to power of a group that is determined to liquidate this dependence in order to be free to pursue a consistent policy of development.

In many cases, the entire bureaucratic machinery of a modern state must be newly created as well. This applies where the former colonial power has barred the "natives" to the very end from access to senior administrative and military posts and from responsible participation in political decisions; it also applies where an indigenous traditional regime of the autocratic or oligarchic type has failed to develop any modern machinery of state.

5.) Finally, *the people's sense of belonging to a common political unit, the emotional identification with the new state and the will to participate in its affairs, must also often be created anew.* Without such a sense of belonging and participation no modern state is possible, let alone a state with comprehensive tasks of development. But in many developing countries, this sense is missing. The period of traditional autocracy or colonial rule has not accustomed the population to think of the state as its own affair; and the prolonged isolation of the village has preserved a situation in which the narrower units of clan and tribe, of caste, sect, or language group are still the only ones to which the rural masses feel actually tied by their experience, while the concept of the state, if known at all, appears as a pale abstraction by comparison. Hence the nationalism of the developing countries is often the expression not of a sense of nationhood actually existing among their masses, but of the determination of groups of intellectuals to create such a single sense of national identity, on the basis of the given state and despite its linguistic and cultural pluralism, because it is considered an indispensable factor in the process of development.[9] Such an enterprise is difficult, but not a priori impossible. Even the sense of identity of the ancient Western nations has not existed from time immemorial but has developed historically; it is easy to think of European ethnic groups that would identify themselves with other national affiliations today if history had taken a slightly different course—nor is there a lack of cases in which the course of history has been "helped" by conscious political measures, above all by means of compulsory school education.

For all these reasons, *the effort to use political means for catching up with the technical, economic, and cultural development of modern societies begins regularly with the assumption of power by a new regime—with a revolutionary act.* It is revolutionary, not necessarily in the sense of a violent overthrow of the constitutional order but in the sense of a clearly marked break in the continuity of the elites running the state, of the principles by which they legitimize their rule, and of the tasks they set themselves. Whether the break is constituted by emancipation from a colonial regime or from indirect forms of dependence or by the overthrow of an indigenous, traditionalist form of government, the victory of a "regime of development" is the precondition for a comprehensive attempt to tackle the tasks we have enumerated.

"DEVELOPMENTAL" AND "ANTI-DEVELOPMENTAL" REGIMES

The question of the prospects of different forms of government in the developing countries, to which this essay is devoted, may now be rephrased as follows: How effective have various forms of government proved in accomplishing the tasks of a "regime of development," or what specific advantages and weaknesses have they shown if viewed in relation to those tasks? Here we must begin with a word of warning. *In the developing countries, systems of government that are identical or closely similar in their constitutional forms may serve as a framework for the rule of totally different social groups pursuing diametrically opposite aims;* hence the political scientist must beware of confusing the effects due to the ruling group's positive or negative attitude to the goals of development with the effects due to the form of government as such.

Thus there still exist today a number—though a quickly diminishing number—of authoritarian regimes legitimated by tradition (as in Saudi Arabia or until recently, Ethiopia) whose ruling aristocracies, for all the compromises they may feel forced to make with the modern world surrounding them, are in principle seeking to preserve the old order and are thus at least partly opposed to development. Yet in nineteenth-century Japan, the Meiji restoration, also known as the Meiji revolution, brought to power an authoritarian regime with traditional legitimation which was to become the first conscious "regime of development" and to tackle the tasks of modernization in an astonishingly systematic and successful way; and even in our time, such a "modernization from above" by an authoritarian regime with traditional legitimation has been at least attempted, e.g., under Nuri es-Said in Iraq.[10]

Again, parliamentary monarchies or republics with democratic legitimation have frequently been the form of government used by a landowning oligarchy to maintain its rule over a largely illiterate population and to prevent development, e.g., in many Latin American countries since the nineteenth century, in the Middle East after World War I, and in some of the ex-colonial states of Asia since World War II. Yet in India, and more recently also in a few Latin American states, parliamentary democracies with a functioning multiparty system approaching the modern Western model became the framework for clearly conceived efforts at development.

Military usurpers legitimated by plebiscite have often replaced the oligarchic sham parliamentarianism in Latin America, with the change in the form of government producing no more profound social effect than a change of the governing clique within the dominant oligarchy. Yet lately, plebiscitary military dictatorships have repeatedly become the form in which revolutionary movements of the nationalist intelligentsia have won power with a pronounced program for development—particularly in Islamic countries, but in a few cases also in Latin America.[11]

Yet if the correspondence between the form and the function of government in the underdeveloped countries is by no means strictly regular, it is not a mere matter of chance either. On one side, the developing countries have in our time produced a series of new political forms that occur only in "regimes of development," such as the regimes of dominant nationalist-revolutionary parties with a tolerated opposition, the nationalist-revolutionary party dictatorships with suppression of all political alternatives, and the Communist type of totalitarian party dictatorship. On the other hand, attempts to repeat the "Japanese road" of modernization from above under an autocracy legitimated by traditional authority seem to become exceptional and to have much smaller prospects of success than their nineteenth-century model. Probably the principal reason is that the intelligentsia whose active cooperation is now crucial for the creation of a modern state and the execution of a program of development is no longer prepared to obey a traditional authority and to act in its name: the nationalism of this stratum today means to them not only an obligation to serve their own people, but a need to be legitimized by the people's will.

Of course, such "democratic legitimation" does not necessarily require a Western-type democracy based on the rule of law; it is merely *one* of its elements, and by itself is just as compatible with various forms of plebiscitary military dictatorship or even with a totalitarian party dictatorship, because all these forms of government claim to represent the will of the people and make the necessary arrangements to be confirmed by it—but it is really incompatible with traditional authority "by the grace of God." Hence the regime of Nuri es-Said, despite its realistic program of development based on favorable economic conditions, failed, owing to its inability to win the cooperation of the nationalist intelligentsia for the implementation of that program.

The practically relevant range of possible regimes of development thus appears confined to governments of revolutionary origin claiming to represent the will of the people.

It extends from a development-oriented democracy of the Indian type at one extreme via the various forms of one-party predominance, military dictatorship, and one-party dictatorship, to the ideological dictatorship of a Communist Party regime at the other extreme. We now turn to a comparison of the favorable and unfavorable effects of the forms of government within that range on the process of development.[12]

THE COMMUNIST MODEL OF DEVELOPMENT

In any such comparison, the first thing that strikes the eye is the tested efficiency of the Communist model. In its Stalinist form, Soviet Communism has proved itself as a gigantic engine of development. Indeed, in surveying the basic measures taken by the Soviet government in the course of forty-five years of "socialist construction," we find that they have been concentrated precisely on the tasks we have just enumerated: the forced accumulation of capital by the state; the planning of investment by the state; the mobilization of the masses for the development goals set by the state and for loyalty toward the regime by a political movement embracing every stratum of the population; and the use of this movement for re-educating the masses in a cultural revolution by struggle against superstition and illiteracy, for disciplined work according to plan. No wonder the modernistic, nationalist intelligentsia of all the developing countries is fascinated by the Soviet model!

Yet the same groups of nationalist intellectuals are also becoming increasingly aware of the extraordinarily high price the Soviet government and the peoples of Russia have paid for this achievement—a price that was only partly inherent in the task of development but was raised far beyond necessity by Communist ideological dogma. The dogma of irreconcilable hostility to the "capitalist" world has barred any form of Western development aid to the Communist countries and forced them to squeeze the needed capital funds exclusively from the bones and muscles of their own peoples. The same dogma requires that absolute priority be given to the buildup of heavy industry in order to achieve complete military independence from the "enemy" as quickly as possible: this needlessly prolongs the period during which the efforts and sacrifices of industrialization bear no fruit for the people's standard of living. The dogma that declares state planning to be incompatible with private ownership of means of production results in the needless rejection of the collaboration of the all too few industrial entrepreneurs available in the developing countries, hence in needless dealy in the training of the necessary number of qualified technical and economic cadres. The dogma that declares planning to be incompatible with a market economy—so far fully revised only by Yugoslavia among Communist states—leads to the senseless attempt—particularly absurd in the conditions prevailing in underdeveloped countries—to have every detail of production centrally regulated by an immense bureaucratic machinery, hence to inflated costs, to graft, to interruptions of supply, poor quality of output, and continuous discrepancies between the type of goods produced and that demanded. Most crucial of all, the dogma of agricultural collectivization, originally imposed on the peasants as a means to enforce delivery of their produce at state-fixed prices, has caused agriculture miserably to lag behind industrial development in all those Communist countries that still cling to it, again unnecessarily depressing the standard of living.

To this considerable economic cost of the Communist raod of development a political price must be added. A Communist dictatorship is not, after all, content to proclaim the realistic goal of modernizing its own country—an aim limited in space as well as time; it justifies itself by the utopian goal of the worldwide victory of the Communist order, the achievement of a classless terminal stage of history. The world-wide aim implies indefinite continuation of an unbridgeable conflict with the non-Communist world; the classless Utopia requires indefinite preservation of the party dictatorship at home, which can only "wither away" once the unattainable terminal stage has been reached. The choice of the Communist road of development thus has to be paid for by the rise of an *ideological* dictatorship that tends to cling to power by maintaining a state of permanent external and internal tension even after the original task of modernization has been completed.[13]

It is becoming increasingly evident even for the nationalist intelligentsia of the developing countries that *the specific advantages of the Soviet model are due to the comprehensive tackling of the tasks of development proper and to the organized concentration of economic and political power, while the specific disadvantages are due to the dogmatic narrowness of Communist ideology.* Hence the tendency, manifested by other "regimes of development" with growing frequency, to copy the organizational forms of central investment planning, and even of the one-party state, but to reject Communist ideology in favor of an eclectic combination of nationalist and socialist ideas with native traditions while deliberately limiting their practical program to the modernization of their country.

THE WESTERN DEMOCRATIC MODEL

Among the "regimes of development," the opposite extreme to Communist ideological dictatorship was until recently represented by Indian democracy. Its achievements, if measured by the short time of its existence, the level of poverty on which it started and the intensity of population pressure, were no less impressive. Its methods of combining internal accumulation with the acceptance of economic aid from both power blocs, central planning of investment with a market economy giving scope to private enterprise, promotion of the voluntary formation of agricultural cooperatives with the fostering of peasant initiative, and the authority of a leadership tested in the struggle for independence with democratic freedom for opposition and public criticism under the rule of law, were also studied and admired in many other developing countries; but they were rarely imitated. This is due first of all to the fact that the working of the Indian political system is linked to conditions that are absent in most developing countries, but also to the evidence that even in India, the real advantages of parliamentary democracy had to be paid for with specific drawbacks—a fact by no means ignored but rather consciously accepted by the Indian leaders.

To mention first the special conditions favoring Indian democracy: India's entrepreneurial middle class, though much weaker than in the advanced Western countries, is much stronger than in other developing countries in Asia and Africa. Owing to the gradual evolution of self-government during the long period of British rule, India's Western-educated stratum in general and her political and administrative cadres in particular were at the beginning far more numerous than in any other ex-colonial country and far more homogeneous in their outlook than in most of those underdeveloped countries that had never come under colonial rule. The breadth of this political and administrative elite group made it less difficult for India than for other "nations in formation" to attempt the integration of multilingual and culturally pluralistic populations not by imposing a brutal supercentralism, but by a federal system of decentralized administration; and the federal constitution long proved a solid foundation also for political pluralism. The high value placed on toleration and the deprecation of violence in the Indian religious tradition are further favorable conditions which account for the fact that despite the ignorance of the masses, freedom of criticism only rarely led to excesses; while the British tradition in turn left behind a respect for the independence of the courts as the natural protectors of individual rights which is rare in the developing countries. Finally, the uncontested authority enjoyed by Nehru and the Congress Party as the creators of Indian independence made it possible for this ruling party to cling to democratic methods of government at a time of immense difficulties of economic development and of national integration, without running any serious risk of being replaced in power by any opposition party or combination of parties, while within the Congress, the special authority enjoyed by Nehru and his companions from the nationalist-socialist intelligentsia long enabled them to determine the broad lines of party policy, although there were spokesmen of landowning and capitalist interests in many important positions who regarded this policy as too radical and still have the will and the economic power to oppose it.[14]

In developing countries in which few or none of the above conditions are present, the institutions of Indian democracy could not fulfill the functions of a regime of development: Either the interests of the economically privileged groups would prevail unchecked, leading to an oligarchic degeneration of democracy and a failure to tackle the tasks of development, as traditionally in Latin America or Egypt and more recently in South Korea or the Philippines, or the struggle between the parties and the separate organs of power would assume such unrestrained and anarchic forms that the ruling group would either founder in the general dissolution of the state or would itself suspend the democratic constitutional guarantees and introduce some form of "guided democracy" or open dictatorship, or finally would be overthrown in a *coup d'état* in which the military proclaimed itself as the guardian of public order and national unity. In the many developing countries that have won sovereignty under democratic constitutions since the end of World War II, we have seen examples of each of these varied forms of the collapse of democracy.

But even where a combination of favorable conditions long allowed a democratic regime of development to function as in India, the important advantages which this form of government assures for the personal freedom as well as for the longer-term political education of the citizens have to be balanced against the social cost of having measures necessary for development slowed down by the opposition of vested interests. The implementation of land reform and of important elements of the economic plan, particularly in the field of taxation, were long seriously impaired by the resistance of the representatives of landowning and capitalist interests inside the Congress Party and particularly inside the provincial ministries and administrative offices staffed by this party. Moreover, the appearance of such obstacles is not accidental but inherent in a democracy operating under the rule of law: a process of state-directed development requires that powerful interests that are linked to the old order or to its remnants must be hurt, and the resistance of such interests may of course be broken more speedily by the methods of revolutionary dictatorship than by methods involving respect for minority rights, for strictly democratic procedures of decision-making, and for a division of powers assuring the rule of law.

It is a fact well known to political science that even in such old, highly developed industrial countries as the United States and Great Britain, recurrent dangers of political stagnation, of a paralysis of decision, arise from the nature of a pluralistic democracy under the rule of law—dangers that must each time be overcome by special impulses, such as the pressure of a major crisis or unusual qualities of leadership. Where the need for modernization is as urgent as in the developing countries, the problem is even more serious. It may indeed be stated that *within a certain range, there exists for these countries a dilemma of choice between the extent of pluralistic freedom they can afford and the pace of development they can achieve.* It is not a dilemma of absolutes which would force them to choose between the extremes of total dictatorship or total stagnation, but a continuous line of alternatives where *every degree of increased freedom has to be paid for by some slowing down of development, every degree of acceleration by some loss of freedom.* In the nature of the process of state-directed development this seems inevitable.

THE NATIONALIST "DICTATORSHIPS OF DEVELOPMENT"

Because this is the case, the large majority of genuine "regimes of development" has so far shown a preference for forms of government that lie between the extremes of pluralistic democracy under the rule of law and the totalitarian ideological dictatorship of the Communists. Here we intend first to distinguish the main types of these intermediate forms of government, and then to point to their common features.

Closest to pluralistic democracy is the system of *nondictatorial one-party hegemony.* It combines a democratic constitution—usually of the presidential, more rarely of the parliamentary type—with a situation in which the formation of opposition groups is not hampered by legislation or police action, but where the incomparable authority of the governing party, based on its leadership in the national revolution, leaves no effective chance for the development of political alternatives.[15] Such regimes, among which the rule of the Partido Revolucionario Institucional in Mexico[16] has proved the most stable, seem to differ only in degree from the Indian type, yet the difference is substantial. The Indian opposition parties, too, had no real prospect of replacing the Congress Party in the central government, but they are real factors in Indian politics: They were strong enough to give the Congress a serious battle at election times, to exert effective pressure on government policy, and to force the formation of various types of coalition governments in a number of provinces. By contrast, the opposition groups in the countries just mentioned are too weak to play an effective political role in that sense; the importance of their admission lies primarily in keeping a safety valve open for free criticism, and indirectly in giving a chance for the democratic struggle of tendencies *within* the governing party itself. In creating "regimes of development," the national revolutionary mass parties typically rely on a network of "mass organizations"—trade unions, peasant leagues, student associations, etc.—representing members with different interests, whose leaders are at the same time influential party officials. Where the ruling party has proclaimed the principle of a single-party regime, it must also prevent the free struggle between these partial interests within its ranks and must thus subject the mass organizations to political directives under centralist discipline (*Gleichschaltung*), as the risk of a factional split in the party cannot be safely eliminated in any other way; but where opposition groups outside the ruling party are admitted in principle, partial interests may also enjoy greater freedom of expression within that party. The evolution of such regimes into true pluralistic democracies may thus take place not only by the growth of the early marginal opposition groups, but also, and perhaps more easily, by the growing differentiation of tendencies and interests within the predominant party.

Much closer in form to the totalitarian regime of the Communists (as well as to that of the National Socialists) are the nationalist *single-party states* proper that have arisen in a number of developing countries. Their ruling groups have the conviction in common that the solution of the problems of development requires a concentration of power to a degree incompatible with the admission of organized opposition or the free representation of partial interests; in such a case, it is of no account whether the formation of other parties is forbidden by law or whether their activity is only gradually paralyzed by persecution, as at first in Ghana—what matters is that the regime regards any form of opposition as "sabotage." But while these single-party states share with the totalitarian regimes proper the decisive rejection of institutional pluralism and of the rule of law for the period of modernization and industrialization, they differ from them by the absence of an ideological program that would transcend the tasks of national liberation from all colonial dependence, whether direct or indirect, and of forcible national development by political means. Accordingly, state compulsion in these countries is directed to the solution of the immediate tasks of development, not to the enforcement of an all-embracing ideological conformity: *They are "development dictatorships," not ideological dictatorships.*

The first single-party regime of this pragmatic type, the Kemalist dictatorship in Turkey, was created under the direct impression of the Bolshevik revolution and imitated, in deliberate eclecticism, the Communist methods of organization and development without adopting the Communist ideology. Dr. Sun Yat-sen's reorganization of the Kuomintang with the help of Soviet advisers was also based on an eclectic concept of this type, and the Kuomintang regime headed by Chiang Kai-shek actually showed a similar character, at least from his 1927 break with the Communists until the Japanese invasion—a tradition that has been resumed, on a smaller scale and in more favorable conditions, in the present Kuomintang regime on Taiwan. Many new single-party regimes have arisen in the course of decolonization in Africa, beginning with West Africa; there the form has been adopted not only by militantly "anti-imperialist" states like Ghana, Guinea, and Mali, and more recently Algeria, but also on the basis of similar problems, and in part of similar traditions, by leaders more inclined to cooperate with the West like Houphouet-Boigny in the Ivory Coast and Nyerere in Tanganyika.[17]

In developing countries that have never been under direct colonial rule, or have been able to produce a native military elite even under colonial rule, the officer corps may form an important sector of the nationalist intelligentsia—particularly if, as is often the case in Islamic countries, a military career is not reserved to the traditional upper classes. In such countries, therefore, the nationalist intelligentsia often wins power by a military *coup d'état;* the resulting regimes, as in Nasser's Egypt, are *plebiscitary military dictatorships,* seeking, just like the nationalist single-party regimes, to concentrate state power for the tasks of development and to suppress any organized opposition while legitimating their rule by an eclectic mixture of nationalist and socialist ideas defining a pragmatically limited program. Frequently, such military regimes attempt to create a "state party" from above, in order to mobilize the masses for active participation in the tasks of development; but where such a party was not the original moving force of the national revolution, it has regularly proved very difficult to organize it after the event.

Finally, there exists in the developing countries a great variety of *mixed types* of authoritarian regimes, intermediate between limited forms of democracy and the "development dictatorships" of a state party or a military junta. Among examples that do not fit into any general formula I should like at least to mention the "guided democracy" of President Sukarno of Indonesia, and the long reign of Peron in Argentina; both regimes rested on the skill of *a leader balancing a plurality of organized forces not by democratic institutions under the rule of law but by his personal authority.* Sukarno, having eliminated a number of Indo-

nesian parties, pledged the remainder—the Nationalists, the
Communists, and one section of the Islamic traditionalists—
to cooperation under his leadership, but in practice was
chiefly concerned to hold the balance between the army,
the only effective part of the state machine, and the Communists, the best-organized force among the parties; as the
balance was highly sensitive to any changes in the external
or internal situation, the regime proved unstable. Perón
relied for a long time on a similarly unstable balance between the section of the officer corps loyal to him, a party
chiefly based on state trade unions, and the Church, while
ruthlessly suppressing all other forces; he achieved considerable results in some fields of development, but was
overthrown when he tried to shift the balance decisively
in favor of his party and trade-union basis.

All those "regimes of development" which are neither
fully grown pluralistic democracies nor totalitarian dictatorships tied to an ideological dogma, from the regimes of one-
party hegemony with freedom of criticism through the
authoritarian mixed types and the plebiscitary military
dictatorships to the regimes of nationalist single-party rule,
have a number of features in common. All of them have
come to power by the victory of a national revolutionary
movement and are primarily supported by nationalist-
socialist intelligentsia groups whose main concern are the
tasks of development. All are seeking to tackle these tasks
by means of a greater concentration of power than is
normally possible in pluralistic democracies—by methods
that are at least authoritarian and often clearly dictatorial.
*All these regimes therefore have, for the sake of the pace
of development, rejected the attempt to assure a maximum
of freedom from the start.*

But all these regimes, including the outspoken "dictatorships of development," are not tied to an ideological dogma
but remain ideologically open-minded. They are open for
new ideas and influences reaching them from the outside

world, including the old industrial countries of the West, as they do not see themselves as existing in a basically unbridgeable conflict with the outside world.[18] They are, therefore, also open for further evolution of their own political systems as advances are achieved in the political solution of the immediate tasks of modernization. *None of these regimes, then, in contrast to the totalitarian dictatorships, has for the sake of the pace of development renounced an indispensable minimum of freedom*—of freedom of thought and of freedom to determine the direction of its further political evolution. Even when they are dictatorial, they do not erect dictatorship into a principle; and it is certainly no accident that the historically first among these pragmatic, nationalist "dictatorships of development," the Turkish regime founded by the Kemalist revolution, has fulfilled its promise to abandon power in free elections. For though it is in the nature of dictatorial power that its holders will seek to preserve it even when the task that originally justified it has been solved, it is difficult in practice to prolong a dictatorship whose task was defined from the start not by utopian and therefore unlimited goals, but in concrete, pragmatic terms.

CONCLUSIONS

I should like in the end to draw some conclusions from this survey of the functions and forms of government in the developing countries. I have tried not to judge the various political systems of those countries by measuring them against the yardstick of our Western democratic values, but to investigate their chances objectively by asking how they can serve the present needs of those countries as conceived by their politically decisive stratum. But inasmuch as we can influence these chances, they depend in part on our own actions. Effective political action, however, is not the same thing as wishful thinking: It cannot consist in simply giving preference to those types of political system which, on the basis of *our* experience, we should prefer in *our* conditions—without regard for the effect in the different conditions of those countries, and particularly for the prospects for the stability of such systems.

The central objective of the decisive stratum in the political life of these countries, of the intelligentsia, is their politically forced development—the overcoming of traditional stagnation by political means. The central objective of Western foreign policy in these countries must be to keep their future evolution open, to avoid the impasse of a totalitarian solution tied to Communist dogma. Experience has shown that the nationalist intelligentsia in those countries will be the less inclined to such a dogmatic solution the earlier it attains power and the more successful it is in tackling the tasks of development by different methods.

If we remain conscious of the dilemma of choice between the pace of development and the degree of freedom, we shall not try in those countries to oppose Communist dogmatism by ultra-liberal dogmatism. Rather, we shall seek to serve the long-term prospects of a liberal-democratic evolution by promoting in each particular case what appears as the most promising alternative to stagnation on one side and to totalitarian dictatorship on the other—whether this alternative turns out to be an imperfect democracy or an undoctrinaire, open-minded "dictatorship of development." For in those countries, maximum approximation to a pluralistic democracy under the rule of law, as we know it in the West, can only be the result of a process of development successfully completed: It can never be its precondition.

2

The Soviet Model
of One-Party Rule
and Its Impact

From an early date, the Communist model of modernization in its Russian form has enjoyed great prestige among the modernizing intelligentsia of the underdeveloped nations. Even where the movements and regimes created by this group did not accept the doctrinal framework and the egalitarian and internationalist ultimate goals of Communist ideology, they were impressed by Communist performance in terms of the more immediate goals of modernization and national independence. Consequently, many of them have tried, with greater or lesser success, to find ways of using the model selectively.

The following chapter was originally written for a volume of essays dealing with the impact of the Bolshevik Revolution on the outside world, on the occasion of the 50th anniversary of the revolution. It analyzes first the origin of the modern single-party state in its totalitarian Communist form, and then looks at the transformations this model has undergone as it came to be "selectively imitated" both by nationalist modernizing regimes in underdeveloped countries and even by the fascist opponents of communism in more or less advanced societies.[1] *For the present version, the section dealing with the "nationalist modernizers" has been considerably updated.*

THE ORIGIN OF THE MODEL

Fifty years ago, the Bolshevik Party seized power in Russia in the name of the Soviets of Workers' and Soldiers' Deputies. For months before, "All Power to the Soviets" had been their central political slogan. For many years afterwards, they propagated the "Soviet system" as the specific political institution of the new regime—the only adequate political form for the rule of the working class, the 'dictatorship of the proletariat' envisaged by Karl Marx. The new Russia was proclaimed a "Soviet Republic" and soon extended into a "Union of Soviet Socialist Republics." When the Communist International was founded in 1919, it was to the Soviet banner that it rallied the most militant revolutionaries of Europe, and it was for the creation of Soviet rule on the Russian model that Communists were subsequently to fight and die in Germany and Hungary, in the Balkans and the Baltic States, and even in distant China. But the Soviet system did not, in fact, spread to other countries—not even to those which came, after the Second World War, to form part of the "Soviet bloc"; and even the Chinese Communists, who had copied the institution in the shifting rural areas controlled by them after 1928, did not in the days of their final triumph restore the name which they had abandoned under their 1937 anti-Japanese alliance with Chiang Kai-shek.

   This failure of the efforts to spread the "Soviet system," and the ultimate abandonment of those efforts by the Russian Bolsheviks themselves, did not, however, prevent the political forms of their new state from having a worldwide impact; only it was a very different set of political institutions that proved of major historical importance as an international model. It is as the first totalitarian single-party state, rather than as the first Soviet state, that the new type of government developed by the Bolsheviks has attracted imitators—not only among those who share their ideological goals but also among their most bitter enemies and among people who are quite indifferent to those goals. For while the Bolsheviks, in stressing the Soviets as their most important political contribution, selected the institution that expressed most clearly the *legitimation* of their power by its alleged social content, the course of history has selected the institution that embodied the *reality* of their power—independent of any social content.

In the completed form which it reached in Russia from about 1921, and in which it has made its impact around the world, the totalitarian single-party state may be defined by four main institutional characteristics. The first is the monopolistic control of the state by the ruling party, excluding the toleration of other, independent parties in opposition or even as genuine partners in coalition, and leading logically also to a ban on the formation of organized tendencies or "factions" *within* the ruling party; this amounts in effect to a monopoly of political initiative and decision for the inner leadership of that party, and ultimately to a monopoly of decision for a single leader. The second is the party's monopolistic control of all forms of social organization, depriving these organizations of their role as independent interest groups as exercised in non-totalitarian, "pluralistic" societies and converting them into as many tools for the mobilization, education, and control of their members by the ruling party; this enables the totalitarian regime to supplement the levers of the state bureaucracy for controlling the actions of its subjects "from above" with a network of organizations enveloping them from cradle to grave, while preventing the formation of any independent groups. The third is the monopolistic control of all channels of public communication, from the press and other mass media to all forms of education, of literature and art, with the aim not merely of preventing the *expression* of hostile or undesirable opinions by a kind of censorship, but of controlling the *formation* of opinion at the source by planned selection of all the elements of information. The fourth is what Lenin himself used as the definition of dictatorship—"the removal of all legal limitations on state power," in other words, the possibility to use state power in arbitrary and terroristic ways whenever this is deemed expedient for the purposes of the regime. It is essentially the combination of these four characteristics which has enabled the totalitarian regimes of our time to extend the effectiveness of state power beyond anything that was deemed possible before 1917.

This institutional scheme had not been conceived by the Bolsheviks in advance. We may apply to it the words of J. L. Talmon about another regime with which their rule has often been compared: "Jacobin dictatorship was an improvisation. It came into existence by stages, and not in accordance with a blueprint. At the same time, it corresponded to, and was the consequence of, a fixed attitude of mind of its authors, intensified and rendered extreme by events."[2]

In the Bolshevik case, however, this attitude of mind had long created its appropriate body in the centralistic organizational structure of the party that seized power on 7 Novenber 1917. Lenin had consciously created his "party of a new type" as an instrument for the revolutionary conquest of power; and even though, in writing *What is to be Done*, he had been far from envisaging the concrete forms that party's domination was to take fifteen or twenty years later, the possibility of a totalitarian party dictatorship was implied in the shape of that instrument. Without the pre-existing "party of a new type," the first state of the new type could not have been built up; with that party once victorious, the tendency for its leaders to establish dictatorial, monopolistic rule was given—to be brought out "by events."

To understand how the truly epoch-making new system of government became possible, it is therefore necessary to recall how unusual were the basic features of Lenin's concept of the revolutionary party. Up to 1902–3, a party had been generally understood to be the organized expression of a part, a section of society—of a particular economic or social interest or current of ideas. Even the socialist parties of western and central Europe that based themselves on the revolutionary teachings of Karl Marx were supposed merely to express the actual ideas and aspirations of the industrial working class of their respective countries; in Marx's own view, his theories could be gradually assimilated by these parties only in the course of their experience, and it was for each of them to draw its own conclusions on the best road to power in accordance with national conditions. Yet Lenin, in writing *What is to be Done* as a platform for the reconstruction of the Russian Social-Democratic Party organization in 1902, and in forming his own "Bolshevik" faction over the question of centralized control during its 1903 congress, started from the assumption that no mere "interest group" of the industrial working class would be able to overthrow Russian Tsarism; that the coalition of all discontented classes and groups necessary for this crucial task could be forged only by a conspiratorial organization of professional revolutionaries specifically devoted and adapted to the conquest of power; and that this organization needed links in all oppositional classes and groups as well as in the state machine, even though the industrial workers must furnish its main base. Such a party, being not an expression of a social current, but the instrument of a will to power and of a strategy for achieving it, could not grow democratically from its roots, but must be planned

and built "centralistically" by its founders. Its local committees must be appointed by the central leadership, its
members admitted only after scrutiny by the local committees, selection from above rather than election from below must be its principle all along the line: only thus could
the historically conscious, "scientifically" Marxist leadership use the party to carry out its strategy and bring about
a result which the historical process might fail to yield
"spontaneously," that is, without such planned intervention.

As Lenin's Marxist critics—Plekhanov, Axelrod and Martov,
Trotsky and Rosa Luxemburg—protested at once, this
concept of the party had its roots not in Marxism, but in
the tradition of the Russian revolutionary conspiracies of
the nineteenth century, and partiularly in the theories of
those of their members who professed so-called "Jacobin"
principles, that is, the primacy of the conquest of power
and the need to adapt the revolutionary organization to
this overriding purpose. In reply, Lenin proudly accepted
the model of such revolutionary organizations as the *Narodnaya Volya* and its predecessor, the (second) *Zemlya i
Volya,* pointing out only that they did not confine themselves to conspiratorial activities, but combined those
activities (such as the infiltration of the state machine and
the preparation for armed insurrection) with open revolutionary propaganda; and he also defiantly accepted the
Jacobin label, going as far as to define the revolutionary
social-democrat of his dreams as "a Jacobin inseparably
linked to the working-class movement."[3] The view that
both the Leninist party and the Bolshevik dictatorship were
largely re-enactments of the earlier model set by the Jacobin
Club and the rule of the Comité du Salut Public—a view
equally widespread among the apologists and the critics of
Bolshevism, and also encountered among historians and
political scientists—goes back to those early debates; but

this interpretation overlooks the fact that all the parties to the dispute confused the historical reality of Jacobinism with the later legend created by F. M. Buonarroti, and as a result gravely underestimates the true originality of the Bolshevik achievement.

In fact, and contrary to that legend, the dictatorial climax of the French Revolution was not, and could not be, a party dictatorship of the Jacobins, because the Jacobin Club never was the kind of disciplined, centralized, and ideologically homogeneous party that could have played that role.[4] It started as a broad forum for politicians ranging from liberal monarchists to intransigent republicans; it became more radical by the secession or expulsion of the more moderate elements just as the National Assemblies changed their political color; the secretary in charge of correspondence with the provincial clubs changed frequently and had no power to enforce conformity with the views of the center; and when cnetralized dictatorship did in fact develop, it spread from the centralization of government—through the *commissaires en mission*—to the clubs and not vice versa. The idea that the clubs should control state appointments was voiced by the Hébertists but rejected by Robespierre, and a temporary majority in the Jacobin Club did not protect the Hébertists from being wiped out by the holders of the real power, the Committee of Public Safety. Conversely, the rule of that committee was eventually overthrown in the Assembly by deputies who belonged to the Jacobin Club— although Robespierre had not previously lost his majority there.

But while the French Revolution never produced the reality of a party dictatorship, it did produce the idea. That idea arose among the defeated extremists in the prisons of the Thermidor: the concept of the "revolutionary vanguard" was born as a dream of the defeated rearguard of revolutionary extremism. The first attempt to put the dream into practice—to create a party and a regime which would avoid the "weaknesses" of the Jacobins and of Robespierre—was made in the conspiracy of Gracchus Baboeuf; and it was a survivor of that conspiracy, Filippo Buonarroti, who later launched the legend that Robespierre and the Jacobins had themselves set the example for that attempt.[5] From Buonarroti, the concept of the conspiratorial revolutionary party aiming at an "educational" dictatorship passed to Louis-Auguste Blanqui and to the Russian "Jacobins" of the nineteenth century, notably to Blanqui's friend Peter Nikitich Tkachev. It was in that sense that the founder of Bolshevism was accused of being a Jacobin, and that he accepted the label.

Even so, Lenin at first sincerely rejected the implication that he was aiming at a party dictatorship in Russia. We do not know just when he came to regard such a regime as the necessary political form for the "dictatorship of the proletariat," but we do know that up to the First World War he considered that a dictatorship of the proletariat was not yet on the agenda of Russian history. During the revolution of 1905, he aimed at the overthrow of Tsarism by an alliance of workers and peasants, and at the formation of a coalition government of Social-Democrats and Social-Revolutionaries as its political expression. It was only the shock of the war of 1914 that convinced Lenin that a socialist revolution had become an immediate task internationally, and that it was therefore the duty of socialists even in backward Russia to go beyond the overthrow of Tsarism and the establishment of a "bourgeois-democratic" regime and to set up the power of the proletariat in order to contribute to the fulfilment of the international task.

When Lenin, after his return to Russia in April 1917, began to propagate this new concept, first within and then beyond his party, he did so under the slogan "All Power to the Soviets." Yet while he emphasized the Soviets as the direct organs of proletarian rule, the opposition of all other socialist parties to this programme convinced him that the establishment of that rule depended on the Bolsheviks acquiring control of the Soviets first. In the course of 1917, the Bolsheviks ceased in Lenin's mind to be merely the most enlightened and energetic representatives of the interests of the Russian working class and became, to him, the *only* party of the Russian proletariat; and this implied that the "dictatorship of the proletariat" must in fact take the form of a Bolshevik party dictatorship.

This crucial identification of party and class appears as a matter of course in all Lenin's writings during the months immediately preceding the seizure of power. It becomes most explicit on the very eve of victory in his pamphlet *Can the Bolsheviks Retain State Power?*, in which the Soviets—the directly elected representatives of the workers, soldiers, and peasants—are openly and unceremoniously treated as the new "state apparatus" by means of which the victorious Bolsheviks will exercise and maintain *their* power and carry out *their* policy. It was a consequence of this outlook, not yet understood at the time even by many leading Bolsheviks, that Lenin after 7 November consistently rejected all proposals for a coalition with the Mensheviks and accepted as temporary partners in the new regime only those Left Social-Revolutionaries whom he regarded as representing the peasants in the process of agrarian revolution. It was another consequence that he dispersed the Constituent Assembly, elected *after* the Bolshevik assumption of power, when its large non-Bolshevik majority refused to vote a blanket endorsement of all the revolutionary measures already enacted by the new regime.

By the time of the October Revolution, then, Lenin was determined to establish a revolutionary dictatorship of his party. But this did not mean that he had, even then, a plan or blue-print for a totalitarian single-party state. What was clear in his mind was the last of our four characteristics of such a state—the rejection of any legal limitations on the revolutionary power. This was sufficient to enable him to suppress resistance to his policy as the need arose. But as resistance developed into civil war, determination to break it was no longer enough: to maintain and defend the revolutionary government, a new state machine had to be created.

It had been an essential part of Lenin's revolutionary programme, explained most fully in his pamphlet on *State and Revolution* and based on Karl Marx's analysis of the Paris Commune, that the victorious proletariat could not use the bureaucracy, army, and police which had served its exploiters as a machine of oppression, but must smash them. Before 7 November, he had also followed Marx in arguing that the new proletarian regime had no need to put another *professional* state apparatus in their place: part-time workers' delegates in the soviets, part-time voluntary organs of workers' control in economic life, a part-time workers' militia would be enough. Yet after victory, and especially with the spread of civil war, the creation of a new, revolutionary army, police, and bureaucracy became imperative if the Soviet regime was not to follow the Paris Commune also on the road to defeat. The new, professional state machine had to be staffed with reliable cadres at least in the key positions; and in the conditions of party dictatorship, reliable cadres could only mean Bolsheviks. From being the leading force in the soviets and the government, the party thus developed into the backbone of a new state machine: its monopolistic control of the new State became entrenched in practice before it was proclaimed in theory. In fact, as Leonard Schapiro has shown,[6] the party was so little prepared for this task that its provincial organizations were temporarily almost paralysed by the absorption of the most active cadres in the work of the new Soviet bureaucracy. When the need for central control of the assignment of party members to state jobs was recognized by the spring of 1919, the central party apparatus was still quite inadequate for this new role: it had to be expanded from a mere 15 persons to 600 within two years.

Even so, during the entire period of the Civil War, the Bolsheviks never argued in principle that they should be the only legal party; nor was there any hint of that doctrine in the constitution of the RSFSR adopted by the fifth All-Russian Soviet congress in July 1918. But they did argue that they would not tolerate any bourgeois parties opposed to Soviet rule in principle, nor parties working for the armed overthrow of the new regime, even if they professed a socialist programme; and they claimed that the central and local organs of Soviet rule, including the Cheka, must not be hampered by any legal safeguards in deciding whether any party, newspaper, or individual was guilty of such counter-revolutionary activity. In practice, this led not only to the suppression of parties and groups that were actually supporting armed insurrection against the Soviet power—such as the Right Social-Revolutionaries when they set up a counter-government in Samara in June 1918 in the name of the dissolved Constitutent Assembly and under the protection of the Czech legionaries, or those leaders of the Left Social-Revolutionaries involved in the assassination of the German Ambassador and the abortive Moscow revolt of July of that year; it also produced a cat-and-mouse game of arbitrary harassment of parties and groups that explicitly and consistently placed themselves on the ground of the new Soviet Constitution and the defense of the Soviet regime, but claimed the democratic rights of competing for influence and criticizing the authorities on that basis, such as the Mensheviks led by Martov and some breakaway groups from the Social-Revolutionaries. In the absence of legal standards, the only maxim underlying that practice was clearly that no party, however loyal to the "Soviet system," must be allowed to become strong enough to endanger the effective power of the Bolsheviks: whenever and wherever that seemed to threaten, newspapers were shut down, opposition candidates arrested on the eve of elections, newly elected soviets with opposition majorities dispersed, elected trade union boards replaced by appointed Communists—and it was a mere matter of expediency whether the arrested leaders would quickly be released again, deported by administrative order, or—in rare cases—brought to trial on trumped-up charges.[7]

Yet while the Bolshevik regime of the Civil War years was clearly a terrorist dictatorship—"Red Terror" was officially proclaimed as a policy after the attempt on Lenin's life in August 1918—and while the dictatorial party increasingly merged with the new state machine in process of construction, it did not yet create a totalitarian single-party state as we have come to know it since. As late as 1920, there were many hundreds of Mensheviks in the provincial soviets, and Martov himself was able in the Moscow soviet to voice their protest against the arbitrary suppression of "working-class democracy" and to advocate their programme for economic recovery that anticipated the later New Economic Policy of the Bolsheviks. Important trade unions were still under Menshevik control, and the Bolshevik leaders were fully aware that the influence of their critics among the workers was increasing as the Civil War drew to a close. Discontent and indiscipline had moreover affected so many of the Bolsheviks' own militants that spontaneous co-operation between Mensheviks and those undisciplined Bolsheviks produced surprise majorities against the "party line" in soviets or trade unions more than once. It was only after the end of the Civil War, in early 1921, at a time of growing unrest among both workers and peasants culminating in the Kronstadt rising, and simultaneously with the decision to introduce the New Economic Policy, that Lenin decided to put his regime on a more secure institutional basis. To understand the decision that produced the first modern totalitarian regime, we must try to envisage the problems that faced him.

The classical tasks of a Jacobin revolutionary dictatorship had been fulfilled. The counter-revolution had been defeated, the power of the former ruling classes broken for good. But the expectation that the Bolshevik victory in Russia would be the immediate prelude to socialist revolutions in the advanced countries of Europe had not come true: the "dictatorship of the proletariat"—in fact of a minority party claiming to represent the proletariat—had remained isolated in a backward country in which the proletariat formed a minority, and in which, as Lenin knew and recognized, the economic and cultural preconditions for a socialist system were lacking. To overcome the discontent born out of economic paralysis, to begin the work of recovery after the devastations of war and civil war, major economic concessions to all the remaining non-proletarian strata—to the peasant majority above all, but also to the traders and technicians—were inevitable; the "war Communist" fantasies of a straight leap into Utopia had to give way to a policy of patiently creating, in cooperation with all classes, the productive resources which elsewhere had been created by capitalism, and which alone could eventually form the basis for a socialist economy. It seemed the typical situation for a "Thermidor"—for liquidating the revolutionary dictatorship that had done its work; and that was indeed what the Mensheviks suggested with growing confidence in their own judgment.

Yet Lenin drew a different conclusion. He agreed on the need for a break with utopian dreams, for material concessions to all productive classes, for shifting the emphasis in Russia from political revolution to economic evolution; but he insisted that the "proletarian" dictatorship must be maintained during the new phase as well, in order to ensure that evolution was accomplished by what he termed state capitalism—under the control of a state which would maintain Russia's independence from the capitalist world and prevent the restoration of a class of capitalist owners, even while accomplishing the task which capitalism had fulfilled in the advanced countries, and would thus preserve the foundations for the later transition to socialism as well as a stronghold for the international revolutionary movement. The Bolsheviks must hold on to their dictatorial power—no longer primarily as a revolutionary dictatorship, but as a special type of a dictatorship of development. It is from this decision that the truly unique course of the Russian Revolution begins; it is from this decision, too, that the need to create a system of totalitarian institutions has resulted.

The new need, as Lenin saw it, was no longer the comparatively simple one of fighting the class enemy arms in hand: it was to harness the economic energies of non-proletarian classes for a constructive task, to grant them a place in society for a whole period—yet to prevent them from influencing the direction of economic and social development. As Lenin had once conceived the "party of a new type" as an instrument to make the social forces of discontent converge in a revolutionary direction which they might not otherwise take, so now he conceived the state of a new type as an instrument to guide the millions of independent peasants, the private traders, the industrial technicians of bourgeois origin, in a socialist direction which ran counter to their natural tendency to evolve a capitalist social structure. To foil that tendency, it was not enough that the state kept firm control of the "commanding heights" of the economy; the alien classes must be permanently excluded from any possible access to the levers of political power. The unique purpose of forcing an entire society to develop not in the direction corresponding to its inherent trend, but in the direction dictated by the ideology of its ruling party, required a unique institutional form, closing all channels of political expression to the existing social forces: no plurality of political parties, however vestigial; no organized interest groups or publishing media free from party control; and finally, as a logical extension of this principle, no plurality of organized tendencies *within* the ruling party, as in the absence of opposition parties such factions would tend to become the channels for the pressure of non-proletarian class interests.

Oddly enough, no formal ban on all remnants of non-communist parties was passed even then. But mass arrests of their central and local leaders destroyed their organizations for good in the early months of 1921, so that in the summer of 1922 even the Menshevik leadership, by then in exile, explicitly renounced any further attempt to put up candidates for Soviet elections. Moreover, a formal ban on factions within the ruling party *was* passed at its tenth congress in March 1921—the same congress that introduced the NEP—on Lenin's proposal, and explicitly based on the grounds stated above—thus showing that the final destruction of the other parties at this moment was a deliberate decision. By November, on the fourth anniversary of the Bolshevik seizure of power, Zinoviev could state publicly that the Bolsheviks had been "the only legal party" in Russia for some time past. The remaining Menshevik-controlled trade unions were "reorganized" under appointed Communist leaders during the same year, thus proving that the regime could in fact not afford to tolerate the independent advocacy of the interests of the industrial workers any more than of any other class; and by the time of the twelfth party conference of the Bolsheviks, in August 1922, the need to extend the principle of *Gleichschaltung* to all "so-called social organizations," as well as to the universities and publishing firms, was proclaimed on the ground that otherwise those legal channels could be used by the now illegal "anti-Soviet parties" for their dangerous propaganda.[8]

The first totalitarian state thus did not arise either as an automatic result of revolution and civil war, or as a mere instrument for the accelerated economic development of a backward country: it was the product of the decision to use the dictatorship resulting from the revolution in order to twist the development of society in the preconceived direction indicated by the ideology of the ruling party. As Lenin saw it, however, that politically directed development would henceforth proceed by evolutionary methods, without further violent upheavals. The emphasis in the writings of his final years was on the need to raise the economic and cultural level of the Russian people—including in particular the cultural level of the new bureaucracy—by steady, patient efforts within the given political framework; Lenin's last pamphlet on the agricultural co-operatives in particular, which Bukharin was later to describe as his political testament, pointed to the growth of co-operation rather than capitalist differentiation in the countryside as decisive for the evolution of Russia in a socialist direction, but envisaged that growth as taking place voluntarily on the basis of the peasants' material self-interest, parallel with the progress of the agricultural machine industry on one side and of the peasants' educational level on the other.

This evolutionary vision of the state-guided development of Russian society was also generally accepted by Lenin's heirs, at least as long as the problem of post-war recovery dominated economic life. As for Stalin in particular, he continued to oppose the idea of reviving the internal class struggle against the peasants for several years after first Trotsky and then Zinoviev and Kamenev had called for it. When, in 1925, he undertook to define the task of the totalitarian regime in terms of a distinction between the "bourgeois" and the "proletarian" revolution, he explained that the former had only had to remove the pre-capitalist "political superstructure" after the new capitalist economic and social "basis" was already fully developed, whereas in the case of the latter the political seizure of power—the creation of the new "socialist" superstructure—was a *precondition* for the development of the new basis, the socialist economy and society.[9] But while this formula brought out with striking clarity the originality of the task bequeathed by Lenin and the extent of his departure from the Marxist tradition, it contained no hint that the creation of the new basis would require further crises of a revolutionary character.

Yet as the period of recovery drew to a close and the problem of financing Russia's industrialization—of the primitive socialist accumulation of capital—pressed to the fore, the hidden, inner contradiction of Lenin's vision of the guided socialist evolution of a society containing a majority of small, independent producers became obvious and confronted his heirs with a dilemma. The financing of socialist industrialization by peaceful, evolutionary methods—by encouraging the peasants to earn surpluses and to lend their savings to the state—as advocated by Bukharin, was *economically* possible and indeed rational; but, as experience showed by 1928, it was bound to increase the *social* weight of the individualist peasantry and to lead to a growing dependence of the formally all-powerful party-state on the informal but effective organizations of the village, typically led by the most efficient, near-capitalist peasants.[10] The more successful the evolutionary road in terms of production and savings, the less likely was it to lead in the desired direction of preventing a capitalist development of the village and its growing impact on Russian society as a whole—the more it would therefore undermine the purpose and ultimately the power of the totalitarian regime. Conversely, the alternative road of financing socialist industrialization at the expense of the peasants, by syphoning off their surpluses more or less forcibly, as originally advocated by the "Left Opposition," might effectively stifle the tendency towards capitalist development in the village and maintain the course required by the regime's ideology; but it was bound to provoke peasant resistance to an extent that could be broken only by the massive use of state power—in other words by the abandonment of peaceful evolution.

In launching the "liquidation of the kulaks as a class" and the forced collectivization of agriculture, which he himself later described as a revolution "equivalent" to that of October 1917, but distinguished from it by being "accomplished from above, on the initiative of the state,"[11] Stalin decided in favor of the primacy of the totalitarian regime and its ideological goal: he recognized what Lenin had not foreseen—that a totalitarian regime can fulfil its task of diverting the development of society from its "spontaneous" course in an ideologically preconceived direction only by repeated recourse to revolutionary violence. The dynamics of the permanent, or at any rate recurrent, revolution from above as developed by Stalin are the necessary complement to the ideological goals set and to the totalitarian institutions created by Lenin: they, too, were not part of a blueprint, but they grew out of a fixed attitude of mind—and out of the institutions in which it had been embodied— under the pressure of events.

There is no need for us at this point to discuss the later development of Soviet totalitarianism under Stalin and its post-Stalinist fate; for it is the form given to the single-party state in the final years of Lenin's rule and the early period of Stalin's that has become effective as an international model and that is still regarded as "classic" in the Soviet Union today. What concerns us here is the degree of success obtained by the Bolsheviks by means of those institutions in achieving their objectives, the impression made by that success in different regions of the world, and the reasons both for the domestic success and for the spread of the model.

To begin with a negative statement: the Bolsheviks clearly did *not* succeed in achieving the goals that had originally inspired their revolutionary dictatorship—in establishing the social power of the proletariat or in approaching an egalitarian society. Both ideological goals were, of course, strictly incompatible with the immediate task of state-directed primitive accumulation, which required massive material sacrifices on the part of all productive classes, including the industrial working class; and the ruling party, being potentially independent of its original proletarian basis by its centralistic structure, used its dictatorial power to impose these sacrifices on workers and peasants alike, and to identify itself in outlook and composition increasingly with the "new class" of bureaucrats and technicians who were both indispensable for the process of state-directed industrialization and few in numbers, and therefore had to be privileged.

But the Bolsheviks *did* succeed in achieving the goals that had inspired their transformation of the original revolutionary dictatorship into a totalitarian single-party state: in maintaining their own dictatorial power, far beyond the revolutionary crisis that had enabled them to seize it, by turning it into an engine for the state-directed modernization of their country, and in changing the direction of Russian social development to a considerable extent from the course it would otherwise have taken. Their experience showed that even the most powerful state could not force society to conform to aims that were inherently utopian; but it also proved that a new type of state specifically geared to the purpose of directing social development could alter the "natural" course of that development far more effectively than had previously been believed possible.

Ever since, in the eighteenth century, the first Western thinkers began to conceive of the economy as a self-regulating mechanism, and of the development of society as following immanent historical laws, modern thought about the relation between state and society had been dominated by the concept of the limits of political force. However much Liberals and Marxists might later disagree about the *content* of the laws that controlled social life, they did agree that these laws were objectively given and could not be altered by political fiat; nor did either school show much awareness that their supposedly universal laws were in fact generalizations based on the experience of modern western societies alone. Conservative thinkers, too, while more wary of this type of generalization, tended to minimize the "manageable" element in society by their emphasis on the limits of legislation and on the necessary ineffectiveness of any attempt to interfere with the organic growth of a historical entity. To all of them, the Bolshevik experiment seemed foredoomed to failure—because it violated the canons of economic rationality, because it tried to leap ahead of the stage reached in Russian social development, or because it was contrary to the character and traditions of the Russian people.

Yet the Bolshevik regime, by following political investment priorities and by brutally forcing the mass of the people to bear the cost of its often grossly irrational economic methods, succeeded in building up the industrial apparatus of a modern great Power with remarkable speed—at the price of depressing the standard of living of the Russian people for decades. By deporting millions of "kulak" families to break peasant resistance, it succeeded in suppressing the inherent tendency of the individualist peasantry to competition and capitalist differentiation, and in shepherding the bulk of the rural population into state-controlled collectives—at the price of causing a catastrophic loss of livestock and condemning Russia's agriculture to abysmal stagnation for a quarter of a century. By exposing an entire generation to a combination of harsh bureaucratic pressures, based on the threat of dire penalties for trifling offenses against labor discipline or for failure to fulfil the delivery quotas, with intense educational remoulding through an all-embracing network of party-controlled organizations and publications, it succeeded in changing the "Russian character," the typical attitudes to work and leisure, to rationality and superstition, to family and state, far more quickly than the combination of Reformation, Counter-Reformation, and Enlightenment with the brutalities of early capitalism had brought about comparable changes in the West—at the price of creating a "reserve army" of state slaves in its labor camps and of drastically narrowing the mental horizon of the entire nation.

Moreover, the unprecedented concentration of political, economic, and ideological power by the totalitarian institutions (which caused Trotsky to write at the end of his life that Stalin could truly make the claim *"La Société c'est moi"*), did not only enable the ruling party to create a social structure of a completely new type, consisting of the four classes of the ruling and managing bureaucracy, the state workers, the collective peasants, and the labor slaves in the camps. It also enabled it to combine the prevention of any organized resistance to state-imposed sacrifices and party-directed mental remoulding with the active mobilization of the people to share in the society's transformation and their own. The party-controlled soviets, trade unions, and other mass organizations, long deprived of any independent role as organs of self-government or of the advocacy of group interests, proved effective organs for broadening mass participation in the administrative execution of decisions handed down from the top; the institutions of the Union Republics and the smaller national units, barred from attempting independent national policies or even from developing a true cultural autonomy at the risk of countermeasures ranging from wholesale purges of political and intellectual leaders to the verge of genocide, proved nevertheless effective in giving large numbers of members of these nationalities, including not a few who had been illiterate only yesterday, the chance to learn to help administer their own affairs in their own language—always in accordance with central directives. In the end, totalitarian oppression proved compatible with, if not conducive to the growth of a truly felt "Soviet patriotism," a genuine allegiance of the citizen to the state in whose greatness his blood, sweat, and tears had been invested by the rulers.

Last and not least, the party regime has succeeded in maintaining for half a century, in the face of several crises of leadershp succession, dramatic policy turns, murderous purges, and the supreme test of a world war, both its power over its subjects and its internal cohesion. No ancient or modern dictatorship of revolutionary origin can boast of a similar record. The Russian achievement has been all the more remarkable because, while the nature of the totalitarian single-party state requires a single leader with uncontested authority (so as to stop the inevitable disagreements within the inner circle from leading to the growth of organized factions), the nature of Communist ideology has prevented the Bolsheviks from admitting this need and seeking an institutional solution for the problem of succession. Yet on the other hand it is that same ideology, the common faith inspiring the cadres of the ruling party, that must be regarded as to an important degree responsible for the longevity of the regime—not only because it has helped again and again to maintain its *political* cohesion in the face of crises, power struggles, and tyrannical crimes that would have been intolerable to non-believers, but also because it has helped to maintain its *moral* cohesion in the face of the innumerable temptations of dictatorial rule. Soviet bureaucracy, including the party bureaucracy, has of course had its full share of the corruption inseparable from the exercise of arbitrary power, but a comparison with some other modern dictatorships will at once show the vital difference of degree: in fifty years of Bolshevik rule, corruption has never reached the point of endangering the cohesion of the system. For an ideology that has had to be adapted to such far-reaching changes of situation, policy, and generation as the Communist one, that, too, is a remarkable achievement.

The experience of the first totalitarian regime has thus shown that the impact of the political will, of modern state power wielded in the service of an ideological faith, on the development of society, can be far more profound than either liberal, Marxist, or conservative thinkers had believed possible before the 1920s. The "limits of political force" could be stretched far beyond the imagination of the nineteenth century by a revolutionary party in power—on three conditions. It must be inspired by an absolute, unquestioning belief in its idea and determined to act on it with the utmost ruthlessness. It must know how to utilize the new totalitarian engine, to combine the employment of a state machine freed from legal restrictions with a monopoly of political, organizational, and educational activity, in order to prevent the formation of independent social groups and to mobilize the people in its service. And it must know how to make hard choices when the necessities of maintaining power come into conflict with some aspects of its ideological beliefs, and yet preserve its ideological cohesion.

For the stretching of the limits of political force did *not* mean, as it might have appeared at first sight, that *anything* was now possible to a skilled and ruthless political manipulator. Limits still did exist, and they had repeatedly forced the Bolshevik leaders to change their policies and revise their ideology accordingly. As we have seen, it had proved inherently impossible to create in any real sense the dictatorship of the proletariat which they had set out to establish. It had proved impossible to combine the forced industrialization of Russia with an approach to egalitarianism, or the imposition of sacrifices on all classes with freedom of discussion and organization. The Bolsheviks survived in power because, under Lenin as under Stalin, whenever they were confronted with the dilemma of choice between the needs of forced modernization and the vision of Utopia, they gave preference to the former: they succeeded in extending the range of the possible because they did not persist in attempting what was really impossible.

It may be seen as a reflection of this feature of the Bolshevik achievement that the impact of the totalitarian institutional model on the working-class movement of the advanced industrial countries has on the whole been less durable and far-reaching in its consequences than has been the impact on the nationalist elites of non-western countries with major unsolved problems of development, and even the impact on the anti-democratic and anti-labor extremists of some western countries in the throes of major social crises. Communist ideology might well hold out the example of the October Revolution to Western proletarians in a temporary mood of acute despair and utopian expectation, but the very strength of such expectations tended to act as an obstacle to successful imitation of Leninist practice in periods of potentially revolutionary crisis; and as with the lapse of time the essence of Leninist-Stalinist totalitarianism as an engine of forced modernization of a special type became increasingly obvious to Communists and non-Communists alike, it also began to appear increasingly irrelevant to the needs of the working classes of advanced industrial societies. In the course of half a century, no Communist party beholden to the Bolshevik model has succeeded by its own strength in winning power in a western industrial country; and the only remaining western communist parties of importance, those of Italy and France, are by now so convinced of the hopelessness of the attempt that in recent years they have issued programmatic statements to the effect that they no longer regard the model as applicable in advanced western countries with democratic traditions.

By contrast, some non-Western nationalist leaders have been far ahead of the Western Communists in recognizing the importance of Russian party dictatorship as an engine of state-directed social development, and in viewing this instrumental function as completely separable from the egalitarian and internationalist goals of the Communist ideology with which these institutions had been historically bound up in their Russian origin. It was nationalist leaders of this type who were to make the first attempts at a selective imitation of the Russian model of the single-party state.

THE NATIONALIST MODERNIZERS

Kemalist Turkey

Kemal Ataturk is generally considered the first national leader to have successfully practised such selective imitation of the Russian model—to have built up a single-party dictatorship without accepting the Communist ideology. As he proclaimed his intention to found the "People's Party" at the end of 1922, shortly after his decisive victory in a "war of national liberation" in which the Soviets had given him substantial support against the "imperialists," the assumption that he was consciously learning from the system of government of his erstwhile allies is indeed plausible, and there is ample evidence that the ideas and institutions of revolutionary Russia had been much discussed in revolutionary Turkey during the war years.[12] Yet in contrast to what was to happen shortly afterwards in the case of the Chinese Kuomintang (and also to a legend occasionally found in print),[13] there was no direct Russian advice to Kemal on the building of his state.

In fact, Kemal could build in part on the indigenous foundation of the Young Turk conspiracy, the Committee for Union and Progress, of which he had been a member, and of its later party rule, of which he had been an increasingly bitter critic. They had been the first to unite the modernizing elements of the officer and civil servant class with the most active part of the urban intelligentsia in a political organization around a programme of national salvation by constitutional modernization on the western model; and, finding that growing opposition in the country threatened their parliamentary rule, they had suppressed their critics step by step until, by 1914, they ended up with a single-party parliament. But the outcome had not then been a revolutionary party regime, but rather a wartime military dictatorship, and it collapsed as a result of military defeat in the First World War.

When Kemal Pasha decided in 1919 to engage his military prestige in starting a national resistance movement not for the recovery of the decayed Ottoman empire, but for the sovereignty of the Turks on their national territory proper, the Association for the Defense of Anatolia and Rumelia formed under his leadership was largely based on the same type of notables, and not infrequently on the same individuals, who had formed the backbone of Union and Progress in the provincial towns. But he made them forswear any attempt to revive that defunct party, explaining that they must have no programme narrower than the defense of the national territory; and it was only on the ground that the Sultan was in enemy hands and no longer a free agent that he brought the Association, and the Grand National Assembly based on it, to commit themselves in the srping of 1920 to the principle of popular sovereignty. To the end of the war, the Association saw itself not as a political party with a common ideology and discipline, but rather as the organ of a non-party provisional administration set up to deal with a national emergency—as the civilian arm of the army of resistance, whose members might hold widely different ideas on the future form of state and society.

Throughout this period, revolutionary Russia was important to Kemal chiefly as an example of successful struggle against the victorious Western "imperialists" and as a powerful potential ally against them. It was their common interest in eliminating the independent Caucasian states as a focus of western influence in the area that formed the basis of their early establishment of diplomatic relations in 1920 and of their treaty of friendship of March 1921; and it was arms supplies and international support rather than advice on his system of government that Kemal requested, and received, from the Bolsheviks during the remainder of his struggle for national survival.[14] Indeed, when the Russians did send a group of Turkish Communists along with their first diplomatic mission, the Kemalist authorities had them drowned in January 1921; and though a Turkish Communist Party was authorized in March 1922, during the period of closest Russo-Turkish military co-operation, it was suppressed again in October, immediately after the war had been won.[15] Conversely, Kemal's decision to move towards a single-party state of his own, though evidently inspired by the Russian model, was taken during the critical months of the Lausanne peace negotiations, at a time when relations with Russia had cooled considerably, and without any assistance from Soviet experts.

It had been victory in the war of liberation that, by ending the national emergency, had put the future of Turkey's system of government on the agenda. To many of Kemal's wartime associates, a return to traditional legitimacy by a compromise with the Sultan-Caliph seemed the obvious solution. But to Kemal, the national revolutionary and unbelieving rationalist, the wartime conduct of the Defender of the Faith had been the final proof that the Turkish nation could be renewed and modernized only by a radical break with the monarchy and indeed with Islamic traditionalism. Under the fresh impression of his military triumph, he forced the National Assembly to take the first step by voting the abolition of the Sultanate; and the initial resistance he encountered among the deputies convinced him of the need to transform the Defense Association into a disciplined political party, pledged to a programme of national modernization and unity under his leadership against all "traitors," and apt to become the instrument of the secularist revolution he intended. Now Kemal understood clearly that the only alternative to a traditionalist regime deriving its title from the will of God was a revolutionary regime deriving it from the will of the people; yet while wishing to mobilize the people for the struggle for modernization and for the democratic legitimation of the regime, he also feared that a pluralism of political parties and organized interests would be dangerous to national unity, or rather to the speedy achievement of his revolutionary goals. To a leader thus seeking to combine democratic legitimation with a refusal to permit freedom of organization, the Russian single-party state offered, by the turn of 1922–3, a ready-made prescription.

Thus Kemal toured the country in the early months of 1923, calling on the local committees of the Defense Association to transform themselves into units of the new party and to broaden their membership; in February he summoned an Economic Congress of traders, farmers, artisans, and workers, and used it to appeal for the concentration of all efforts on the economic development of the country and to give warning against a class war which Turkey could not afford; he combined this campaign of mobilization with a series of repressive measures, tightening control of the press, banning public meetings, and even seeking to lift the Assembly members' immunity from arrest. When the Assembly, defending its rights and rebelling against Kemal's obvious attempt to prolong his dictatorial powers beyond the term of the wartime emergency, sent a deputation asking him to give up leadership of the new party because "the head of state must be above party," he replied openly that the People's Party he had founded must be the *only* party because of the continuing need for national unity, and that it was a point of honor for him to combine leadership of party and state.[16]

The new system, however, proved more difficult to create than Kemal had expected. Elections to the new

National Assembly took place in June, before the party was properly organized; the first party congress was held only in August, on the eve of the Assembly's first meeting; and though it adopted the principle of voting discipline on penalty of expulsion from the party, it could not assure uniformity in the new Assembly. When, at the end of October 1923, Kemal asked the Assembly formally to proclaim the republic and to adopt a presidential system of government making him independent of its confidence, the proposal was voted only by 158 out of 286 deputies—40 per cent of the elected representatives abstained.[17]

It was on this precarious basis that Kemal and his party, now named the Republican People's Party, began the new phase of the revolution, the struggle for the secularization of the country, with the abolition of the Caliphate and of the religious courts and schools in March–April 1924. Within a few months, the convergence of economic and religious sources of discontent proved so strong that Kemal found himself unable to prevent the formation of an opposition party, the Progressive Republican Party, led by the opponents of his personal power within the Assembly.[18] Attempts to intimidate the opposition by terrorist acts, including the murder of a deputy by the chief of Kemal's bodyguard, backfired so badly that Kemal had to break up that formation and to appoint a government of conciliation before the end of the year; a motion drastically to reduce the presidential powers was only narrowly defeated in the Assembly. Only the outbreak of a major rising of the Kurdish minority, led by religious fanatics, in February 1925, enabled Kemal to rally the bulk of the nation against all "traitors," to get dictatorial emergency powers voted by the Assembly, and to use them for dissolving the opposition party, setting up emergency tribunals, and closing down the religious orders. Even so, resistance among the leaders of his own party still prevented him from impeaching the leading opposition deputies, some of whom had been among his

closest comrades-in-arms during the national war. It took
the discovery of a murder plot against him in June 1926 to
give him a chance for show trials in which these former
military leaders were discredited and driven from public life,
while a number of other opposition leaders were hanged.

By 1927, the single-party dictatorship was at last complete. The new National Assembly elected in that year
consisted exclusively of members of the Republican People's Party bound by strict discipline, and it extended the
dictatorial powers for another two years. A party congress
to which Kemal gave a triumphant account of his road to
power in the famous "six-day-speech"[19] elected him leader
for life; it also resolved that all public appointments in the
political, economic, social, and cultural fields, down to the
village headmen, should henceforth be subject to the approval of party inspectors.

In step with this decisive political breakthrough, the
secularist revolution made further major strides. The famous
campaign to abolish the fez was forced through under extreme pressure. The western calendar and clocktime were
introduced. Most important, the introduction of the Swiss
civil code in 1926 finally replaced the religious laws on
matters of marriage and divorce, and by legally ending
polygamy and repudiation laid the foundation for the
emancipation of women. By 1928, the constitution had
been amended to remove the last references to Turkey as an
Islamic State. Parallel with these measures, an educational
movement to develop the Turkish national consciousness,
going back in part to pre-war efforts, had since 1924 been
encouraged to found "People's Houses" in the provincial
centers and had held a first national congress in 1927. In
1928, a further major step both to cut the links with Islamic
tradition and to increase literacy was taken with Kemal's
introduction of the Latin alphabet for the Turkish language,
based in part on the alphabet that had been introduced a

few years before for the Turkic-speaking peoples of the Soviet Union.

By the beginning of 1929, the legislative programme for the secularization of Turkey had been more or less completed; and it now became apparent that the ideology of nationalism and modernization, as so far developed by Kemal and the Republican People's Party, comprised no further revolutionary task. In the circumstances, continuation of the party dictatorship no longer appeared justified to Kemal himself: by March, the emergency powers were allowed to run out, and after some preparation an old friend of Kemal's was encouraged in 1930 to start a Republican Liberal Party as a loyal opposition. Yet the popular response showed quickly that a few years of forced enlightenment might transform the political, legal, and educational system, but could not break the hold of religious traditions on a large part of the people; and in a situation when the world economic crisis led to a drastic fall in Turkish export yields and forced a corresponding tightening of imports, economic misery easily combined with religious opposition to form a powerful counter-revolutionary potential. Toleration of criticism thus quickly led to riots and risings, and within a few months the emergency powers had to be restored and the loyal opposition dissolved itself.

The experience convinced Kemal that, compared to the legislative and bureaucratic aspects of modernization, both the economic and the educational had been neglected, and that in both respects he could still learn from the model of Russia, just then in the throes of its first five-year plan. By 1931, the slogan of "etatism," defined as the responsibility of the state for speedy economic development as a vital interest of the nation, was listed among the basic principles of the Kemalist movement;[20] and the practice of the following years made it clear that while Kemal continued to reject the Communist programme of wholesale nationalization

and particularly of agricultural collectivization, he had resolved to go beyond the piecemeal mercantilist measures of
the early period and to try to supplement the insufficient
private initiative of the Turkish middle class by planned
state investment in the creation of new industries. A first
Turkish five-year plan came into force in 1934, and a Russian loan contributed to it.

During the same period, the party was reorganized to
broaden its social composition and adapt it more effectively
to tasks of mass education as distinct from pure administration. The People's Houses were taken over by the party in
1931; recruitment among the lower classes was pushed more
actively leading to the election of some ninety members
listed as workers, artisans, and shopkeepers to the new
National Assembly in the same year; and special women's
and youth organizations of the party were developed. On
the other hand, the party made no attempt to form workers' or peasants' organizations under its control, while
tolerating no autonomous trade unions up to 1947.

In this way, the Kemalist regime continued as a dictatorship of economic development by "etatist" methods and of
nationalist and secularist education until the death of its
founder in 1938, and under his successor Ismet Inönü to the
end of the Second World War. The party's monopoly of
political activity and its monopolistic control of social organizations were maintained for more than twenty years, and
they accomplished profound changes in the country's economic and social structure, its legal system and its educational level. But, to the end, Kemalism remained different
from the totalitarian model of Bolshevik Russia not only
in its concrete political goals, but also in its institutional
means.

First of all, being exclusively concerned with a task limited
in time and space—the establishment of a modern society on
the national territory—it did not have to work out an all-

embracing ideological system and did not need a monopoly of information to enforce conformity: the political censorship it imposed remained compatible with some freedom of discussion in the intellectual sphere. Second, the party sought to combine administrative with educational tasks, but never struck strong roots in the villages and succeeded only to a limited or even marginal extent in activating the lower social strata; the official classes and intellectuals continued to form its backbone throughout, and their relation to the masses always remained somewhat paternalist—a factor which limited the depth of the party's impact on the countryside.[21] Finally, in contrast to all true totalitarians, the Kemalists never idealized their single-party rule as the only true democracy, but insisted on its provisional and educational—or with the term first used by Dr. Sun Yat-sen, its *tutelary* character; and this enabled (and to some extent compelled) them eventually to repeat the attempt to end the monopoly and admit opposition parties in 1946, and this time to go through with it to the free elections of 1950 which ended their rule.

Even so, the renunciation of single-party rule was not, of course, achieved without concrete pressures from without as well as from within. The victory of the Anti-Hitler alliance in a war in which Turkey had preserved its neutrality almost to the end, and the subsequent need to rely on Western backing against Soviet territorial and military demands, made the one-party system appear anachronistic in international terms on the morrow of its wartime achievement in preserving national independence. At the same time, the very success of state-directed industrial development had led to the rise of a new class of industrial and commercial entrepreneurs opposed to the bureaucratic controls of Kemalist "etatism," while the core of the ruling party around President Inönü, based on army, bureaucracy, and intellectuals, was unwilling to abandon those controls and socially moving to the left with the adoption of a land reform law. As the opposition "Democratic Party" was permitted, it thus started with a program of free enterprise and rejection of the land reform, but as the campaign unfolded it came increasingly to appeal also to the religious traditionalism of the small town populations and the village elders. It was the combination of this appeal with the promise of cheaper imports for the countryside that gave it victory in 1950 and also in subsequent elections.

The result has been a rather faster development in some sectors of the economy, combined with an increase in social tension and a partial reversal of the achievements of the Kemalist "cultural revolution." It is this marked unevenness in the process of modernization that has since led to repeated crises of the new pluralist democracy and to relapses into military rule. The degree to which Kemal's and Inönü's "Republican People's Party" has achieved the goal of its "dictatorship of development" may thus be disputed in the light of later events. It appears nevertheless impressive in comparison with other Middle Eastern Islamic nations that started on a similar level. But their most remarkable contribution to the history of systems of government consists in the proof that a single-party dictatorship may voluntarily surrender its monopoly of power—provided that it has founded its legitimation not on worldwide, utopian goals, but on a task that is by definition limited in space and time.

Kuomintang China

While Kemal Ataturk founded his monopolistic party in order to transform the military power he held as a wartime national leader into a peacetime revolutionary dictatorship, Dr. Sun Yat-sen had to go the opposite way: he had to transform the organization structure of his long-established, revolutionary party, the Kuomintang, in order to enable it to gain at last a military power base under its secure control. Having repeatedly failed, despite his immense prestige as a patriotic leader, to build up a stable governmental structure by his own devices, Dr. Sun thus needed not only Soviet diplomatic and military support against the "imperialists" and the Chinese warlords linked with them, but Soviet advice on the problem of revolutionary political and military organization. Yet in seeking to learn from the Russian model of the single-party state, he wished to reject the Communist goals and the doctrine of the international class struggle, and to replace them with his own programme of national sovereignty and modernization; and it was in part the example of Kemal that convinced him that such selective imitation was possible.[22] The Soviets in turn, who had accepted a Kemal *in* power as a valuable ally even if he suppressed the communists, were able to use their support of the Kuomintang's struggle *for* power to press for a legal role for the Communists in its regime—with the result that this regime carried from birth the contradiction between a single-party concept and a two-party reality.

Dr. Sun Yat-sen had first become known as the leader of the nation-wide conspiratorial movement against the Manchu dynasty, whose programme of national sovereignty, republican constitution, and agrarian reform he had propagated from his Tokyo exile, and had become the first president of the Chinese republic after the monarchy was overthrown. But the legal National People's Party (Kuomintang) which he founded after resigning his office to Marshal Yuan Shih-kai had quickly eluded his control as many of its office-seeking representatives made their individual compromises with the military power, and Sun withdrew into exile and renewed revolutionary plotting in 1913. Returning to Canton in 1916 after Yuan's death, he became by September 1917 head of a counter-government opposed to Peking's entry into the war; but when his military "subordinates" settled their differences with Peking in May 1918 they abandoned him and a third term of exile began. It was on 10 October 1919, the eighth anniversary of the overthrow of the monarchy, that he refounded the Kuomintang in Shanghai, in the midst of the ferment of national protest against China's impotence and her humiliation by the imperialists that had been aroused by the decision of the Versailles Powers to hand the former German protectorates in China to Japan. In the following years, both before and after his acceptance of the invitation of the general in control in Canton to assume the presidency of the regional government there, he began to develop his political ideas into a system, to look for the lessons of his political disappointments, and in particular to take a growing interest in the Russian Bolshevik Revolution, the apparent kinship between its anti-imperialist spirit and his own, and the reaons for its success.

Dr. Sun's famous "three people's principles"—national sovereignty, popular power, and people's welfare—had been sketched out by him before, but were now elaborated in the light of recent Chinese and international experience. He came to see the struggle for China's national unity and for the abolition of the unequal treaties as part of a common anti-imperialist struggle of the exploited nations. The programme of a democratic constitution with an elaborate division of powers was now interpreted as a final stage, the realization of which must be preceded first by the military unification of China and then by a limited "tutelary" period of educational dictatorship by the revolutionary party. The plan for raising the people's welfare by a policy of modernization and social justice, on the other hand, was given greater precision in conscious contrast to the Marxist idea of class struggle and to Communist policies of wholesale nationalization: state ownership of natural resources, banks, and transport, and state investments for development were to be combined with a moderate agrarian reform by taxation, rent control, and promotion of co-operatives, and with a general redistributive social policy designed to promote class harmony in a framework of predominantly private property.

Dr. Sun's contacts with the Soviets clearly influenced the elaboration of his doctrine both positively and negatively. A first letter from Chicherin, the Soviet Commissar for Foreign Affairs, suggesting friendship, trade relations, and anti-imperialist co-operation, reached Dr. Sun in June 1921 when he was president of the Canton government; and his reply, dated August, contained an urgent request for detailed information on the organization of the Soviets, the Red Army, and particularly on Soviet methods of political education: "Like Moscow, I should like to anchor the foundations of the Chinese revolution in the young generation, the workers of tomorrow." He was to receive some of the information he desired in two conversations later that year with the Dutch Communist Sneevliet, then one of the Comintern's leading experts on Asian revolutionary movements under the party name of Maring; and Maring was the first to urge Dr. Sun to transform the Kuomintang into a disciplined mass party and to set up a military academy for the technical and political education of a new type of officer in order to create a politically reliable armed force. Before Dr. Sun could act on this advice, its soundness was borne out: the revolutionary ideologue was once more toppled from nominal power by one of the formally subordinate generals on whose support he had hitherto always depended. The Canton commander who had made him "president," embarrassed by Dr. Sun's plans for a military expedition to unify China, overthrew him in June 1922.

It was when he arrived in Shanghai in mid-August, once more a powerless fugitive but still the nationally famous leader of a party of some 150,000 members, that another Comintern official offered him a united-front pact with the tiny Chinese Communist Party, which had just agreed at its second congress to co-operate with the "bourgeois nationalists" of the Kuomintang on a basis of mutual independence, as suggested in Lenin's theses of 1920. This Dr. Sun rejected: if the Communists wanted to support the national revolution, they were welcome to enter his party. Now Maring once again took a hand and persuaded the Chinese Communist leaders to try the policy which came to be known as the "bloc within"—joining the Kuomintang as individuals without concealing their continued membership in a separate Communist Party. By the end of the month, one of the Communist founders, Li Ta-chao, made a test application and was accepted. Other leaders followed, and the new policy was officially confirmed by the fourth congress of the Communist International in November 1922, and by the third congress of the CPC in June 1923.

Meanwhile Dr. Sun made a first attempt to reform the Kuomintang in the sense suggested by Maring—that of the Bolshevik model of a disciplined, centralistic party with links to a net-work of "mass organizations." A committee in whose work the Communist Party secretary Chen Tu-hsiu took part published a new statute for the Kuomintang on 1 January 1923; yet in the absence of an effective party machine operating from a secure power base it hardly reached the membership. But the conditions for a real transformation improved decisively when later in January a visit to Dr. Sun by a representative of the Soviet government, A. A. Yoffe, led to a formal pledge of Soviet political support for the Kuomintang and to an informal promise to send advisers, and when just at that time the general who had expelled Dr. Sun from Canton was overthrown by other generals who recalled the exile and asked him to form a "national government" in their city. By July, a Kuomintang delegation headed by Chiang Kai-shek, Dr. Sun's personal chief of staff, left Canton for Moscow, where it was to study Soviet military and political institutions; and in early October, a group of forty Soviet advisers arrived in Canton to help Dr. Sun to reorganize his party and to establish a military academy. It was headed by Mikhail Borodin, who had previously worked for the Comintern but was now accredited by deputy foreign commissar Lev Karakhan as representing the Soviet government, and it included the Soviet general Blucher (Galen).

The first effect of Borodin's advice was Dr. Sun's decision to call the first party congress ever held by the KMT, and to charge a provisional executive committee of nine, including one Chinese Communist, with drafting a new party programme and statute for submission to it. Borodin took a prominent part in its deliberations; and after the outlines of the reorganization plan had been published in mid-December, he was officially appointed "adviser to the KMT." The congress, composed of 113 appointed and 83 elected delegates, met on 20 January 1924 in an atmosphere of friendship and admiration for Soviet Russia. It adopted a manifesto which criticized the party's past failures as due to insufficient "links with the masses" and called on the Chinese workers and peasants to join its ranks; it combined a programme of national unification and democratic and social reform with a clear warning that a democratic constitution could come into force only after the complete victory of the revolution, and that while it was in progress its opponents would not enjoy democratic rights. The new party statute closely followed the model of Bolshevik "democratic centralism." New entrants were to be sponsored by two party members and to pledge themselves to disciplined execution of party policy; local, district, and provincial units were each to elect an executive committee and a control commission, while the national congress, to meet annually, was to decide policy, to elect a Central Executive Committee (CEC) and a Central Control Commission; the CEC in turn had power to give binding instructions to all regional and local units and to fix the method of delegation to the congress; it was also to set up central departments for dealing with various types of activity, including organization, propaganda, mass organizations, and military affairs. There was one major deviation from the model, however: Dr. Sun was made lifetime leader of the party by statute, with the right to preside over both the congress and the CEC, to veto any decisions of the latter, and to demand obedience from all members—a role familiar from Bolshevik practice but never admitted by Communist theory.

The Chinese Communists played an important part in making the "new model Kuomintang" work. With only 300 members at the time, compared to the KMT's 170,000, they not only gained substantial representation in the Central Executive Committee; despite the misgivings uttered by some old KMT leaders before, during, and after the congress, the communists succeeded with Dr. Sun's help in occupying positions of great importance for the transformation of the party organization and its link-up with a network of 'mass organizations'—notably in the central departments dealing with personnel appointments, with the peasant movement, and to a lesser extent with the trade unions. As the national revolutionary movement expanded in the following years, the control of those key positions greatly helped the Chinese Communists to turn the "mass organizations" into their strongholds.

Meanwhile the creation of another vital element of KMT power, the "party army," began with the new military academy which opened in June 1924 under Chiang Kai-shek's direction, combining military and political training for enthusiastic volunteers from all over China. Here Russian military experts introduced the Russian model of organization, including the dualism of commanders and political commissars; Russian funds had to finance an institution which the local generals regarded with understandable suspicion; and Russian arms arrived at a crucial moment to permit the newly trained cadres to form the first units under their command. But the Chinese commanders, political commissars, and teachers at the academy were in the main non-Communist, and the CPC never succeeded in gaining a major share in the new army's control. It was in October, in a clash with a "Volunteer Corps" armed by Canton merchants, that Chiang Kai-shek's cadets first made use of their training and their Russian arms to put a reliable force at the disposal of Dr. Sun, securing for him undivided control of the city; and in February 1925 they defeated for the first time the mercenaries of a provincial general and brought much of Kwantung province under the rule of the KMT. After Dr. Sun's death in March, during a visit to Peking, some other generals rebelled in June and the performance had to be repeated—no longer in the name of the leader, but of the primacy of his movement. Chiang's renewed victory proved beyond doubt that the "new model army" had at last established a solid basis for the power of the "new model party."

Dr. Sun had undertaken his last journey in a vain attempt to persuade a new ruling group in Peking to join him in summoning a broadly representative 'national convention' for the peaceful unification of the country; when it failed he reaffirmed his revolutionary concept in a "political testament" and in a message to the Soviet authorities which he signed on his deathbed. The CEC of his party reacted to his death by two major changes. It decided not to invest any of the survivors with the powers of lifetime leader, but merely to elect a technical chairman of the collective leadership in the person of Wang Ching-wei; and it proceeded to replace Dr. Sun's personal rule by the creation of a formal government designed to administer the territory under the party's control and to claim authority over the whole national territory in its name. The ministries of defense, foreign affairs, and finance, which formed the nucleus of the new state apparatus, were staffed with KMT members and remained responsible to the party as the only organ of popular representation.

In May and June 1925, a series of clashes between striking Chinese workers and Japanese and British police in Shanghai and Canton led to a nationwide mass movement of strikes, demonstrations, and boycotts directed against the unequal treaties, in which the KMT successfully took the lead. This breakthrough to the masses, and the part played in it by anti-imperialist slogans and Communist organization techniques among the workers, helped to strengthen the influence of the left-wing revolutionary nationalists in the Canton leadership and to increase the misgivings of the more conservative leaders, many of whom left Canton for Shanghai or Peking during the winter of 1925–6 and even attempted to set up their own rival "KMT" in the North. Chiang Kai-shek, riding with the left wave, used it to achieve the unification of all the Canton government's armed forces into a "National Revolutionary Army" under his command; by the time of the second KMT congress in January 1926, this army controlled the whole of Kwantung province.

The congress was marked by enthusiasm for the Soviet alliance and anti-imperialist world revolution, as well as by the emphasis put on winning the active support of the workers and peasants, and it led to a further strengthening of Communist positions in the central party machine. By this time, moreover, some of the Soviet military advisers had assumed positions of direct command, while the Chinese Communists controlled the armed workers' militia created to enforce the anti-British boycott and had begun to gain positions as political commissars at least in some army units. This led to the first crisis of the alliance when Chiang, soon after the congress, began to prepare for a military expedition to conquer Central China which the Soviet advisers regarded as premature. Taking advantage of Borodin's temporary absence, Chiang suddenly moved on 20 March 1926 to arrest the Communist political commissars and disarm the workers' militia, keeping the Soviet officers under house arrest during the coup; he subsequently assured Borodin on his return of his continued loyalty to the Soviet alliance, but asked and obtained the recall of the "interfering" Soviet officers. The simultaneous departure of his civilian colleague Wang Ching-wei for a health cure in Europe left Chiang in sole control of army, party, and government, and he used it to remove Communists from key positions and to demand from them pledges to refrain from any criticism of Dr. Sun's ideas and to submit all their party instructions to a mixed committee.

The Northern expedition, begun in July, soon yielded major victories, and by October Wuhan on the middle Yangtse had been taken. Yet while success increased Chiang's military power and prestige, it also led to the incorporation of entire non-political army units under unregenerate local warlords into the Revolutionary Army, when their commanders came over for opportunist reasons; at the same time, Communist-controlled peasant leagues and trade unions that had helped to disorganize the enemy rear acquired growing influence. Soon Wuhan, where the government had been transferred on Chiang's own prompting, became the center of a coalition of communist and ex-warlord forces led by famous names of the KMT Left and directed against Chiang's dominant position in the name of the primacy of civilian party power. In March 1927, when Chiang was on the point of taking Shanghai and Nanking, a CEC plenum held in his absence in Wuhan asked for and obtained his resignation from the leadership of the central party organs and for the first time entrusted two Communists with ministries, those of agriculture and labor.

By this time, however, Chiang Kai-shek had made up his mind to shake off all dependence on the Soviets, to break with the Communists, and to use the leverage which control of Shanghai, China's economic center, would give him for achieving recognition by the other Great Powers. Hardly had a Communist workers' rising delivered the city into his hands when Chiang proclaimed a local state of siege, imposed a ban on unauthorized arms-carrying, and encouraged the formation of an anti-Communist "movement for the protection of the party and the salvation of the nation" throughout the region controlled by forces loyal to him; and on 12 April 1927, he began to disarm, dissolve, and massacre the organizations of the Communist Party and the Communist-controlled trade unions from Shanghai right down to Canton. He followed this up by forming a counter-government to Wuhan at Nanking, in the name of a purified KMT which would embody the only true alternative to either warlordism or foreign-inspired red terrorism, and by stating that co-operation with the Soviets was justified only so long as it could be conducted on the basis of equality and non-interference in Chinese internal affairs.

The Wuhan government, now led by the returned Wang and backed by a majority of the CEC including the Communists, had first reacted to Chiang's moves by "expelling" the members of the Nanking counter-government from the party. But the conflict with the Communists, which both they and Wang wanted to avoid, was forced on Wuhan as forcible land seizures by the peasant leagues and equally violent counter-actions by local military commanders and secret societies spread on its territory. When at last the Communists reluctantly moved, in agreement with the even more reluctant Stalin, to press for the adoption of a revolutionary land policy and the punishment of the commanders in question, Wang and his associates realized that they would have to break with the CPC unless they wanted to lose that part of the army on which they had so far relied. By the end of June, army units disarmed the workers' militia in Wuhan and the Communists withdrew from the government; by mid-July, they were expelled from the Kuomintang—and Borodin was sent home.

The Communists expected that Chiang's and Wang's "betrayal" would end the Kuomintang's role as bearer of the national revolution. The KMT leaders expected that the crushing of the Communists would open the road to a true nationalist single-party State. In fact, the élan of the movement for national unification was not broken, and the KMT gradually did succeed in unifying China in the following years; but the break with the Communists changed the structure and composition of the party once again as drastically as Soviet advice and Communist co-operation had changed it before.

Henceforth, the mass organizations became suspect objects of restrictive control, permitted to engage in little more than professional training, with the result that in many areas they dwindled into insignificance; local party branches were largely reduced to groups of notables from the landowning and official classes, while the party machine suffered from a persistent shortage of civilian full-time cadres which the creation of a central party school could mitigate but never overcome. As national unification came to appear rather as the result of military campaigns and military bargaining than of an ideological and social revolution, the role of the military within the leadership of party and government was bound to increase correspondingly—carrying with it the seeds of a new military regionalism *within* the Kuomintang regime. The bitter regional conflicts of the following years were different from the earlier warlordism in that all the rival commanders now had to base their claims on the common principle of party legitimacy; but this was possible because the political leaders themselves were so divided into rival factions and clans that party legitimacy could again and again be interpreted in a variety of ways. Centralist discipline remained the party's constitutional rule in theory, but in practice the unity of will, the authority of the single leader, and even the monopoly of legitimate force were achieved only gradually, with repeated setbacks, and incompletely. Under the cloak of single-party rule, regional and factional pluralism retained so much vitality that the one-party state of the KMT was never completely one-party, and perhaps never completely a state.

The immediate consequence of the break with the Communists was a compromise between Nanking and Wuhan, negotiated by the more conservative second-rank military and political figures on both sides with little regard either for their leaders or for party legitimacy. Chiang resigned all his offices to demonstrate that he would not stand in the way of unity, and Wang withdrew in protest with his left-wing followers when leadership was transferred to a "special committee" of all factions including right-wingers he had once helped to expel from the party. But this group proved unable either to cope with the unrest from below, fomented not only by ill-prepared local communist risings but also by Wang's demand for a new plenary session of the "legitimate" CEC elected by the 1926 party congress, or to provide effective leadership against the warlords who still dominated China north of the Yangtse. As the demand for Chiang's return as commander-in-chief grew, he made the resignation of the "special committee" and the recall of the CEC a condition of his acceptance and achieved both at the turn of 1927–28; but by then, the abortive communist rising of December 1927 in Canton, Wang's stronghold, had so much weakened the Left that the CEC session now confirmed not only all anti-Communist measures, but also the dissolution of the KMT's department for mass organizations, the cancellation of all earlier pro-Communist resolutions, and the readmission of those on the right who had earlier been expelled for their premature anti-communism.

It was thus an army commanded and a party and government dominated by Chiang that resumed the Northern expedition at the beginning of March 1928 to achieve national unity under Kuomintang rule; but it was also an army, party, and government that had been able to preserve their own unity only by granting considerable autonomy to the most important regional military leaders through the creation of "regional bureaus" of the Central Political Council. Full and final victory over the Northern warlords was achieved within three months; in early June, Chang Tso-lin withdrew to his Manchurian domain only to be assassinated there, and Kuomintang troops entered Peking. The military campaign for the unification of China was over, and by December the decision of Chang Hsue-liang, the son and heir of Chang Tso-lin, to join the Kuomintang and accept its rule in Manchuria, put the seal on its success.

Now the creation of effective political institutions—the "educational dictatorshp" conceived by Dr. Sun—and the recovery of external sovereignty by the revision of the unequal treaties became the principal tasks. Chiang did not envisage their solution as a continuation of the revolutionary process depending on the active participation of the people, but as a work of constructive reform legislation from above within China, and of patient diplomatic negotiations without; so he rejected all proposals from the Left for reviving the mass organizations and accepted the ideas of Hu Han-min, the most conservative among Dr. Sun's principal lieutenants, for the provisional organization of the State. Dr. Sun's plan for the creation of five parallel organs of the central government—the executive, legislative, judiciary, examining, and inspecting bodies—was to be carried out immediately; but when the new "Organization Statute of the Republic of China" was completed in October, it showed that the composition of all these organs was to be decided by a single Council of State, whose chairman would act both as chief of State and as commander-in-chief: thus the technical division of labour between the five organs would not in fact amount to a political division of power. Moreover, the "Principles of Educational Dictatorship" adopted at the same time made it clear that the theoretical sovereignty of the people was to be exercised for that entire period by the ruling party, represented between congresses by its CEC and entitled to give policy directives to the government: in fact it was the CEC that appointed the first Council of State, with Chiang as chairman.

The substitution of party dictatorship for popular sovereignty, characteristic for all single-party regimes but disguised in most of them, was thus openly admitted by Kuomintang China from the start—admitted, that is, as a temporary necessity pending the education of the people for democratic self-government. Yet the regime as now constituted showed little aptitude or inclination for promoting such education in practice. At the third congress of the KMT held in March 1929, 285 out of 399 "delegates" had been appointed, not elected; small wonder that the majority rejected the left-wing view that the needed social reforms could not be carried out by bureaucratic methods alone, without organized popular activity, and approved the principle of confining all "mass organizations," in the interests of social harmony and internal peace, to tasks of professional training. The new CEC consisted of a solid majority of followers of Chiang and Hu, with regional generals and politicians making up the minority.[23]

In fact, while the party dictatorship was overt, party centralism was still largely fictitious. Outside the territory occupied by Chiang's own "central army," agreements on the proportional demobilization of all regional armies after the end of the civil war were being ignored; so were central directives aimed at preventing arbitrary tax extortion by local authorities or at stopping landlords from passing on the tax burden to their peasants. It was at the same third congress that Chiang gave the first sign of his determination to come to grips with this new intra-party warlordism. On his demand, three generals from Kwangsi were expelled as "rebels" for having deposed a provincial governor who had dared to pass on taxes to the central government. When he had driven them from most of their territory within three months after the congress, Chiang openly proclaimed his intention to centralize the government: he now dissolved the regional bureaus of the Central Political Council which he had conceded on the eve of the decisive battle against the old warlords. It was the beginning of a new series of armed conflicts, but this time between Chiang and other generals belonging to the KMT and claiming to fight for its true principles.

Between May 1929 and January 1930, Chiang defeated five successive regional rebellions, all claiming to act in support of Wang Ching-wei's "left" faction and its demand for a new, genuinely elected party congress, but all in fact representing little more than the struggle of various regional commanders to maintain their independence. But as all the rebels used the slogans of the Left, Chiang came to treat all propaganda of the real Left, and indeed all public criticism, as if it were armed rebellion, and his increasingly harsh repression provoked increasingly bitter opposition among the intelligentsia. In the atmosphere thus created, Chiang's military rivals and civilian critics from both left and right finally coalesced in the spring of 1930 into a common front against what they regarded as his personal despotism. They formed a joint High Command in April, set up a rival party leadership under Wang in Peking in July, and finally a counter-government on 1 September. But Chiang had already defeated the Southern branch of the rebellion by mid-June; in October he triumphed over his most formidable opponent in the North, Feng Yu-hsiang, and in November the coalition dissolved.

By the end of 1930 Chiang was thus completely victorious and in effective control of almost all China; but he was also shrewd enough to realize that repression had passed the point of diminishing returns. The most articulate part of the nation, the intelligentsia, had for the first time begun to turn from a party that seemed increasingly identified with the rule of the army and the bureaucracy; during the summer of 1930, Wang had responded to that mood by calling for an end not only to Chiang's despotism, but to the "educational dictatorship" of the party, proposing instead the early election of a national convention with open competition between several parties. The consolidation of the communist "Soviet Areas" and partisan armies in spite of the repeated "annihilation campaigns" by Kuomintang troops, amounting to the revival of a danger that had seemed totally crushed in 1927, was another indication of the weakening popular basis of the regime. So Chiang decided to launch his own programme for carefully controlled liberalization—a limited political amnesty and the summoning of a national convention with broad non-party participation which was to draft a new provisional constitution. The next plenary session of the CEC, which crowned the victory of centralism and laid the foundation of financial reform by at last abolishing all internal customs, also approved the calling of the national convention; the electoral law, announced on 1 January 1931, was based on a kind of corporative franchise, with candidates to be chosen not only by the party, but by all legal professional bodies, including registered trade unions and peasant leagues as well as educational associations and universities. The amnesty, however, was crippled by the resistance of Hu Han-min, who successfully insisted on excluding from it not only Communists, but all "ringleaders of rebellion" so as to prevent a possible reconciliation between Chiang and Wang. By the time Chiang broke with Hu and forced his resignation by putting him under house arrest, the chance of a genuine relaxation had passed; the basis of the regime had, in fact, further narrowed.

Even so, some 40–50 million voters are said to have participated in the elections of March–April 1931; moreover, these elections, though obviously managed to a high degree, did not take place on a single-list system, and the deputies elected included known critics of Chiang. In its one and only session, held on twelve days in May, the convention passed a new "Basic Law for the Period of the Educational Dictatorship" which set out the stages for the gradual building of local and regional self-government from below, with the introduction of full constitutional democracy as the final stage. In the meantime, the party dictatorship was to continue in the form of a presidential regime.

By the time this law was passed in Nanking, a new coalition of Chiang's political opponents, backed by a group of Southern generals, was once more forming in Canton; at the end of May, they proclaimed a counter-government headed by Wang. But this time, the country's disgust with civil wars had become so strong that each side hesitated to march against the other; instead, they began to compete with promises for a new party congress and protestations of their desire for a true national reconciliation. After the Japanese occupation of Manchuria which started with the "Mukden incident" in September 1931, the pressure for compromise became overwhelming. In October, negotiators from both sides agreed to hold separate congresses in their respective territories, to form a new party executive in agreed proportions, and to reorganize the government on a more collective basis. The Nanking congress promptly ratified these terms; in Canton, some of Chiang's military enemies at first resisted, and agreed only on condition of his resignation, which took place in December. But once the new executive was formed at the turn of the year, Wang and his followers began to side with Chiang's men against their former regionalist allies. A personal reconciliation between the two leaders followed quickly under pressure of the double threat from Japan and from the popular clamor for a war for which both knew China to be unprepared; by March 1932, a true division of power was established between them, with Wang as Prime Minister and

Chiang as chief of staff and chairman of the Military Committee. In this form, the party regime was to last without major crisis until the eve of open war with Japan.

It would be wrong to conclude from the foregoing that during its early years, the Kuomintang regime had produced nothing but victory over regional rebellions and some constitutional fictions of doubtful practical importance. On the contrary, in the midst of all its political troubles, the government found the time and energy to frame a number of modern legal codes and make them effective at least in the major urban centers of the south and east; to reform the tax system and abolish the internal customs; to unify and improve the standards for higher education; and to recover control over the external customs and reduce greatly the extra-territorial and extra-jurisdictional privileges enjoyed by the imperialist Powers (with the exception of Japan). But general economic progress was hamstrung both by the lack of internal peace and by the shortage of funds; and major changes in the social structure were excluded by a regime which lacked an administrative machinery distinct from the economically privileged groups, and was afraid to mobilize the masses. This applied above all to the crucial issue of land reform: a moderate but useful reform law was passed early, but its execution was delayed pending an 'implementing law' that was held up until 1935; moreover, the land of all holders of public office and all serving officers was exempt in principle.

With all this, the party members, bureaucrats, and officers—and the latter two groups now made up a vital part of the party membership—could still feel that they were truly serving the rebuilding of the nation. The Japanese occupation of Manchuria marked a turning point by cruelly showing up the national impotence of the regime; it thus came into conflict not only with the social aspirations of the masses, but with the nationalist emotions of the very elites on which it most wished to rely.

The establishment of the Chiang-Wang duumvirate had been welcomed as promising a change in the character of the regime which would leave greater scope for public discussion and criticism. In fact, while Communist activity continued to be mercilessly suppressed as far as the power of the government reached, non-revolutionary opposition groups and even "parties" were henceforth permitted, in an effort to restore the dialogue between the regime and the intelligentsia. Beginning in 1932, a number of them quickly developed among the professors and students of Peking, Tientsin, and Shanghai—the same groups that had started the nationalist movement of the 4th May 1919, and with largely similar anti-Japanese, liberal, and modernizing slogans. But now their nationalism led them to attack the Kuomintang government for failing to offer effective resistance to Japan.

Prima facie, the charge was justified. Chiang Kai-shek and Wang Ching-wei had been driven together not only by the common threat of Japanese invasion, but by their common conviction that China lacked as yet the strength for a war against the only Great Power in East Asia. As their appeals to the League of Nations proved the unwillingness of the western Powers to restrain Japan, while the Soviets were prepared to encourage Chinese resistance by the resumption of diplomatic relations but not to offer substantial support, the Kuomintang adopted a policy of yielding to Japan under protest and looking for some accommodation with the moderate elements in the Japanese government: it refused to recognize the Japanese puppet State of Manchukuo, it even authorized armed resistance when the Japanese attacked in Shanghai, but it preferred to react to each local defeat by concluding a military armistice rather than by a war that might spell the collapse of all it had achieved so far. In the opinion of Chiang and Wang, the paramount need was to delay all-out conflict while building up Chinese strength and consolidating national unity—and this included the destruction of the "Soviet Areas": it was necessary to defeat the communists before a serious confrontation with Japan.

But this was not the kind of argument to convince Chinese nationalist intellectuals or even many of the younger officers. When the government called a "National Emergency Conference" in April 1932 to discuss its response to Japanese aggression with its intellectual critics, a number of the latter refused to attend, some representatives of the Shanghai bourgeoisie among them. New nationalist opposition groups mushroomed, and though their membership remained small, their influence among the students and through them on public opinion kept growing. Moreover, their anti-Japanese demands were given constant public backing by the Canton regional government under Hu Hanmin.

It was an even more serious warning sign when in the autumn of 1933 the 19th Army, nationally famous for its resistance to the Japanese in Shanghai and now stationed in Fukien province, rose against the Kuomintang and called on the left-wing nationalist leaders of the socalled "Third Party" to form a counter-government around a programme of resistance to Japan, political democracy, and radical social reform, offering military co-operation to the communist partisan armies. Despite a preliminary agreement, the communists never implemented that co-operation, and the revolt was crushed within two months; but it had demonstrated how dangerous a weapon anti-Japanese nationalism, once abandoned by the regime, could become in the hands of its opponents.

Nevertheless, Chiang and Wang were not to be shaken in their determination to crush the "internal enemy" first. In the cities, the three parallel political police oranizations of the regime—one of them, the dreaded "blueshirts," directly dependent on the headquarters of the KMT—were remarkably successful in hunting down communists. In the countryside, where several campaigns against the "Soviet Areas" had failed, the government revived in 1932 the system of universal registration, under which groups of families were held responsible for mutually checking on each other's loyalty—a system first used by General Tseng Kuo-fan in fighting the Taiping rebellion in the nineteenth century.

But Chiang and his immediate circle were well aware that the regime could not in the long run maintain its cohesion and destroy the communist partisan forces by repression alone—without an ideology which would give a moral backbone to its officials, a sense of mission to its officers, and hope for progress to the peasants in the contested areas. It was this search for an ideology that brought a number of the younger generals trained by Chiang to form the "Rebirth Group," and it was one of them who started in 1933 the first "special force" of volunteer officers for fighting the communist partisans by political as well as military means: they were to ensure the pacification of reconquered areas by combining refugee relief, educational and health work, and control of the army's conduct towards the population, with their police and intelligence duties. The special forces thus felt themselves to be a true political and moral elite of the army, and they scored considerable initial successes.

The young generals of the Rebirth Group, being Nationalists engaged in fighting communism, were inclined to take inspiration from the Japanese militarists and from the victory of national-socialism in Germany. But Chiang, while impressed with what appeared to him as the spirit of community and national sacrifice displayed by the fascist states, finally decided against adopting a variant of their ideology. One reason for this was that the Rebirth Group recommended the fascist model chiefly on account of its 'leadership principle', appealing to him to abolish the committee system in party and government in favor of open one-man-rule for life, as once established by Dr. Sun Yat-sen. But during the years in question—1934–36—Chiang was more convinced than ever of the need to maintain unity with the important regional leaders by negotiation and compromise, and he regarded committee leadership in party and government as a tried and proven method for achieving this purpose in Chinese conditions—all the more so as his prestige assured his ascendancy in any committee.

Another, more fundamental objection was probably that an ideology of the fascist type required the open exaltation of militant nationalism, and that was incompatible with the tactical flexibility Chiang's diplomacy required at the time: an anti-Japanese nationalism would have prevented a continuation of his efforts to secure a modus vivendi with the aggressor and precipitated war, while an unconditional commitment to pro-Japanese nationalism would not only have been extremely unpopular, but would have disarmed the Kuomintang on the eve of its most serious attempt to reach a settlement with Tokyo. In fact, during the second half of 1934, parallel with Chiang's final offensive against the Kiangsi Soviet area, the KMT leaders hinted to Japan that they were willing to support her in any future conflict with the West or with Russia, if only Japan would respect China's territorial integrity and treat her on a basis of equality. The negotiations resulting from this offer dragged on far into 1935, leading as a by-product to government measures against the anti-Japanese movement, until the determination of the Japanese military leaders to create a series of protectorates on Chinese soil finally ended this prospect.

Whatever the reasons, the fascist type of ideology was finally rejected by Chiang in favor of a neo-Confucian revival that was more comparable to the ideas of the Moslem Brotherhood, or even to an Asian version of Moral Rearmament: an effort to ensure the devotion of officials and officers to a programme of national discipline and orderly reform from above not by a commitment to any sort of revolutionary nationalism, either Kemalist or fascist, but by a moral regeneration based on a new interpretation of the values of the Chinese tradition. This was the essence of the "New Life" movement launched by Chiang in the spring of 1934. Its origin was linked closely with the largest, and ultimately successful, military campaign against the principal Soviet area in Kiangsi: it was the "special forces" that were charged with training students from all over the country to become "leaders towards rebirth." As their basic text they were given a pamphlet written by Chiang himself, which outlined the qualities needed by the elite that was to regenerate China—honesty and social justice, respect for authority, discipline and self-discipline, cleanliness and dedicated activism—and derived them from the classical Confucian virtues. By July 1934, the movement had become organized on a nationwide basis with Chiang as leader, and the official cult of Kung-tse was reintroduced during the same year. Campaigns to clean the houses and the cities and to fight the sale and consumption of opium followed, the latter supported by anti-drug legislation specially directed towards curing officials and officers of the habit.

The adoption of this ideology set the seal on the Kuomintang's alienation from the modernizing intelligentsia. Despite its reformist elements, the movement was essentially conservative and quite incompatible with nationalism of the Kemalist type; it was thus less suited to a new-style party dictatorship aiming at the re-education of the people and their active participation in the reshaping of society than to an old-style authoritarian regime based on the bureaucracy and the Army. Yet this was what the rule of the Kuomintang, under the impact first of the conflict with the Communists and then of its inability to fight the Japanese invasion, had in fact largely become by the middle thirties. Of the 1.2 million members to which the ruling party had swollen by the time of its fifth Congress in 1935, some 700,000 were in the Army; of the remainder, it is safe to assume that about half were party and government officials, including state-employed teachers, and most of the other half urban and rural notables from the same families from which the bulk of the officers and civil servants were drawn. Far from controlling the army and the bureaucracy, the party no longer had a separate existence from them: it was now simply the meeting ground where the various military and bureaucratic cliques made their deals.[24]

It was characteristic of this transformation of the regime that during the same years, Chiang increasingly relied on concessions to regional leaders to avoid conflict and promote national unity. At the CEC meeting in December 1934, which celebrated the liquidation of the Kiangsi Soviet area, agreement was reached to increase the power of the provincial governments in the execution of national laws, the maintenance of local forces, and the selection of officials. The policy was successful in reducing friction, and a final revolt of Kwantung and Kwangsi generals after Hu's death in 1936 was quickly reduced without serious fighting; but it meant that when the 'implementing law' to the land reform was finally passed in 1935, it left the fixing of maximum holdings to the provincial authorities—with the result that nothing serious was attempted except in parts of Chekiang and the reconquered areas of Kiangsi.

The fifth congress of the Kuomintang met in November 1935 under the impression of new Japanese attempts to create "autonomous" areas in Inner Mongolia and North China, and of a rapid expansion in the scope of the anti-Japanese movement. Before the congress, Wang Ching-wei had offered his resignation in an effort to commit Chiang to a continuation of the policy of appeasement, but as he was seriously hurt in a nationalist attempt on his life, he could not attend; and Chiang, while calling for priority for internal construction and patient efforts for an understanding with Japan, gave a first hint that there were limits beyond which he would not yield to pressure. In the following weeks, anti-Japanese mass demonstrations, centered in the universities, culminated in the formation of a "National Salvation Union" which called for an end to the civil war with the communists, a government of national unity, armed resistance to all further Japanese encroachments, and a speed-up of armaments; and Chiang thought it wise to meet the delegates of this organization and plead with them. Yet efforts to negotiate with Japan were continued, in increasingly hopeless conditions, to the middle of 1936, and some of the student associations that had organized the demonstrations were dissolved as late as April.

The turn towards resistance seems to have begun with the Japanese proclamation of a "Military Government of Inner Mongolia" at the end of June 1936. By August, Chiang had fixed for himself the point beyond which he would not yield, even at the risk of national catastrophe, and by mid-November that point had been reached with the occupation of parts of Suiyuan province by Japanese auxiliaries: the privince was reconquered on Chiang's orders by units of the central Army while Japan was warned of the acute danger of war. Yet even then, the KMT leaders strove to complete their monopoly of internal power first: Chiang ordered a new offensive against the communists in Shensi, where they had organized their new base after the "Long March," even though they had by then made a number of offers for a united anti-Japanese front—including offers to "dissolve" the Soviet government and subordinate themselves to a national government following national elections. Seven leaders of the National Salvation Union were arrested in Shanghai late in November—a move that contributed much to the later rapprochement between the communists and the intellectual opposition.

The famous "Sian Incident" of December 1936, in which Chiang was arrested by the regional commanders he had ordered to attack the communists—headed by the Manchurian exile Marshal Chang Hsue-liang—showed the risks of this policy in the new conditions. But the rallying of opinion against the coup, and the recognition by the Soviets, and in their wake by the Chinese Communists, that Chiang's authority was indispensable for mobilizing united national resistance to Japan, forced Chang to release his captive and submit to his discipline, so that Chiang emerged once more with a free hand for his future policy. He subsequently dissolved the units that had revolted, and at the next CEC meeting in February still repeated his readiness to negotiate with Japan on a basis of Chinese equality and territorial integrity, and his demand for the liquidation of the Chinese Soviet government and Red Army and for the cessation of all "class struggle." But as the Communists were by then offering to turn their territory into a regional government, and to subordinate their army to any national government that would resist Japan, without any longer insisting that a "democratic" reconstruction of the government must precede that move, Chiang's demands seem in fact to have been the prelude to secret negotiations with them—though even then the negotiations were accompanied by the transfer of loyal elite troops to the neighborhood of the communist base. It was only the Japanese attack on Peking in July 1937 that finally persuaded the KMT to conclude new agreements both with the Soviet Union and with the Chinese Communists—after a break of ten years.

When the war with Japan, which the leaders of the Kuomintang had striven so long and so hard to avoid, was forced on them at last, it did not bring the total collapse of Chinese statehood which they had feared; but it did finally foil their hopes of ever completing their programme of internal reconstruction.

On the most formal level, this was shown in the indefinite postponement of their plans for ending the "educational dictatorship" and passing to the "third stage" envisaged by Dr. Sun Yat-sen—full constitutional democracy. In fact, the bureaucratic, authoritarian regime had in the intervening years made no real progress in creating the conditions for such a transition laid down in the provisional constitution of 1931—the fostering of local and provincial self-government. Nevertheless, various government bodies had been working on the draft of a democratic constitution since the spring of 1934 and had adopted a final version in May 1936; it provided for a national assembly to be elected once in six years and to elect in turn a president for the same period who would appoint and head his government, while the assembly would select the legislative and inspecting bodies and meet at rare intervals as a revising chamber. The debates on this draft and the plan to hold elections to the first national assembly in November 1936, then in November 1937, sounded curiously remote from reality in view of the lack of progress on the lcoal and regional levels and the real pressing problems of those years; when war broke out, the "educational dictatorship" was prolonged for the duration.

On the level of actual organization, the war brought a further narrowing of the leadership by the defection of Wang Ching-wei, and a vital weakening of the administrative structure by the transfer to the front of the young officers who had been the only promising cadres for reform from above. With the economic strain of war added to the other unsolved problems, the lack of a civilian elite now led to a rapid growth of bureaucratic corruption and a corresponding loss of political attraction and cohesion for the regime.

Finally, on the level of real power, the understanding with the Communists meant the *de facto* renunciation of the Kuomintang's monopoly of power at the very moment when it was *de jure* extending the period of its "educational dictatorship"; for though the communists had nominally accepted the subordination of their territory and their armed forces to the National Government and High Command, it was obvious that Mao Tse-tung was unwilling to carry out this pledge and Chiang unable to enforce it. Henceforth, a Kuomintang and a Communist government were in fact developing side by side, first in limited cooperation and then in increasingly hostile mutual toleration, on different parts of China's territory—in addition to Wang Ching-wei's pro-Japanese government which both were fighting.

While the Kuomintang started the competition with a vast advantage in the extent and wealth of the territory controlled, the size and equipment of its armed forces, and the recognized legitimacy and national prestige of its leader, the Communists were enabled gradually to neutralize this advantage in part owing to their greater capacity for survival in fighting the superior Japanese enemy by prolonged partisan warfare in primitive conditions, and in part owing to greater ideological cohesion of their cadres. When, after the victory over Japan, talks about a national coalition were started between the two rival one-party regimes on the initiative of the Great Powers, neither had the slightest belief in the possibility of such a solution; and the inevitable outcome was the renewal of their civil war, in which an effective Communist one-party regime finally defeated a degenerated non-Communist one.

As this account would seem to suggest, that outcome was neither due to an inherent inferiority of national revolutionary regimes, nor a purely external effect of the damage inflicted on the fabric of Chinese society by Japanese aggression: it was primarily caused by the successive deformations produced in the Kuomintang first by the initial participation of the Communists and the scars of the break with them, and then by the period when it had to avoid an open stand against Japan. The first crisis crucially weakened the modernizing and socially progressive aspects of the ideology of Sun Yat-sen's party, the second its nationalist aspects, until it had lost the substance of the mass appeal on which a modern one-party state can alone be built.

The Doubtful Case of Mexico

The Mexican party that, from its foundation in 1929, has ruled the country under different names to this day was not discussed in the original version of this essay for two good reasons: it never established a formal single-party monopoly, and its original creation was in no way influenced by the model of Bolshevik Russia. Yet it may well be argued that this model did influence the transformation of the structure and function of Mexico's ruling party at a crucial stage in 1937–38; and this point may claim an increased interest owing to the importance that has come to be attached to Mexico's form of government in recent comparative discussion of "established one-party systems."[25]

The Mexican revolution that overthrew the rule of Porfirio Diaz in 1911 and broke the dominant role of the landowning oligarchy, the old army linked to it, and the clergy in a series of civil wars in the following years, was not led by any party, but by individual liberal landowners and more radical middle-class intellectuals, who were backed at critical junctures by armed peasant risings and armed workers and quickly learned to weld a broad popular following into new armies. The Constitution of 1917 expressed the resulting broad majority consensus on the goals of achieving independence from foreign capital by nationalization of natural resources, social justice by distribution of land to the tillers and assurance of union rights for workers, and limitation of personal power by a ban on re-election of the President. Between 1920 and 1928, the country took some major strides of development on these lines under two reforming presidents, Obregón and Calles, who had first established their prestige as leaders of the new constitutional armies. Sectional parties of Agraristas and Laboristas had formed in the meantime; yet the Presidents were not their exponents, but saw their role in holding the balance between them.

The weakness of this regime lay in the absence of an established procedure for the nomination of the powerful President: the temptation for the actual holder of that office to impose his successor by use of the government machine, and for rival political-military leaders to turn to armed insurrection was ever-present. In 1928, when Calles had pushed through the return of Obregón as his successor, the latter was assassinated at the victory banquet. Now Calles was not content to put in a substitute nominee of his: he decided to crown the period of major reforms—which he regarded as closed—by the achievement of institutional stability. It was for this purpose that in a message to Congress on September 1, 1928 he proposed the creation of a party comprising all organizations that supported the broad aims of the revolution—both regional political machines, professional associations, and other economic and functional interest groups. Within this loose confederation, they should both argue their policy proposals and put forward their candidates for office under the implicit primacy of the President. In fact, a convention of all the invited groups, except one group of trade union leaders and the Communist Party, met at Querétaro in March 1929, founded the PNR (National Revolutionary Party), and concluded a "Pact of Union and Solidarity" binding them to the new procedure. Though at first corporative rather than democratic, this did in fact work both to legitimize the presidential succession and to ensure to Calles, in his new role of party leader, the decisive influence on it for the next six years. By 1932, the new party had sufficiently grown together for another convention to abolish the confederal structure with its "parties within the party" and create instead a system of individual primary voting by members to state and national nominating conventions; the bulk of the members at that time were government employees.

It will easily be seen that the PNR, as conceived by Calles, owed nothing to the Bolshevik model either in function or form. It was not meant to serve as an instrument of accelerated social transformation: Calles started it at a time when he was turning conservative and putting a stop to land distribution. It was not intended to prevent open argument between interest groups: it was originally founded as a confederation of autonomous groups. It claimed no monopoly of organization: groups that stayed outside were branded as lacking in loyalty to the revolution, but not banned— even the Communists, who after supporting the common cause against the counter-revolution were, during the Left period of 1929, dreaming of armed insurrection against the government, were only temporarily crushed but not permanently outlawed. Its main purpose, indeed, was one on which the Bolshevik model was notoriously weak—to ensure smooth and legitimate leadership succession. With the adoption of primaries on a territorial basis in 1932, the PNR began distinctly to resemble quite a different model—that of the large American parties.

A new turn toward radical social transformation began in 1934 with the election of President Lazaro Cardenas, whose nomination Calles had approved so as to reconcile growing left-wing discontent within the party. Cardenas used the election campaign to create an independent popular base for his program of resuming the advance toward the proclaimed national and social goals of the Mexican revolution, and he acted accordingly during his period in office, which coincided with Roosevelt's New Deal, with the West European Popular Fronts, and with the Spanish Civil War. In the course of six years, twice as much land was distributed as under all his predecessors and the total of beneficiaries doubled; unionization of the masses of the workers and collective contracts improving labor conditions were favored by the government; and the nationalization of foreign-owned estates and railway stocks were followed by the expropriation of foreign oil companies (without major conflict with the U.S.) in reply to their refusal to accept government arbitration in a labor dispute.

These policies were accompanied by moves to mobilize the masses for more active participation in political and social life, beginning with a broadening of the ruling party's membership to almost one million by recruiting of workers and peasants in 1936. A public attack by Calles on the government's toleration of strikes drew no response from the army (as had been the apparent intention) but led to the formation of a Committee of Proletarian Defense, and the defeated old leader went into exile in April 1936. Even before, a new organization of mass trade unions to supplement the old craft unions, the CTM—comparable to the CIO in the United States—had been formed under the leadership of Toledano. After that, party and government actively set out to organize the *ejido* farmers—the collectives of peasants settled on distributed land—in leagues within the various states and merge these in a national confederation, the CNC.

Mass mobilization in a framework of social transformation inevitably raised anew the question of the role of the ruling party, and particularly of its relation to the new mass organizations. Early in 1937, Toledano, who had strong Communist sympathies, proposed the formation of a Mexican Popular Front, which would comprise the PNR, the trade unions and peasants leagues, and the Communist Party. But Cardenas had no intention of giving the mass organizations the status of potential rival parties by concluding a formal alliance with them—he preferred to incorporate them within a reorganized party. The Communists, who had voluntarily stayed outside when the PNR was founded in 1929, now would have gladly come in and accepted the all-inclusive party as the Mexican equivalent of a Popular Front—but now they were kept out, in part because of the army's distrust of them and in part because a "party within the party" would not have fitted the new corporate structure.

In December 1937, Cardenas called for the formal dissolution of the PNR and the creation of a new PRM (Party of the Mexican Revolution), committed to socialism and a workers' democracy and based on four "sectors." The agrarian sector would consist of the CNC with automatic membership of all *ejido* farmers—there were now two million of them. The Labor sector would comprise all trade unions, with no monopoly for any trade union federation and no compulsory membership in any of them. The "popular" sector would take over the old individual party members as well as the federation of government employees' unions and the organizations of the liberal professions; it amounted to a representation of the urban middle class, Mexican style. A fourth sector was to represent the army, that is, the officers' corps; yet the latter disliked this separate political status, and by 1940 this sector was abolished and its active members transferred into the "popular" sector. Henceforth, the nomination of candidates for the state and federal parliaments was to take place by allocation among the sectors; the presidential candidate would need the support of three out of four—later two out of three—national sector organizations.

The reorganization in fact made the party more centralistic (as the local sector leaderships depended more on the national sectors than on the party's state leadership) as well as more nearly monopolistic (the permitted opposition parties had no chance to compete against an "official party" which incorporated all mass organizations). The idea of a state party of the Bolshevik type which would "control" all forms of social organization had clearly influenced Cardenas's thinking, as he considered how to maintain effective leadership in the presence of such strongly organized interest groups: in practice, the President would both control the appointments of the sector leaderships and arbitrate between them. Yet the concept of arbitration itself, which presupposes the legitimacy of open and organized conflict of interests within certain limits, did not spring from the totalitarian model: it sprang from the Mexican tradition of corporate compromise within the "revolutionary coalition," made possible also by the loose, non-dogmatic and non-utopian character of the official ideology.

This system has continued to permit a peaceful alternation between periods of conservative consolidation and major transformation; the last of the latter, under Lopez Mateo after 1958, brought the distribution of 16 million hectars of land. There have also been further struggles within the party between the advocates of direct individual primary voting on a territorial basis and of corporate sector voting. The critics of the latter could argue both that the sector system was too crude for the increasingly differentiated interests of an increasingly modern country, and that it favored the bureaucratic machines at the expense of individual participation, most obviously in the case of the agrarian sector based on "automatic," that is, compulsory membership. As the pressure of the active membership of the "popular sector" grew stronger with the growth of the middle class, a new party reform, enacted in 1946, renamed the party PRI (Party of the Revolutionary Institutions) and restored nomination by primaries, over the bitter protests of some Labor leaders including Toledano who left the party; the sectors were to be retained for economic and social issues only. However, the approach of the first new primaries in 1950 led to serious inner-party conflict, so that nomination by sectors was restored at the last moment. Finally, in 1959, another method to reduce the power of the sector bureaucracy was introduced: local groups may now initiate their own nominating lists subject to central approval.

On the whole, then, the Mexican form of rule by a dominant rather than monopolistic party has shown not only remarkable longevity but considerable capacity for adaptation to the social changes it has brought about; it is that capacity that has made it appear to some American students as a model of the successful "institutionalization" of one-party rule. Yet the conclusion that the growth of a similar degree of institutionalized pluralism within a single party could by analogy be expected in countries under Communist Party rule seems unwarranted, in view of the non-monopolistic, non-dogmatic, and quasi-corporative features present in the Mexican case from the beginning, yet absent in the Leninist tradition.

The New States of Black Africa

After a long interval, the model of the single-party state as an instrument of development returned to the agenda of history with the emergence of a number of ex-colonial states in Africa in the second half of the fifties. Most of the creators of the parties in question probably did not plan from the outset to establish a party dictatorship, but they were consciously influenced by the Communist type of party organization and at least by some aspects of Communist ideology—notably the Leninist doctrine of imperialism and of the need to organize democratic revolutions against colonial rule. On the other hand, none of these "Afro-Marxist" parties was Communist in the sense of accepting the doctrine of class struggle and the leading role of the proletariat for their own countries, of identifying themselves as proletarian class parties, or of wishing to submit to the leadership of an international Communist center.

Though, after the achievement of independence, most of these parties sooner or later created one-party regimes, only part of them retained the "Afro-Marxist" outlook while a number of others sought gradualist modernization with Western aid and without mass mobilization in a more or less conservative framework. Correspondingly, some of these parties turned into a form of the rule of notables or, more effectively, into something akin to "machine-parties" in the American sense. As will be seen, even those African ruling parties that retained the aspiration to modernization of a "revolutionary" or "mobilizing" type mostly failed in practice to create the "Bolshevik" kind of organization recommended by their ideology. At any rate, we shall confine our present discussion to some outstanding examples of those parties that made the attempt.

The first parties of the new type were created from 1946 onwards in French West Africa; they had their common origin in the *Rassemblement Démocratique Africain* founded in that year at Bamako by Félix Houphouet-Boigny and his associates with the active assistance and advice of the French Communist Party. It was from the Communists that the RDA and its regional sections, notably the *Parti Démocratique de Guinée,* the *Union Soudanaise* and the *Union Démocratique de Cameroun,* (as well as Houphouet-Boignys own *Parti Démocratique de la Cote d'Ivoire,* which later turned moderate), learned the need to base their struggle for self-government and eventual liberation on a mass organization with professional organizers and propagandists and with branches formed, if possible, down to the last village.

The alliance between the new parties and the French Communists had been concluded at a time when the latter formed part of the metropolitan government and were able directly to aid their progress. But when in the course of the Cold War the French communists turned to violent and embittered opposition, the tie with them was transformed from an advantage into a handicap, and by 1950 the RDA preferred to ensure its future legality by a clean break with the PCF. Its type of organization, however, was not affected by this development, and it continued to gain in electoral strength whenever the colonial authorities gave an opportunity for voting.

Of the one-party regimes that eventually arose from this development, the most important in our context has been that of the PDG in Guinea. Its peculiarity is based on the fact that Guinea, alone among the States emerging in the former territory of French West Africa, has a semi-revolutionary origin: Sekou Touré and his party were alone successful in rejecting membership of the new French *Communauté* during the 1958 plebiscite, and paid the penalty in the form of a sudden and complete withdrawal of French administrative cadres, assets, and aid. As a result, the new sovereign State of Guinea had to be built up from scratch by the victorious party; the new administration was simply the party organization under another name, and there was never any question of permitting other parties. According to the official doctrine, the state has no existence separate from that of the people, and it is the party that organizes and leads the people.

In fact, there was originally no selection procedure for party membership, and a very large part of the adult population became nominally party members, though the organizational skeleton appears to consist mainly of intellectuals and semi-intellectuals. The party is organized on the communist principle of democratic centralism with strong emphasis on "collective leadership." While Sekou Touré's unique position as party leader is undisputed, he has not permitted the type of "personality cult" in which Kwame Nkrumah used to indulge, but the collective principle seems most important in the intermediate and lower committees as a safeguard for ensuring disciplined execution of central directives.

All "mass organizations" are controlled by the party in conformity with the communist model. It was an attempt at Communist infiltration of two of these organizations, the youth league and the teachers' union, that led to a crisis in Guinea's relations with the Soviet Union in December 1961. Since then, the Soviets have made it clear that they will not support any competing Communist parties in "progressive"

African one-party states of this type. On the basis of this assurance on one side, the general renunciation of the principle of single-centred international discipline by Moscow on the other, loose, semi-fraternal relations have since developed again between the PDG, the CPSU, and some other Communist parties, as shown by mutual representation at party congresses. In November 1964, Touré carried out a large-scale purge of "petty-bourgeois factions" aimed at making the party less all-inclusive and more nearly an effective cadre party; an attempt to react to this by the formation of an opposition party was crushed in the following year. The PDG, for all the instability noticeable above all in its foreign policy, has thus become the most lasting of the African single-party regimes influenced by the Bolshevik model.

Fraternal relations also existed between the CPSU and the *Union Soudanaise* which ruled Mali until November 1968 and whose regime appeared to come closest to the earlier phase of the PDG in its type of organization and ideology: the two parties shared not only the early Marxist training of their leading cadres, but also the origin of their states in conditions of conflict. In Mali, the break of its original federation with Senegal left, though to a lesser degree, similar traumatic effects as did Guinea's break with the *Communauté*. But the leader of Mali's ruling party, Modibo Keita, rejected the Guinean device of purging the party to make it more effective, apparently from fear of isolating it. Instead, he began in 1967 to combine a radicalization of economic policies, stepping up the pace of nationalization and collectivization, and a campaign for greater "political mobilization" with moves for an increasingly personal rule, dissolving both the Politburo of the "*Union Soudanaise*" and the National Assembly and seeking to govern with the help of a newly appointed "Committee for the Defense of the Revolution."[26] The success of the army leaders in overthrowing Keita in November 1968 so as to end the "Marxist radicalization" of his regime was thus facilitated by the fact that he had himself broken the cohesion of the party regime and more or less abandoned such legitimacy as it had acquired.

The Communist model of organization has also played an important role in the development of the party that created the first of the new African States—the Convention People's Party of Ghana. In this case the model first made its impact not through any direct inter-party relations at an early stage, but through the formative personal influence which an ex-Communist, George Padmore, exerted on Kwame Nkrumah during his years in Britain. In converting from communism to Pan-Africanism, Padmore had rejected Moscow's authority and the communist class analysis for Africa, but had retained anti-imperialism and a belief in the communist technique of organization. On his return to the Gold Coast in 1947, Nkrumah carried this plan with him, and it was his attempt to transform the then most representative party of that colony, the United Gold Coast Convention, from a party of notables into a militant mass organization, that led to a split and to the formation of the CPP.

Independent Ghana, however, was not born as a single-party State. The transition to sovereignty was peaceful, and as the administration remained intact and was only gradually africanized, the party never completely merged with it. Rival parties were at first tolerated, generally on a tribal basis. Nor was the CPP itself originally monolithic: its very success was as much due to the features of an American machine party, which Nkrumah had observed during his student days in the USA, as to centralism of the Bolshevik type; and for years after it had formed the government, its congresses and press showed open factional differences which were reflected in government policy. On the other hand, Nkrumah was from the start imbued with an unshakable sense of his unique personal mission; even before his return from Britain he had formed an inner circle of followers sworn to personal loyalty to him as leader, and such "circles" or "vanguards" remained a feature of his style of leadership to the end.[27]

Thus as the young state experienced its inevitable economic and political difficulties, Nkrumah reacted to every crisis by a tendency to crush the opposition, and his authority and the power of his party were strong enough to accomplish this. Between 1959 and 1961, the opposition parties were gradually harassed out of existence, their leaders driven into exile or arrested. Parallel with that, control over the mass organizations was tightened to the point where they lost all separate identity; in 1960 they were given formal representation in the party's central committee; in 1961 the membership cards of the trade unions, peasant organizations, women's and youth organizations, etc. were abolished and exchanged for cards directly issued by the party. While the party thus reached a nominal strength of more than two million, it became more amorphous rather than more effective; this was shown in 1961, when a combination of economic difficulties and government infringement of trade union rights led to a spontaneous general strike called against the will of the official union leaders. The suppression of all parliamentary and trade unionist opposition was followed by acts of terrorism and by an all-pervading fear of plots, for which various right-wing and left-wing factions within the CPP and the government were held responsible.

Hence when in 1964, the party monopoly had at last been embodied in the Constitution, the party itself had also become formally monolithic by the elimination of all potential opponents of Nkrumah's personal rule, while the glorification of the leader as a semi-divine savior of his people assumed an increasingly central part in official propaganda. As this transformation of the regime was not accompanied either by success in the solution of the country's problems or by an effective adjustment of the party's organizational structure to the growth of its nominal membership, what developed in fact below the facade of monolithic despotism was a widening gulf between the regime and the people. When in 1965 Nkrumah was overthrown, during his absence in Peking, by a military coup, the almost total lack of resistance showed that the party regime had long ceased to be a reality and that he had created a void around himself. It also showed that the Afro-Marxist ideology which Nkrumah had propagated in his own peculiar version had penetrated rather less deeply in Ghana than in Guinea.

By the time the bulk of the new African states obtained independence in 1960, the model of single-party government appeared to be well established on that continent, not only by the West African precedents discussed above, but also by some of their conservative rivals; hence, it was no longer considered as necessarily linked to its origin in the Communist world. More and more of the new African leaders came to regard single-party rule simply as a convenient means of national integration and mobilization during the period of development, without linking it with Marxist or Leninist ideological tenets. In some cases single-party rule first developed by the party that had played a leading role in the struggle for independence winning all or almost all seats in a fairly free election, or even by the weaker party voluntarily joining the stronger in order to ease the transition.

On the other hand, the absence of an initial struggle for power with all its ideological concomitants often meant that the need for effective organization based on reliable cadres was not grasped in the early stages, and this led to a weak and unstable power structure. However, this weakness could be remedied with time and experience, and the influence of the Bolshevik model thus come to manifest itself at a later stage, as the case of the originally extremely broad and loose Tanganyika African National Union shows. Under the leadership of the open-minded Julius Nyerere, whose early concept of an African "Ujamaa-Socialism" owed nothing to Marx and much to an idealized view of traditional African society, TANU had, only as a result of its overwhelming electoral success and of experiences in other states, begun in 1963 to consider establishing permanent one-party rule, and actually embodied it in the constitution of Tanzania after the merger with Zansibar in 1965. During the same period, the entry of some Communist-influenced activists from the Afro-Shirazi party of Zanzibar and some conflicts with Western countries contributed not only to the growth of "Afro-Marxist" elements in the party's ideology, but to the decision of 1964 to give the party a much more thorough, centralized organization to increase its effectiveness. Finally, the programmatic "Arusha declaration," adopted by the party in January 1967, combined a specifically African emphasis on self-reliance in development with a concrete catalogue of measures to prevent future exploitation by nationalization of the banks and key resources and by the systematic promotion of cooperatives. As a result, Tanzania has come to be recognized as a "revolutionary democracy" by the Soviets and to receive substantial aid from Communist China without renouncing its independent and non-aligned position in world affairs.[28]

Summing up, we may say that the net effect of the Bolshevik model of the single-party state on the new states of Black Africa has been much less sweeping than may have appeared at the time of their foundation. Most of the nominal one-party regimes founded there, whether of the more conservative or of the would-be revolutionary variety, have turned out to be poor instruments for either mobilization or modernization, or even national integration: they have frequently failed to make their policies effective in the tribal areas of rural subsistence economy, in part because of the absolute shortage of non-traditional cadres and of their own inability to win and unwillingness to rely on the traditional ones; they have as frequently failed to produce sufficient ideological cohesion to prevent flagrant corruption and nearly as flagrant in-fighting among their own elites; and they have consequently frequently been unable to win a statewide legitimacy corresponding to their formal monopoly of power. As a result, a number of them have been overthrown by military coups in the later 1960s, while some of the surviving "conservative" specimens in the former French colonies of West and Central Africa bear as little resemblance to the "model" as some of the nominally parliamentary governments established in Latin America in the 19th century and in parts of Asia in the 20th bear to Western democracy.[29]

In short, the degree of underdevelopment of most of the new African states appears to have been too severe for the Bolshevik type of "engine" to be applicable. Nevertheless, the impact of the model has been considerable not only on the thinking of radical intellectual elites, but also on the orientation of the few apparently stable and successful cases that have emerged—even though none of them has shown any inclination to renounce its new-won national independence for the sake of an outright Communist allegiance.

THE ARAB WORLD

Beginning with the middle 1950s, regimes describing themselves as nationalist one-party systems have become an increasingly prominent feature of the Arab world. Yet, in nearly all of them, single-party rule was either conceived from the start as a subordinate instrument, if not a mere facade of military rule (as in Egypt and later in the Sudan), or turned out to become subordinate to the military in course of time, as in Algeria and in the governments of the Baath party in Syria and Iraq. The one important exception is the rule of the oldest of all the governing Arab parties, the *Parti Socialiste Destourien* in *Tunisia*. In part, the exception may be due to the fact that in contrast to the Middle Eastern regimes mentioned, the PSD under its earlier name of *Néo-Destour* was the creator of its state, the champion of the struggle for independence from France, while in contrast to the Algerian FLN it achieved this goal in the main peacefully, without major military action: the FLN owed its political victory to the attrition of the French will to hold on to *Algérie Française* by years of bitter, organized fighting in which an army was born before a party assumed organized structure; and the Baath, always a minority party in the states of the Fertile Crescent, only came to nominal power in one or the other of them by the *coups d'état* of groups of army officers that might sympathize with it or even belong to it, but were never willing to obey its civilian organs for any length of time. But, there seem to be other deeper factors underlying the Tunisian exception which may also account for the degree of its success, in terms of institutional stability and effective progress in modernization, that is remarkable not only by Arab standards.[30]

The Néo-Destour had been founded in 1934 by splitting away from the more traditionalist older Destour (constitution) party over the willingness of its young leaders—a group of French-educated intellectuals with no vested interest in the traditional order—to combine the struggle for independence with the acceptance of a measure of Western-style modernization, including a modernist interpretation of Islam. It developed at first as a democratic opposition party, using the ideals of the enlightenment to extract political concessions from the colonial power, and quickly won the support of the French-educated intelligentsia, gradually expanding its influence also over the Arabic-educated youth at the expense of the old Destour. Originally, it had no "centralistic" structure and no vision of single-party rule.

But, after the Second World War, it quickly learned from the evolving Communist competition the need to control its own "mass organizations" and created one federation each for artisans and traders, for farmers and for workers, of which only the last, the *Union Générale des Travailleurs Tunisiens* (UGTT), developed a real life of its own. By the middle 1950s, on the eve of independence, the Neo-Destour had become a mass party of 100,000 members; the UGTT counted 150,000.

The granting of independence in 1956, negotiated by its leader Habib Bourguiba, brought decisive victory for the party in the elections to the Constitutent Assembly. The Communists only got 1.3 percent of the votes; the old Destour stopped publication of its paper the following year. The only serious challenge had come from within, when Bourguiba's deputy Salah ben Youssef broke with him in October 1955 over the residual ties with France Bourguiba had accepted in the negotiations, and started a campaign against the agreement on extremist pan-Arab, anti-French, and also anti-modernist lines which had little appeal to the party cadres but dangerous potential appeal to the crowds. When the crisis was overcome and the rebel exiled in 1956, the victorious party was faced with the need to build a new state machine from its own cadres, which led to frequent cumulation of offices in party and state. That was the beginning of the evolution to inner-party centralism and single-party monopoly.

Within two years, the creation of larger provincial units was used to replace the 41 elected leaders of district federations of the party by 14 appointed commissioners for the new provincial organizations. During the same period, the demand of the able and ambitious trade union leader Ahmed Ben Salah for economic planning under trade union leadership led to his removal by a party-organized scission and subsequent refusion of the unions, and to his replacement by a member of the party's Politburo. By 1959 the party's mission was declared "permanent." By 1961 it was the party itself that turned to economic planning and renamed itself "Destour Socialist Party," and Ben Salah was put in charge of the new planning machinery—but not on behalf of the unions: the party now formed its own industrial branch organizations first to control, later increasingly to replace the unions and help in executing the plan. This led to another conflict with the new, less ambitious but still independent-minded trade union leadership: in 1963 and 1965, two successive trade union chiefs were overthrown by party pressure and official manipulations, leading to general apathy and a drastic loss of membership. Also in 1963, the provincial governors were made ex officio presidents of the—otherwise elected—provincial party committees. In 1966, this evolution toward a centralistic, monopolistic state party culminated in the creation of a Council of the Republic composed of the members of the government and the Politburo, which in the following year was officially charged with designating the successor to the head of state when needed.

Parallel with this growth of a party dictatorship that left no room for factions or autonomous interest groups, however, there has proceeded a steady effort to rejuvenate the party cadres and raise their quality and to broaden consultation beyond the party. The party centralization of 1958 was used to dismiss from office, with appropriate material compensation, many party veterans with little aptitude for the new tasks of economic construction, and most provincial governors were replaced after the transition to economic planning—the majority now have university degrees. The Politburo itself has been largely rejuvenated by Bourguiba's steady pressure, in part by the device of shifting the older notables to a broader Central Committee or to prestige positions without power. On the lower levels, the younger, educated element appears to predominate in the industrial branch organizations and to play a growing role in the provincial Coordinating Committees which are biennially reelected—under central control—to play their role in the suggestion of provincial investment plans for the national budget: it is these committees that are most active in consulting both party members and outside experts through a variety of commissions and seminars. The latter, together with the rural production and service cooperatives, also seem to be the main recruiting grounds for new activists.

The success of this system in the self-chosen direction of economic, educational, and legal modernization appears on the whole impressive. Soon after independence, Tunisia became the first Arab country to abolish Islamic *shariya* law on personal status, a measure of great importance for the position of women. School attendance has risen decisively. Economic growth has approached an annual rate of 4 percent. The effectiveness of planning is indicated by the fact that the budget has reached the unusually high share of 32 percent of the GNP.

Together with the stability so far shown by the Tunisian regime, these results qualify it as the most successful so far among the single-party states created by nationalist modernizers. Apart from the undoubted personal gifts of Habib Bourguiba, this success appears to be due in no small measure to the importance of rational, enlightened elements and the absence of worldwide and utopian goals in its ideology from the start. In contrast to Communist regimes, the PSD has never been committed to a concept of "permanent revolution," and has not had to overcome it in bitter internal conflicts—nor have major conflicts resulted from the need of each post-revolutionary regime to replace the elite of revolutionary veterans by an elite of post-revolutionary technocrats. Suffering from no major contradiction between its official ideology and its real tasks, it also seems to encounter no serious difficulty in attracting activists of good quality from the young generation, and no serious doubts in its own legitimacy. In contrast to the nationalist regimes of Kemal and the Kuomintang, on the other hand, it has benefited from the tradition of a mass party in opposition and from its continued willingness to draw the broadest strata of the population into its activity.

There remain, however, two great question marks over its future: the succession of the founder and uncontested leader is bound to produce a crisis testing the cohesion of the leadership; and the development of the economy will make it increasingly difficult to maintain rational planning without the granting of autonomy for the major interest groups. The first of these question marks is amply illustrated by the past of the Soviet model—the second by its present.

No peaceful road to independence had proved possible for *Algeria,* owing to the political resistance of the strong French settler community and to the fixation of successive French governments to the constitutional fiction that Algeria was "part of France." Eventually, a group determined on armed insurrection broke away from the more radical of the legal Algerian parties and succeeded by 1954 in winning the support of Nasser's Egyptian government for their *Comité Révolutionnaire d'Unité et d'Action* (CRUA). Operating first from Cairo, later from the neighboring countries of the Maghreb, they gradually built up a strong fighting movement in parts of Algeria, supported by specialized civilian organizations among workers, peasants, and students all over the country, and a rapidly growing "frontier army" on its borders; the whole movement came to be known as the *Front de Libération Nationale* (FLN), and in September 1958, its leaders proclaimed themselves as a government in exile, the *Gouvernement Provisoire de la République Algérienne* (GPRA). As they were fighting against a Western power and receiving arms and money not only from Arab, but increasingly also from Communist countries, their revolutionary nationalism naturally assumed an increasingly anti-imperialist and anti-capitalist tinge; this was reflected by a conference held on the eve of victory at Tripoli, which proclaimed a socialist Algeria led by the peasants and workers as its goal. At the same time, the FLN rejected the belated offer of the Algerian Communists, who had originally opposed armed struggle, for a "united front": instead, it declared its intention to become the only party of the new Algeria, to form the government as its organ, and to accept Communists only as individual members, but not as organized partners.

Yet behind the claim to a party monopoly there existed at that moment no disciplined political organization with a unified leadership and trained cadres.[31] On the contrary, a bitter conflict erupted at the moment of triumph between the GPRA under Ben Khedda and the leadership of the frontier army under Houari Boumedienne, which was by then far stronger than the fighting forces in the country. On the eve of moving to Algiers following the agreement with General de Gaulle on the French withdrawal, the GPRA decided to dismiss Boumedienne and his staff and even tried to prevent them from returning to Algeria at the same time. In ignoring the dismissal and marching home at the head of his troops, Boumedienne had the support of one founder member of the movement who had only recently joined the GPRA after his release from a French prison—Ben Bella. With the help of Boumedienne's troops, Ben Bella succeeded quickly in overthrowing Ben Khedda and was recognized by the army as head of the FLN and president of Algeria.

With the old GPRA leadership removed as tainted by diplomacy and not sufficiently revolutionary, it now fell to the victors to build the institutions of the new single-party state and to shape its social structure. While confirming explicitly the ban on a separate Communist party, the new government decreed in the spring of 1963 the expropriation of the French settlers and the handing over of their land to elected management committees of the laborers; the constitution adopted at the same time confirmed the socialist orientation. As the Army now concentrated on establishing its monopoly of force, using the older fighters it could not retain in peacetime to build a reliable gendarmerie, Ben Bella sought to establish a monopoly of political decision by incorporating the mass organizations of workers and students in the ruling party. But in a party whose members lacked common ideological training, having been previously engaged chiefly in insurrectionary activity, this attempt forced him increasingly to rely on left-wing activists, both independent Marxists who had worked with the FLN and party Communists who now came in through the trade unions and students organizations; during the winter of 1963–64, the Communists, on Soviet advice, accepted cooperation within the FLN as individual members, and the first official congress of that party in April 1964 adopted a programmatic "Charter" strongly influenced by them.

What it all amounted to was that for a time the policy of the FLN was more influenced by the affiliated "mass organizations" than controlling them—nor did the party leader have effective control over the Army: the single-party state was during that period rather less centralistic and more pluralistic than it claimed to be. At the same time, there developed growing mutual suspicion between the two main elements of that pluralism—the army leadership with its commitment to an "Islamic socialism" somehow anchored in native traditions and its distrust of "foreign ideologies," and the left-wing cadres with their fears of a "Nasserist" development and of the growth of a new privileged caste from the military. The issue came to a head in 1965 when Ben Bella, prompted by his left-wing supporters, made preparations for weakening the Army's monopoly of force by the creation of a "people's militia": the army which had put him into office deposed him by another coup on June 19, 1965, and Boumedienne took over sole leadership. Left-wing demonstrations against the coup were soon quelled, and the central organs of the FLN, called only afterwards, endorsed the change: from now on, the Army's Revolutionary Council under Boumedienne was the sole source of power, and the FLN with its mass organizations a mere annex. The Communists in the party were purged and arrested—there was to be no further "licensed infiltration."

The new regime has not bothered to revise the leftist programmatic documents of the preceding years, but neither has it felt bound by them. Workers' self-management on the expropriated estates has been restricted by government-appointed managers and in a number of cases has been replaced by privileged cooperatives of military veterans employing other workers. The promise of a general land reform was only fulfilled, after repeated postponement, in November 1971 by a cautious decree creating farm cooperatives including the existing Algerian landowners as members. Also from 1971, growing emphasis has been given to industrial development, which has not so far been able to absorb the labor surplus so that more than half a million Algerian workers have to find employment in France. Algerian socialism, apart from the effort at planned development and the remnants of workers' management on the expropriated estates, seems now to mean mainly the preservation of a high wage level for the privileged minority of industrial workers employed at home.

Early in 1968, the formal monopoly of the FLN was breached, apparently for diplomatic reaons: the Communist leaders were released from imprisonment and permitted to form their own *Parti de l'Avant-garde Socialiste* outside the FLN. They started once more to concentrate on the mass organizations, with effects the regime found evidently distasteful: by the end of October, the trade union leadership was deposed so as to remove "subversive purveyors of foreign ideologies," and a landowning army officer appointed as trade union chief. The dissolution of the Students' Union for similar reasons in January 1971 has been another confirmation that the military regime has not yet found a way to permit political participation without endangering its control.

The Free Officers Movement that overthrew the Egyptian monarchy in 1952 owed nothing to any political party, though one of the original members of its leadership—the later "Revolutionary Command Council"—belonged to the Moslem Brotherhood and one or two to a Communist group (there was no united Communist party in Egypt at the time). Despite the initial willingness of the parties to support the new regime, the officers decided in January 1953 to outlaw them all; an exception was made at first for the Moslem Brethren as a religious organization. A week later, a so-called "Liberation Front" was created for the express purpose of bringing the existing professional organizations, notably the trade unions and student associations, under the control of the regime. But this front remained a mere coordinating board and never sought to recruit a membership of its own.

The crisis that decided the future character of the regime came a year later, following a clash between Nasser and the Moslem Brotherhood and the refusal of President Naguib to endorse their dissolution. Naguib's threatened resignation alerted opposition also within the Army and on the Left, and in March 1954 the RCC announced its willingness to hold early elections and hand over to a parliamentary regime as Naguib desired. But the announcement had only been meant to mobilize protests, and these came in the form of strikes from the bulk of the officer corps and from the Cairo transport workers organized in the "Liberation Front" under the leadership of an officer, as well as of street demonstrations. As a result, Naguib was defeated and the parties once again outlawed; the final suppression of the Moslem Brotherhood followed later in the year when it opposed the agreement with Britain ending the occupation of the Canal Zone.[32]

The next step was taken in the Constitution of 1956 when the—as yet non-existent—"National Union" was charged with the task of nominating the candidates for a national assembly. But this was still no more than a formal device for creating a sham parliament intended for acclamation rather than consultation. By the time the elections were arranged in 1957, only the executive committee of the National Union existed—and this was apparently considered sufficient for the purpose.

A more serious attempt to create an organization with roots in the country was undertaken after the establishment of the United Arab Republic in 1958. Nasser was unwilling to compromise with the existing political parties in Syria, but realized that he could not simply suppress them as he had suppressed the traditional Egyptian parties—the need for organized links between the regime and the population began to make itself felt. Though the new Constitution provided for the direct appointment of national assembly members by the president, the monopoly of organization of the National Union was proclaimed at the same time, and an effort to build up regional and local committees began in 1959. A national congress of the Union was held in July 1960, and Nasser selected from its ranks those members of the national assembly of the United Arab Republic who had not sat in the previous Egyptian and Syrian assemblies. Similarly, a law concerning local self-government provided for its organs to be composed of a minority of appointed government officials and a majority of representatives to be elected by the local units of the National Union.

Nevertheless, the creation of a genuine political organization by the fiat of the military dictatorship proved extremely difficult; it appears that most of the local committees provided for in the statute never came to life, and that the Union never acquired an active membership. A new start was made when, after the Syrian breakaway and the dissolution of the United Arab Republic in 1961, Nasser took a decisive turn towards a policy of wholesale nationalization of industry. Under a decision promulgated in November of that year, a "national congress of the popular forces" was to be formed by delegates of all professional organizations, to adopt a "National Pact for Revolutionary Action," and then to arrange for the election of new local committees on this basis.

The National Union emerged from this attempt to put new life into it with a new name, the "Arab Socialist Union"; but it remained at first not only an auxiliary of the military regime, which was intended, but a remarkably inactive auxiliary. In addition to the basic difficulty of creating a state party for a regime that was already in power and had developed its bureaucracy without such a party, Nasser seemed to be short of useful ideologists who would be able to justify the pragmatic twists and turns of his international and domestic policies by coherent and convincing systems.

This persistent weakness of the state party despite all its reorganizations, which Nasser increasingly recognized as an obstacle to the national mobilization and re-education needed for successful development, formed part of the background for the new rapprochement with the Soviet Union and the release and subsequent employment of many pro-Soviet Communists after 1963. The Soviets had by then come to accept Nasser's government as a progressive, non-capitalist regime which the Communists should support rather than oppose, and to regard Communist entry into the state party on the Algerian model as the most promising course for their weak Egyptian following. Nasser in turn responded after Khrushchev's visit of 1964 and after the subsequent self-dissolution of the Egyptian Communists of April 1965, by using some of the released Communists in his propaganda apparatus and permitting them to publish a Marxist review in order to stimulate discussion in his stagnating "movement."

The admission of the Communists was, however, accompanied both by official propaganda announcing their surrender to an organization based on Islam and pan-Arab nationalism, and by a new effort to train and activate non-Communist cadres for the ASU, entrusted to Nasser's righthand man Ali Sabri who in October 1965 was transferred from the office of Prime Minister to that of ASU General Secretary. While this in itself marked a rise in the organization's importance, it remained excluded from work in the Army—a clear indication of the continued primacy of the latter.[33]

The moment to attack that primacy seemed finally to have come in 1967–68, after the defeat in the June war with Israel, the purge of the army leadership, and the suicide of Marshall Amer. Demands for making the ASU the inspiring force of a new push for the reform of society and the cleansing of the bureaucratic and military machine were now put forward not only by the Communists: Nasser himself announced in March 1968 a program of further socialist transformation and also agreed to a reorganization of the ASU, starting from the reconstitution of its basic units in May and culminating in a National Congress in September 1968.[34]

But while this reorganization made the sate party more of a reality than it had been at any previous stage and strengthened the position of Sabri to that extent, the events following Nasser's death in September 1970 showed clearly that even now, ultimate power had remained with the Army: Ali Sabri was worsted by Anwar Sadat in the struggle for the succession, and finally purged (together with the former chief of the secret police, Guuma, his successor as head of the ASU) in the crisis of May 1971. Subsequently, Sadat seems even to have considered, in the framework of his deliberate relaxation of police repression and uniformity, whether to maintain a single-party system at all. His announced decision to do so while granting increased autono-

my to the affiliated mass organizations may be intended
to make the official party more alive, but may also create
new problems for its stability.

The only ruling Arab party that originally developed as
an opposition in existing Arab states is the "Party of Arab
Socialist Rebirth," known generally as the Baath Party, in
Syria and Iraq. It received its final name, programme, and
constitution when two separate groups, created by Michel
Aflak and Akram Hourani in the '40s, merged in 1953.
Its fundamental commitment is to the unity and ever new
rebirth of the Arab nation, transcending the particular
states into which it has become divided by the machina-
tions of the imperialists; that unity can only be restored
by a revolutionary movement which must be able to mobilize all strata of the people and therefore must pursue a
socialist policy. As a frontier-transcending movement,
its "regional," that is, statewide, congresses and leaderships or "commands" are subordinated in principle to
"national," i.e., pan-Arab, congresses and the leadership
elected by them; in practice, its activity has been confined
to the countries of the Fertile Crescent, and even there it
has never become an effective force in Jordan. Regarding
nationalism as the supreme value and "socialist" modernization as possible without conflict with the basic tenets
of Islam, the ideology of the Baath is incompatible with
Communist doctrine and indeed has strong anti-Communist overtones; nor was the party originally committed to
the goal of single-party rule or to Leninist principles of
centralistic organization. Yet when the chance came in
1963, it attempted to establish both single-party rule and
an imitation of the corresponding party structure—with the
result of its military overthrow in Iraq and of its transformation in stages by its own military supporters in Syria.
At the time of writing, both the Iraqi Baath regime as
restored in 1968 by General al-Bakr and the Syrian Baath

regime as transformed in 1970 by General Hafiz Assad amount to forms of military rule based on the support of a dominant, but no longer all-inclusive party.[35]

The Baath first gained substantial influence in its Syrian homeland as an opposition to the dictatorship of Shishakly in the early 1950s; having actively contributed to his overthrow in 1954 through its followers in the officer corps, it gained 15 percent of the seats in the Constitutent Assembly elections of that year—a figure it never surpassed in any competitive election. Its influence in the army rose much faster in the following years, but under the parliamentary regime it never achieved complete control; instead, its leaders came to fear a Communist takeover as a result of the country's growing dependence on Soviet support at the end of 1957. Thus it was the Baath that took the initiative in parliament to prepare union with Egypt and prominently shared in the actions of the Army High Command that brought it about in early 1958. No doubt the Baath leaders expected that in the United Arab Republic their party would assume the same privileged place in Syria that the official National Union held in Egypt, and would even influence the latter through its ideology and active cadres. In Iraq, too, the Baath was one of the four parties that supported Kassem's coup overthrowing the monarchy in June 1958. They had one minister in Kassem's first government, and his deputy Aref was close to them in his pan-Arab outlook which caused him to press for Iraq to unite with Egypt and Syria.

Yet the hopes of this first spring of pan-Arabism were to be bitterly disappointed. Nasser took some Baathists into his government, but he was unwilling to tolerate any independent Syrian party and, in fact, treated Syria as a dependent territory. At the National Union elections of July 1959, only 200 Baathists were permitted to stand among more than 9,000 "candidates," and by December all the Baathist ministers resigned, joining the increasingly

disgruntled opposition of the bulk of their Syrian country-
men. Meanwhile in Iraq, Kassem had turned against unity
with Egypt and put Aref on trial before the end of 1958,
and a number of Baathist officers were arrested and their
party outlawed in Iraq for supporting a vision of unity that
was to prove so disappointing to their comrades in the
UAR. In the end, Baathists were almost as active in the
coup of September 1961 that restored Syria's independence
as they had been in the 1958 effort to end it. But in the
somewhat conservative parliamentary regime that emerged
from separation, they were no closer to power than before—
at the elections in December they obtained 14 percent of
the seats.

When a second chance came for the Baath leaders in both
Syria and Iraq in early 1963, they showed that they had
learned two lessons: this time they went straight for total
power in either state, and they were far more wary of
interstate mergers. In Iraq in February, Baath officers were
the core of the military conspiracy that overthrew Kassem
and put Aref—himself no party member—in his place as
head of state, and the Baath took all the key positions in
the new government in which no other party was represented; a Baathist officer also took control of the "National
Guard" which became notorious for the brutal mass persecution of the Communists who had alone risen in defense of
Kassem. In March in Syria, the Baathists took part in a
military coup undertaken under the slogans of Arab unity
and socialism, and received half the government positions
including those of Prime Minister and Minister of the In-
terior. On this basis, a tripartite pact for the creation of a
federal union by stages between Egypt, Syria, and Iraq—
much more cautious than the Union of 1958—was concluded in April; but this time it was the distrust of Nasser by
most of the Baathists as much as Nasser's impatience that
made it fail. The Syrian Baath soon pressed for a purge of
"Nasserites" from the army, and by July had acquired, with

the cautious backing of its Iraqi comrades, complete control under its Defense Minister al-Hafiz; a Nasserite attempt at a coup promptly followed and was suppressed with much bloodshed, and Egypt reacted by cancelling the pact. Parallel with the achievement of effective power in practice came the adoption of the Bolshevik model of the single-party state in theory, at any rate by the committed extremists of the Baath. In Syria, they now began to speak of the need for an "ideological army"; in Iraq, Vice-Premier al-Saadi and Windawi, the commander of the National Guard, tried to turn the latter into an army of the party. In both countries, this wing also combined pressure for radical measures of social transformation with bitter hostility to equally "socialist" Egypt—and in Iraq with fierce anti-communism.

Yet the very radicalization of Baathist claims soon led to serious factional struggles in the party's ranks, and in Iraq to a quick end of its rule. The bulk of the Iraqi officers had either remained non-party or joined the party only nominally; now their professional *esprit de corps* began to resent both the excesses of the National Guard which dishonored the regime and its claim to military independence. Moderate Baathist leaders like Premier al-Bakr supported them in upholding the primacy of the army. While the Baathists quarrelled, the army leadership decided in September to depose Windawi as commander of the National Guard, and he found himself isolated; by November, they deposed and exiled al-Saadi on Aref's orders, and Windawi also had to flee after an attempt at a coup had failed. When the Baath organization, wavering under uncertain advice from the "National Command" in Damascus, still failed to read the signs, the bulk of the Iraqi officers decided to emancipate themselves from party tutelage: on November 18 they disbanded the National Guard and ended Baath rule by a coup, honorably shelving the moderate Baathists and reforming the government under Aref as a plain military regime.

In Syria, where Baath influence had older and deeper

roots, the struggle between "socialist" extremists and moderates continued *inside* the party—and here the "ideological army" remained for years the bastion of the extremists. It was on their initiative that the new constitution of 1964 explicitly put the Revolutionary Command Council above the government, making its president al-Hafiz the head of state. Yet gradually, impressed by economic difficulties and popular unrest caused in part by the extension of nationalization measures to many small enterprises, al-Hafiz began to turn toward moderation and by mid-1965 ordered the return of a number of small firms to their owners—and now the cause of socialist extremism was taken up by Salah Jadid, who combined the offices of Army chief of staff and party "regional" secretary. The crisis came at the turn of 1965–66: al-Hafiz first dismissed Jadid from his Army post and then dissolved his regional party command with the backing of Aflak's "national" command, which accused Jadid both of pro-Marxist tendencies and of Army interference in party affairs; but al-Hafiz could not risk new party elections without purging a number of Jadid's military supporters first—and they forestalled him by a coup that overthrew him in February 1966. From that day dates the "left-wing Baath" regime that under Jadid's effective leadership and with Hafiz Assad as new Minister of Defense, combined a policy of radical nationalization and land reform measures, a semi-Marxist propaganda, a strongly pro-Soviet orientation including the development of party relations with the CPSU, the appointment of a Communist minister without agreements with the Syrian Communist Party, and the campaign for a "People's War" against Israel—the regime that stumbled into the Six-Days-War of 1967.

After that war, the determination of the Army to impose its control on all "popular" armed forces, such as the "workers' battalions" and the Palestinian *fedayin* units, became the starting point for yet another factional alignment: the officer corps under Assad now turned increasingly nationalist and anti-Communist while the party machine under Jadid stuck to its leftist outlook. The struggle dragged on for years, with Assad becoming increasingly independent in Army appointments and even, by November 1968, forbidding visits by civilian party leaders to the once "ideological Army," but unable to overthrow the regional party leadership even by military threats (apparently due to repeated Soviet intervention behind the scenes) while they in turn were unable to force his resignation. Only in October 1970, shortly after the failure of the Syrian intervention in Jordan, Assad reacted to one more attempt to depose him by party decision with a military coup which finally concentrated all power in his hands.[37]

Since then, the Syrian regime has been one of Army rule supported primarily, but not exclusively by an Army-controlled Baath party, since other parties, both nationalist and Communist, have in the meantime been admitted as partners of the Baath in a National Front. This development shows a remarkable parallel to the limited restoration of Baath rule which has taken place in Iraq since July 1968, when the moderate Baathist General al-Bakr succeeded in overthrowing the elder Aref. Al-Bakr has the formal blessing of the former "national" Baath leaders Aflak and Bitar who were exiled from Syria after Jadid's victory, but his power cleary does not depend on any party decisions; nor is he strict in maintaining the Baath's monopoly, as he tolerates Communist Party activity to a limited extent.

If the events of 1958 marked the springtime of Baath pan-Arab hopes and the coups of 1963 and 1966 the high tide of its claims to ideological party rule on the Bolshevik model, the regimes created in 1968 in Iraq and in 1970 in Syria seem to express the twilight of a former revolutionary movement that only serves now as a legitimating cover to a post-revolutionary form of military rule. That transformation can hardly be said to be due to the successful achievement of the movement's original nationalist and modernizing goals. Rather it must be attributed to a succession of failures, due in the first place to the inability of the movement's political leaders to develop a secure, legitimate authority over the growing number of officers in its ranks—the actual or aspiring holders of physical power. The roots of this inability cannot be purely personal—they must be looked for both in the peculiar attraction of Baathist ideology for rising ambitious officers and in the Arabic and Islamic political culture and tradition of which it forms a part.

Indeed, there emerges from our survey a striking proneness of Arab states in the process of modernization to either open or thinly disguised military rule, which causes most of them to introduce single-party government merely as an adjunct to control by a military leader or junta, or at any rate to reduce it to that. This tendency is too general to be explained by the exceptional charisma of the soldiers concerned—on the contrary, the frequent overthrow of the leading military figures by rival leaders and their cliques is a much-noted cause of instability in some of the countries discussed.[38] In short, most of the Arab countries show a remarkable failure to develop rational forms of procedural legitimacy, either of a democratic or of a single-party type, that would be effective in ensuring the submission of ambitious men in control of organized physical force.

Such failures are not, of course, confined to any one nation, culture, or age. They have occurred repeatedly in periods of decay before the emergence of a new order—e.g., in the later stages of Roman Caesarism, in the Caudillo phase in Latin America, or during the rule of the provincial war lords in China. What appears unusual in the case of a number of Arab, and also of some other Islamic countries, is the stage at which the phenomenon occurs—that of an effort at revolutionary modernization that has elsewhere proved more creative of new forms of institutional legitimacy. This suggests that there may be elements in Islamic cultural tradition that are particularly inimical to that procedural aspect of modernity—such as the doctrine that regards any successful seizure of power as legitimated by the *Baraka*, the blessing of Allah. It seems at any rate remarkable that among Arab states only Tunisia, which shows probably the strongest influence of Western-type enlightenment on the intelligentsia, has developed a stable single-party regime, and that among other Islamic nations Turkey after the Kemalist "cultural revolution," while not immune from repeated army intervention in politics, has produced enough military respect for democratic institutions to make its Army reluctant to exercise direct rule for any length of time.

Some Conclusions

I am conscious that the above survey of single-party regimes, or approaches to single-party regimes founded by Nationalist Modernizers, has remained sketchy and incomplete. This applies even to the mere listing of examples. Thus, only a limited number of African single-party states have been considered. The creation of the "Burma Socialist People's Party" by General Ne Win after his second seizure of power in 1962, as a state party formed under the supervision of his "Revolutionary Council" of officers and with the ideological assistance of the Moscow-oriented section of the Burmese Communists, has not been discussed at all.[39] Nor have we tried to examine the respective roles of the party with its official trade unions, the Army, and the church in the borderline case of Peron's prolonged dictatorial rule in Argentina. Yet the experiences presented are sufficiently diversified to permit an attempt to reach some general conclusions.

The first conclusion must be that selective imitation of the Bolshevik model in our sense is possible: even where nationalist single-party regimes were started with Soviet support and a conscious desire to learn from Communist examples, they have generally been able to refuse to adopt Communist goals and to set strict limits to Communist influence and infiltration.[40] The overthrow of Kuomintang rule by the Chinese Communists may be thought a major exception, but it did not happen when the Communists were working within the KMT—only from outside after many years of civil war. A more relevant exception is in one sense the case of Cuba—but there Fidel Castro's conversion to "Marxism-Leninism" occurred before a formal single-party regime, based on a fusion between his original followers and the Communist Party, was installed, and it still remains doubtful how far the result is an effective Communist single-party state or merely the use of the official party as one among several instruments of personal rule.

A second conclusion would appear to be that the success of nationalist single-party regimes in their self-set task of modernization has been rather limited, compared both to the Soviet model and to their own ideological hopes and claims. It should be borne in mind, of course, that the Soviet regime has not only existed far longer than any of its "selective imitators," but that it started on a higher industrial level than any of them: Russia in 1917, though still a predominantly agrarian country, was reckoned one of the five or six leading industrial powers of the world. But the fact remains that even the great developmental "success stories" of recent decades have not concerned national-revolutionary single-party regimes, but countries like Brazil and Iran.

If we look for the reasons for this, one major limitation of success for the countries considered here appears to have been the shortage or one-sided composition of party cadres. While absolute shortage of educated personnel is a limiting factor in many African countries, the predominance of cadres with a military or bureaucratic background *before* the revolution has clearly impeded the capacity both for mass mobilization and for the absorption of new productive elites of the Kuomintang and the Kemalists, and also of the new ruling parties of the Arab Middle East. This is confirmed by the greater success in both fields of the ruling parties in Mexico and Tunisia, who could rely on a broader revolutionary intelligentsia coming from outside the old state machine and have also shown themselves more receptive to the new managerial and technical strata.

Generally, the absence of a utopian dogma could have been expected to benefit the Nationalist Modernizers compared with the Communist-ruled countries in three ways: it freed them from the need for revolutionary upheavals beyond the elimination of real obstacles to development (such as non-investing landowners and privileged foreign companies), for a frontal attack on religion beyond the struggle against obstructive superstitions, and for a lasting conflict with the Western "imperialists" beyond the attainment of political and economic independence.[41] In fact, however, the economic incompetence of some of the nationalist leaders, their military-bureaucratic illusions about the effectiveness of planning by command, and their wavering between the expropriation of small industrial and trading firms or moderately well-to-do peasants and the correction of such steps have damaged the economic development of a number of "national-revolutionary" countries, particlarly in the Middle East and parts of Africa, hardly less than doctrinaire measures of collectivization have damaged Communist countries. The preference for ideological eclecticism over the imposition of an all-inclusive dogma, while permitting more intellectual liberty and avoiding an all-out collision with religious tradition, gave some of the national regimes less strength to fight the danger of bureaucratic corruption in the growing state sector of the economy, as shown in Kuomintang China or Ghana or lately in Egypt, and to impose discipline on ambitious officer cliques, as shown in Syria and Iraq. The unnecessary sacrifices to which the Communist states subjected themselves by their long-term ideological hostility to the West, some of the nationalist states incurred by allowing their foreign policy to be dominated by megalomaniac fantasies or fanatical hostility to neighbors: again the cases of Nkrumah's Ghana and of the Middle Eastern states come to mind. The chance of a more pragmatic orientation implied in the rejection of communism has in fact benefited those who took it—such as Mexico, Tunisia, and Kemalist Turkey in its time; but there have been more nationalist single-party states who failed to take it. Success in the selective imitation of a model seems, after all, to depend not least on the right kind of selection.

THE FASCIST DICTATORSHIPS

In the underdeveloped countries, as we have seen, the Bolshevik model of the "party of a new type" and of the single-party state has been used for a purpose which, for all the differences of doctrine, is historically similar to their function in their country of origin: for mobilizing the masses in the process of modernization and conferring "democratic" legitimacy on a dictatorial regime, while ensuring at the same time a concentration of national energies on its goals by a total suppression of all independent interest groups. The concept of "totalitarian democracy," coined to highlight the links between Bolshevik totalitarian practice and Rousseau's definition of democracy as the rule of an indivisible *volonté générale,* thus applies to all the nationalist modernizers who learned from the Bolshevik model.

The situation is clearly different in the case of parties and party dictatorships of the fascist type, which bear a striking resemblance to the same model in their organizational structure and political institutions, yet are radically opposed in their doctrine to the egalitarian, rationalist, and humanistic values of the democratic tradition. Fascists and National-Socialists believed that it was their historic task to root out the disruptive ideas that had come into the western world since the Enlightenment and the French Revolution, and to destroy all "Marxist" movements, and Bolshevism in particular, as the most pernicious fruits of those ideas.

Yet a closer analysis of fascist ideology will show that the Fascists agree with the Bolsheviks not only negatively in their utter contempt for the liberal aspect of the democratic tradition—freedom of discussion and dissent, protection of minorities and partial interests, security of individual rights under the rule of law—but also in basing the legitimacy of their regimes on the will of the people. The Fascists are not traditionalists content to play an auxiliary role in the defence or restoration of God-given dynastic regimes; they are revolutionaries claiming to carry out the national will in destroying the rule of a conspiracy of alien or separatist interests. That national will is as authentic a derivative of the *volenté générale* as is the "proletarian class-consicousness" of the Communists: as with the latter, it is not to be identified empirically by a counting of votes, but is established *a priori* by the superior understanding of the party and ultimately the leader.

The Fascist Party and the fascist dictatorship, in pursuing their anti-egalitarian and nationalist goals, have thus to solve the same political dilemma as the Communists in pursuing their egalitarian and internationalist goals: how to combine "democratic" legitimation by a mass movement with suppression of freedom of discussion and of the representation of partial interests. It is this similarity of the problem that accounts for the similarity of the forms of party organization and state institutions. But because of the opposition of ideological goals and values, the fascist leaders were not originally conscious of the parallel, and were only gradually driven to adopt the organizational and institutional devices of their enemies.

Italian Fascism

The history of Italian fascism is usually dated either from Mussolini's break with the Italian Socialist Party in 1915, or from the foundation of the *Fasci Italiani di Combattimento* in 1919; but no influence of the Bolshevik model on Italian fascism can be traced before the autumn of 1921, when the movement was transformed into the *Partito Nazionale Fascista* at its Rome congress. The change was more than nominal: it marked the emergence of a new concept out of a crisis both in the practice of the movement and in the ideas of its leader. Benito Mussolini had occasionally boasted that he was the true father of Italian communism because of the prominent part he had played as a leader of the radical wing of the Italian Socialist Party on the eve of the First World War. But the mixture of revolutionary Marxist and syndicalist ideas which he then held, while foreshadowing some aspects of his future in their stress on direct action and their contempt for parliamentary discussion and compromise and for legal procedure, contained no original contribution to the problem of party organization.

In breaking away from the Socialists in order to become an active propagandist of participation in the war, and in reorganizing his followers after the war as a "fascist" movement to resist the militant internationalism and Soviet sympathies of the bulk of Italain organized labor, Mussolini was not at first aiming at creating another party—not even a party of a new type. He rather hoped that his militant movement would give him a basis for concluding alliances with other organizations, notably ex-servicemen's associations, but possibly also with a trade union movement that might emancipate itself from the Marxist internationalist doctrine of the Socialist Party, and that a great new Labor Party would eventually emerge from this alliance.

The actual development of the fascist movement, however, turned in a quite different direction. On one side, the attempts to woo the trade union movement were completely unsuccessful, as Italian labor reacted to the post-war difficulties with an aimless radicalism expressed in theory by admiration for the Soviet system and in practice by an unprecedented wave of strikes, culminating in the famous occupation of the factories by the locked-out engineering workers in August–September 1920. On the other hand, the influx of nationalist and anti-labor former officers, ex-servicemen, and students, gave the fascist "action squads" an increasingly right-wing complexion, and the landowners of the Po valley, hard pressed by agricultural labor unions working closely with the socialist municipalities of the region, began by the turn of 1920–21 to call on these action squads to destroy the "subversive" unions, co-operatives, and municipalities by armed terrorism. A movement that Mussolini had conceived with an ideology combining nationalism and anti-Bolshevism with radical demands for social reform and production control of a syndicalist type, and which up to then had been a marginal factor in Italian politics, thus experienced at the same time both a rapid increase in membership and a transformation of its composition and outlook: between October 1920 and February 1921, the number of local *fasci* rose from 190 to 1,000 and reached 2,500 by the end of that year, but the rapid increase was linked to the role of the new organizations as armed executioners of the labor movement financed by the agrarians.

In the spring and summer of 1921 Mussolini still tried both to exploit the growth of his movement and to change its direction. The elections of May 1921 had enabled the Fascists to enter parliament with a group of thirty-five deputies—a parliament in which the problem of finding a stable parliamentary majority was continually acute, because the traditionally governing liberal groups had lost their majority with the introduction of universal suffrage and proportional representation after the war, while of the two new mass parties, the Socialists and the Catholic Popular Party, the former refused all government participation on doctrinaire grounds.

Mussolini now argued that the "Bolshevik danger" in Italy had been overcome by the successful intimidation of Italian labor, and that the tactics of violence must be ended by a "peace pact" with the tamed labor organizations in order to make fascism respectable and open the road for its eventual participation in the government—preferably in a coalition with both the Catholics and the reformist wing of the Socialists. But when he actually concluded such a pact at the beginning of August 1921, a right-wing opposition based on the strong fascist organizations of the Po valley, and headed by Grandi, Balbo, and Farinacci, denounced him at a regional rally as a "traitor," and opposed the porgramme of a "national revolution" and a corporative state to his parliamentary projects. Within a week, Mussolini had to resign his leadership of the movement.

At this critical juncture, Mussolini was still the fascist movement's only nationally known leader and the owner and editor of its newspaper. He had proved himself an immensely effective propagandist, with great strength of will and ruthless ambition, but he had lost control of his organization; and though he considered breaking with it, he found that he would lose most of his value for possible political partners without its backing, while the organization could not get far without his ability. He emerged from the crisis with the conviction that he would have to adapt himself to the anti-labor instincts and interests of his movement, but at the same time to transform his unruly and generally non-political para-military organization into a disciplined party based on the primacy of the political over the military arm.

It was this that was accomplished at the Rome congress

in November 1921. Mussolini dropped the "peace pact" as "past history," and authorized the resumption of large-scale anti-labor terrorism, thus implicitly abandoning all plans for coalition with the democratic forces. Nationalism and anti-liberalism were made the cornerstones of the platform of the new party. It started with a membership of 320,000, with its cadres recruited largely from the upper and middle classes, among them a large contingent of students, while the lower ranks included the members of many agricultural and some industrial labor unions that had been forced to take refuge with the Fascists after their own leadership had been destroyed.

At the same time, the party's new statute provided for subordination of the action squads to the political leadership at all levels. Local *fasci* were to be founded only with central permission, and were to be grouped into regional federations, whose elected representatives were to form a central committee and a small central directorate of eleven, including one General Secretary, which in turn would supervise the regional organizations. Even the action squads were still supposed to elect their commanders at this time, though these would be subordinate to the "general inspectorate" which formed a department of the party secretariat. Each local *fascio* was to include technical units of specialists in the public services for purposes of strike-breaking; in addition, special organizations for women, students, and young people were to form part of the party.

If this form of organization may be described as "democratic centralism," the democratic element in it was still remarkably strong. The statute of 1921 provided no special position for the party leader, nor did it provide for the appointment of regional and local leaders from above; in fact, despite Mussolini's reconciliation with his opponents at the congress, they still insisted on transferring the headquarters from his seat, Milan, to Rome, and he reacted by refusing membership in the directorate. But they soon found that they could not conduct national policy without him, and the following months saw both rapid progress in the centralization of the local squads into a national fascist militia under a single command, and the beginning of the cult of the Duce. By early October 1922 all commanders were being appointed from above and the principle of strict obedience to superiors was in force. Mussolini had achieved this by arguing the need for centralized action for the conquest of power, though he did not in fact consider armed insurrection: he knew that all the successes in his undeclared civil war had been gained only with the toleration of the army and police, and he remained determined to get into power by legally joining a coalition government—though now it could only be a coalition of the Right. What he really wanted and achieved was a party and a party Army organized not for revolution from below, but for merging with the state machine from above—and this task required even stricter centralization.

The Fascists thus became transformed into a true totalitarian party only during the last year before their "March on Rome" in October 1922, brought off once again thanks to the non-resistance of the King and the armed forces, made Mussolini head of a coalition government. Some of the formal adjustments of the party statute to the leader principle were made even later: the Duce's right to confirm the election of regional party leaders was written in only in October 1923, the principle of their appointment from above transferred from the military to the political organization only in October 1926. The rule that membership in the party was incompatible with membership in a Masonic Lodge also dates from early 1923, the same period when the Nationalist Party, in many ways an ideological forerunner of the Fascists, was finally annexed by them under the euphemistic name of fusion.

The fact that to the Fascists, Bolshevism was a mortal ideological enemy who could not possibly be acknowledged as a model, naturally makes it difficult to judge how far this transformation had really been influenced by a study of the Bolshevik experience. We know, however, that precisely during the crucial period in 1921–22 Mussolini repeatedly referred to Lenin's change-over to the New Economic Policy as proof that the trend of political developments was everywhere to the Right, and that the superiority of the hierarchical over the egalitarian principle had been confirmed even in Soviet Russia. Mussolini detested Bolshevism but admired Lenin as a technician of power; and if he followed Russian developments as he did, he must have been impressed with the effectiveness of the centralized party and its monopolistic rule, which was only finally and formally established during this same period.

At the same time, the origin of the Fascist Party in a political defeat of the leader by the conservative forces indicates a peculiar historical weakness of Italian fascism that was to remain characteristic of it right to the end. Italian fascism was not the creation of Mussolini to the same extent as Bolshevism was the creation of Lenin or national-socialism the creation of Hitler. Mussolini rose to power after abandoning his own original republican and anti-clerical aspirations, not only because this was a tactical precondition for being entrusted with the government, but also because these aspirations were not shared by decisive elements within his own party. Hence, while the compromise with the parliamentary regime, which meant nothing to the party hierarchs, could easily be abandoned in the next major crisis, the compromises with the monarchy and the church remained, to offer a basis of action to Mussolini's enemies in the testing hour of 1943: Italian fascism became the first totalitarian regime to be overthrown from within— because it had never been *fully* totalitarian.

The regime which Mussolini installed after the "March on

Rome" was still a mixture of a parliamentary coalition and an extra-legal party dictatorship. Other parties remained both within and without the government, and even the new electoral law passed in 1923, while providing for a two-thirds majority of seats for any party winning a quarter of the votes, did not eliminate them in principle. On the other hand, the fascist militia was made a state organ without even being sworn to the King, and the terrorism it used against active opponents of the regime, and particularly against the remnants of the labor organizations, became an essential factor in the elections. The contradiction led to an open crisis when the socialist leader Giacomo Matteotti was murdered in 1924, after a speech in parliament attacking the validity of the elections because of widespread intimidation; amidst a wave of nation-wide indignation, the opposition deputies left parliament as a sign of protest.

Mussolini's reaction to the crisis—he offered concessions and hesitated for several months—seems to indicate that he had not made up his mind in advance to regard his coalition as a mere transitional stage to a single-party regime; but he was clearly determined not to abandon power, and by the beginning of 1925 he realized that, as the extremists of his party had urged all along, he had no other alternative. Farinacci was now made General Secretary of the party, and within the next two years the remaining opposition parties were suppressed, their leaders killed, arrested, or driven into exile, the independent papers handed over to fascist editors, and the fascist "trade unions" given a monopoly of organization. New legislation eliminated the parliamentary mandates of the opposition and obliged all civil servants to join the party, while the heads of municipalities were made appointed government officials. The head of government was given both exclusive control of the executive and the right to govern by decree, amounting to the union of executive and legislative power. The list of political offences was extended to "thought crimes," and the penalties were increased by introducing the death sentence and creating concentration camps. Labor relations were based on the principle of the "corporative state," under which the employers' organizations were given the dignity of state organs without a substantial change in their leadership, while the fascist unions, with their appointed leadership, were given a monopoly of labor organization, and co-operation between the two, including a ban on strikes, was imposed.

By the end of 1926, Italy was thus a totalitarian state except for the autonomy of the church and the continued existence of the monarchy, and even the prerogatives of the latter were curtailed by a law of 1928 giving the Fascist Grand Council a voice in the question of succession. At the same time, Italy was unique in combining a totalitarian political organization with an economy run on liberal capitalist principles. It was only the impact, first of the world economic crisis (during which the fascist state took over a considerable number of bankrupt enterprises), then of the League of Nations' sanctions during the Ethiopian war (leading to a number of austerity measures and stimulating the production of substitutes), and finally of the alliance with Hitler's Germany and the Second World War, which forced the gradual extension of state control over Italian economic life.

It is true that some of the early economic policies of fascism, such as the building of motor roads and the efforts to increase the cultivated area by amelioration of marshland, showed aspects of a dictatorship of development; and it may be argued that even the suppression of a militant labor movement which, quite apart from its "revolutionary" ideology, had been too strong for the level of development reached by the Italian economy, may have promoted Italy's emergence from the post-war crisis and its economic growth. But Italy in the middle twenties was not as underdeveloped as Turkey, China, or even Russia in 1917; moreover, the social composition of the Fascist Party made it unwilling to tackle the truly structural obstacles to further development, such as the distribution of land-ownership, particularly in the south. In common with all dictatorships of development, Italian fascism described its programme as that of a nationalist revolution; in contrast to successful dictatorships of development, it directed its dynamism against organized labor rather than against the traditionalist obstacles to development, and toward expansion abroad rather than to the transformation of the economic and social structure at home.

It was this preoccupation with the expansion of Italy's territorial and military power which, by driving the reluctant Duce into an alliance with the much stronger Führer, ultimately led fascism to its doom. In contrast to Hitler, Mussolini had not been willing *a priori* to base his foreign policy on the ideological affinity with nazism; and when the restrictions he had to impose on Italy's economic life in the course of the world crisis made it more urgent for him to obtain spectacular successes in foreign policy, he first thought to gain them by obtaining the toleration of the western democracies for his Ethiopian adventure in return for a measure of co-operation with them in containing Hitler. Yet when the upsurge of anti-fascist and anti-imperialist opinion, notably in Britian, destroyed the basis of this "Stresa diplomacy," Mussolini had no option left but to walk into Hitler's wide-open arms; and in the early stages of the Second World War, his military failure in Greece turned the unequal partnership, which the Axis had been from the start, into *de facto* subordination to Nazi Germany.

By the time of the allied landings in Italy in 1943, the Fascist Party, which had taken power in the name of national greatness, had in fact led its country into a destructive war under foreign control. The manner in which Mussolini's rule was ended by the Fascist Grand Counil, and the latter was abolished by a royal coup, proved that both the leader and his party had completely isolated themselves from the people they governed; and the final revival of the "Fascist Republic" under German occupation had no more political significance than any other Quisling regime.

German National-Socialism

> Supporter of a movement is he who declares his agreement with its aims. Member is only he who fights for it.
>
> The supporter is won for the movement by its propaganda. The member is directed by the organization to co-operate personally in recruiting new supporters from whose ranks new members may arise in turn.
>
> As support requires only passive acceptance of an idea while membership demands its active advocacy and defense, there will always be only one or two members for any ten supporters.

These sentences could have been written as arguments for Lenin's draft of Paragraph 1 of the statute of the Russian Social-Democratic Workers' Party—the draft around which the Bolshevik faction was formed at the party congress of 1903. In fact, they stand in Hitler's *Mein Kampf,* in the chapter entitled "Propaganda and Organization," the central importance of which for Hitler's concept of his party has been rightly stressed by Hannah Arendt. It is true that the second part of the chapter develops a doctrine which is in strict contrast to the Bolshevik theory of organization—the rejection of committee rule in favor of the principle of one-man responsibility at all levels. Yet by the time *Mein Kampf* was written in 1924, that principle had in practice been introduced into the administration of the Soviet state and its economy.

Nothing indeed is more striking about the beginnings of the National-Socialist Party, the NSDAP, than the clarity with which Hitler from the start recognized the basic principles of a centralistic party—even before he developed the clear concept that his party was to become the ruling force of a resurrected Germany, rather than a mere auxiliary of the army. Hitler had been delegated into Anton Drexler's German Workers' Party as a propagandist of the local Reichswehr command in 1919, and it was with Reichswehr funds that Dietrich Eckart bought the *Völkischer Beobachter* for the NSDAP in late 1920. It is highly doubtful whether Hitler consciously aimed at an independent seizure of power by his party before Mussolini's March on Rome set the example in October 1922. Yet it was in July 1921, before the Fascist Party was even founded, and at a time when Mussolini was forced to give in to his regional sub-leaders, that Hitler surmounted his first major inner-party crisis and forced his recognition as party president with unlimited powers by threatening resignation; and at the first party congress, in January 1922, he already proclaimed the principle that his Munich branch was to remain the model and center for the entire party.

For all the radical opposition between Hitler's ideas of a "natural" hierarchy of race and the egalitarian and inter-nationalist goals of the Bolsheviks, and for all the bitter hatred of the "Jewish Bolshevik World Conspiracy" shown by Hitler from the start, the parallel between Hitler's and Lenin's concepts of the party as the instrument of a single will to power, and between their practice in forging that instrument against every kind of resistance, is indeed ex-traordinary—once allowance is made for the difference of conditions in the development of an underground party in Tsarist Russia and of a legal party in the Weimar Republic. Like Lenin, Hitler had in fact to refound his party repeat-edly—notably after his return from the Landsberg fortress in 1925—and to reassert his leadership by threatening or carrying out a split: he broke with the Deutsch-Völkische wing of the party at that time, and subdued the North German faction of the NSDAP with its anti-capitalist and pro-Soviet tendencies in the following year.

Like Lenin, too, Hitler defended the principle of the primacy of the political over the military arm—in a milieu where this was far more unusual and difficult: though some of his best cadres came from the Free Corps and the para-military leagues, he dissolved the SA in 1925 rather than allow it to become a non-political instrument of secret rearmament, organized the SS in the following year as a politically reliable elite unit, and refounded the SA only when its control by the party was assured.[42] Among the anti-democratic nationalists of Germany in the twenties, the idea that the nationalist cause could triumph only by subordinating the para-military organizations to a political party was as novel and startling as the idea that social-democracy could triumph only as a centralist conspiratorial organization was among the revolutionary circles of Russia around the turn of the century.

Yet while the parallel is striking, no direct influence of the Bolshevik model on Hitler can be traced. It is not only that he would naturally have been reluctant to acknowledge any such influence; there is also no indication whatever that Hitler studied the Bolshevik experience, even to the extent to which Mussolini may have done in 1921–22. Hitler's socalled experts on Bolshevism, German expatriates from Russia like Rosenberg and Scheubner-Richter, saw in the Bolshevik regime nothing but the rule of a Jewish gang, based on the extermination of the native elite and the support of Mongol elements, and were quite incapable of even asking what might be the roots of Bolshevik strength; and those sub-leaders who began to recognize that strength and to show an interest in the problem by the middle twenties, like Goebbels and the Strasser brothers, found their ideas scornfully rejected by the Führer.

On the other hand, Hitler's early grasp of the principles of organizational centralism cannot be explained by his military background alone. No doubt it was army experience that had impressed him with the superiority of hierarchical discipline and individual responsibility over democratic election and discussion; but it was not there that he could have learned the importance of the primacy of political over military leadership. Even if the fact is taken into account that Hitler himself held no officer's rank and rose to influence by his gifts as a demagogue, the question remains of what model may have encouraged him to claim a role of leadership over his military betters.

The most plausible answer is to be found in a document the profound influence of which on Hitler's political imagination is beyond doubt: the so-called *Protocols of the Elders of Zion*. Here we have the model of a conspiracy aiming at world domination in the service of a political idea by the ruthless use of all means, but starting without direct control over military forces and making ample use of political intrigue and of the propagandist "rape of the masses." It is no accident that HItler's accounts of the methods of the Jewish all-enemy read so often like a recipe for his own actions: they constitute at the same time a projection of his ambitions and a model for their execution.

But we know that the *Protocols* were forged and used in the circles of the Tsarist secret police and of the ultra-reactionary Black Hundred organization, and that their original purpose was to discredit the Russian revolutionaries as tools of an anti-Russian conspiracy. Much that is said in the *Protocols* about the alleged methods of the Elders of Zion is thus a distorted image of the actual methods of earlier Russian revolutionary organizations, notably of the *Narodnaya Volya*: the Black Hundred were founded in 1881, after the assassination of Alexander II by that revolutionary organization. It was, on the other hand, the real experience of the *Narodnaya Volya* that Lenin took as a model for his theory of organization.

The *Protocols* thus take their place in a series of steps by which the revolutionaries and counter-revolutionaries of Europe may be shown to have learned from each other since the late eighteenth century. The secret order of the Bavarian

Illuminati attempted to use for the aims of the Enlightenment the methods which it ascribed to the Jesuits. The Jesuit critics of the French Revolution sought to explain that entire historical event as due to a conspiracy of the Illuminati and the freemasons, with the Jews thrown in for good measure. The Russian revolutionary societies of the 1870s incorporated in their statutes the formula that "the end justifies the means" which was regarded as a Jesuit motto, and the *Protocols* in turn pretended to reveal the secret international background of those revolutionary societies. Hitler's ideas about the relation of the struggle for power with specific organizational techniques are not derived from Lenin's, but the parallelism between them is not accidental: both were derived from different branches of this interacting tradition.

The common core of this tradition is precisely the combination of "propaganda and organization"—in other words, recognition of the "democratic" need for winning the support of the people, combined with organizational devices for making the party, and later its government, as independent as possible from particular interests and pressures from below.

The experience of Mussolini's March on Rome coincided with a marked acceleration of the German currency inflation and was soon followed by the profound crisis of German society caused by the French occupation of the Ruhr and the German government's decision to finance the policy of passive resistance by means of the printing press. The crisis year of 1923 saw a Hitler who had clearly abandoned all thought of acting as a mere propagandist auxiliary—a "drummer"—for the Reichswehr, and was determined to accomplish a national revolution under his own leadership and with his own party. The crucial months after the fall of the Cuno government in August in particular, during which passive resistance was liquidated while the chief of the Reichswehr, General von Seeckt, was invested with emergency powers, are characterized by Hitler's growing impatience with the various nationalist leaders and military commanders in Munich and Berlin, each of whom was openly hostile to the republic but waiting for somebody else to make the decisive move for its overthrow. Hitler's utterances of this period show his conviction that he alone had the political courage and vision to make this move and establish his dictatorship by a "March on Berlin," but also his recognition that he needed the active support of at least the Bavarian military to ensure that there would be no resistance by the legal forces of order; as one of his advisers, Scheubner-Richter, wrote in a memorandum at the time, the real National Revolution could only start once the police had been brought under the control of the revolutionaries. In short, Hitler had learned from Mussolini both that it was necessary to take full power and that it was possible to do this only with the toleration of the army and the police, but he was not yet committed to the doctrine that this could be achieved only in the forms of "legality."

The events of 8 and 9 November 1923 showed that Hitler had underestimated the strength of the republican institutions and overestimated his own influence on the Bavarian right-wing leaders. As the crisis of state and society was overcome with the progress of economic stabilization, while Hitler disappeared for a time in the fortress of Landsberg, the NSDAP lost at the same time its leader and the respectable allies who had hitherto protected it. It became the prey of factional fights in which Hitler's authority seemed almost completely dissipated, and when he returned he had to start anew by building a secure base in Bavaria at the price of temporary political concessions to the Catholic regional government; it was this opportunism that led to his break with the strongly "anti-Roman" Deutsch-Völkische who had in the meantime merged with his party. The real reassertion of his leadership came in a showdown with those

North German regional leaders who had taken the 'socialist' element in national-socialism seriously enough to wish to support the left-wing parties in their referendum for the expropriation of the former German princes; in forcing them to accept his alternative that the "foreign stock-exchange princes" should be expropriated first, he may have temporarily lost votes, but he ensured his party's chances of "respectable" support in future crises. The successful reassertion of Hitler's leadership was sealed by the new party statute adopted by a full membership meeting held in Munich in May 1926: it not only declared the party programme unalterable; it established the principle that the whole party was an extension of the Munich branch with the Munich leadership acting as national leadership and entitled to appoint all Gauleiters. Under German Association Law, the leader himself could not be made formally irremovable but the statute made his removal dependent on conditions that could hardly ever be fulfilled in practice; at the same time he was given power to appoint the heads of the various departments as well as the manager of the party headquarters, who together would form a majority of the party executive. It was only after this formal establishment of the Führer principle that he started rebuilding the party's para-military force, the SA, but in the changed circumstances he took much greater care than in the early years to keep it within the limits of the law.

By the time the world economic crisis gave the NSDAP its second chance, Hitler's concept of the road to power had clearly matured. He was determined to achieve a type of single-party state in which the party cadres would occupy the nerve centres of the state machine, as was by then the case in fascist Italy as well as in Bolshevik Russia; beginning as early as 1926 and accelerating with the approach of the crisis, the party had created, quite apart from its political organization in the country, a number of specialized central departments preparing plans and cadres for future government policy in such diverse fields as agriculture, education, defense, and "racial health." He was equally determined to take power legally, and particularly with the help of the Reichswehr; but he now realized clearly that the Reichswehr leaders did not want a revolution and would first have to be won over by the argument that the victory of the National-Socialists was the only alternative to that of the Communists. It was the turn of part of the industrial and land-owning classes to renewed opposition to the republic and to active nationalist propaganda which gave the National-Socialist Party its chance to overcome its isolation, from 1929 onwards, by an alliance with Hugenberg's German Nationalist Party, and thus to regain the subsidies and publicity needed for the propagandist exploitation of the crisis along with a new aura of "national" respectability. The first great electoral victory in September 1930 confirmed Hitler on this road and opened a period in which every government crisis was accompanied by his increasingly frantic attempts to find a legal door to the key positions of power. Yet in repeated negotiations he consistently rejected any form of coalition which would have involved him in government responsibility without giving him an effective lever for casting aside his allies and achieving full power. It was for this reason that he allowed the negotiations with the Catholic Center Party to fail and that he wrecked the tentative accord reached between General von Schleicher and his own lieutenant, Gregor Strasser. It was for the same reason that, in finally accepting a coalition with von Papen and Hugenberg in January 1933, he insisted on immediate new elections which would enable him quickly to change the terms of the coalition agreement.

With far greater clarity than Mussolini, Hitler had understood in advance that the legal road to a National Revolution could be opened only by way of an alliance with the conservative forces—army and bureaucracy, landowners and industrialists—against organized labor: while Mussolini had had to be forced on to this course by his sub-leaders at the price of a loss of authority, Hitler forced the same course on reluctant sub-leaders, thereby strengthening his authority. But with far greater clarity than Mussolini, too, Hitler in 1933 formed a legal coalition with those conservative allies with the deliberate intention to transform it into an extra-legal dictatorship of his party.

As Hitler was able to profit from the experience both of bolshevism in 1917–21 and of fascism in 1922–26, he did in fact establish his single-party regime in a much shorter time. Immediately after the formation of the government and the calling of elections, his brownshirts were given the status of an auxiliary police force, so as to prepare the proper climate for the polls. The Reichstag fire of 27 February, though possibly accidental and not expected by the nazis, was at once exploited for destroying the Communist Party and considerably weakening the Social-Democrats by a wave of terror, and for "legalizing" the practice of terror by the "Decree for the Protection of People and State." Though the elections of 5 March still left the Nazis dependent for a majority on their nationalist allies, the cancellation of the communist mandates promptly eliminated that dependence. The enabling law passed by the new Reichstag against the votes of the Social-Democrats removed further legal inhibitions, and within a few months the Social-Democrats too had been outlawed and the bourgeois parties bullied into self-dissolution. With Hugenberg's Nationalists sharing their fate, the coalition was ended and single-party government achieved; a decree of 1 December 1933 formally established the "unity of party and state," thus drawing the conclusions from the new state of affairs and providing the legal basis for the mass entry of party cadres into the bureaucracy.

This penetration of the state machine by the party, though much more thorough than in fascist Italy, never reached the completeness of Bolshevik Russia, where the state machine had to be rebuilt completely after a genuine revolution from below; in different departments of the German government it was accomplished to a very uneven degree, as a result not only of the inertial resistance of the old bureaucracy, but also of the insufficient qualifications of many of the party members aspiring to bureaucratic positions. Success was most nearly complete in the vital area of police control, and here it was entirely due to the SS, which within a short time had developed into a kind of "inner party" with much stricter standards of selection and discipline than the shapelessly swollen civilian party organization. It was the SS that within a few months took over the political police, the guarding of the concentration camps, and the creation of heavily armed mobile police formations; by 1936 Himmler and the regional SS leaders were at the same time placed in charge of the entire regular police force.

The most critical area for the fusion of party and state, on the other hand, was the army. Its wish to avoid a clash with the Nazi movement had been decisive for Hitler's victory, yet at first it still owed loyalty to the non-Nazi head of state, Field Marshal Hindenburg. The ambition of the SA leaders to have their para-military organization integrated in the regular army, and to be established there with ranks corresponding to their SA status, was liable to provoke the solid resistance of the professional soldiers rather than achieve the desired fusion. Hitler brutally solved the problem by the double-edged blood purge of 30 June 1934, which decapitated the SA and broke its ambitions, yet by the assassination of General von Schleicher and of a number of conservative critics demonstrated his determination not to tolerate any political independence on the part of military leaders. By taking the oath of allegiance to Hitler as Führer and Reichskanzler, the Reichswehr a few months later paid for the preservation of its professional monopoly; it was not until February 1938 that Hitler felt strong enough to attack its professional independence and to remove Generals von Fritsch and Beck. Even so, his control of the Army remained less perfect than of other branches of the state machine down to the conspiracy of July 1944.

The purge of June 1934 could not have been carried out without the existence of an armed force tied to no legal rules and owing loyalty to nobody but Hitler: the SS. As proof of the dictator's ability to wield the instrument of terror against a variety of actual or potential opponents at one and the same time, it is said to have profoundly impressed Stalin; according to Krivitsky, it was now the Bolshevik leader who began to learn from the Nazi model for his own impending purges. It is arguable that a similar impact in reverse was also exerted on Communist strategy by the example of the legal seizure of power: the undoctrinaire policy of the anti-Fascist "popular front" in the following years, and the experiments with the "peaceful road" to Communist power encouraged by Stalin after 1945, and used as a basis for a general theory by Khrushchev after 1956, owe more than a little to the successful demonstration of how thoroughly Fasicts and Nazis were able to transform states of which they had taken control by methods which in form had been legal and parliamentary.

Conversely, it is certain that Hitler was profoundly impressed by Stalin's purges, and that by the late thirties he was no longer convinced of the weakness and instability of the "Jewish Bolshevik" regime. He had come to admire its techniques of power and in particular its political control over the army, and during the war he expressed this admiration first by the order to kill all political commissars who were captured on the Russian front, and finally by creating a parallel institution in the shape of the "NS-Führungsoffiziere" in 1944.

As with the Bolsheviks and in contrast to Mussolini, the clarity with which Hitler conceived of single-party rule as a system of total power was linked to the purpose of a total transformation of society in accordance with an ideological vision. But in the conditions of highly industrialized Germany, that purpose could not be connected with the process of modernization, as in Russia and in less developed countries. Here as there, political power was to be concentrated in a single hand in order to overcome a form of social stagnation—but it was not the stagnation of a semi-traditional society, but of an economic crisis resulting in paralysing social conflicts; and the transformation envisaged was the total mobilization for war and territorial expansion and the creation of an empire based on the principle of racial hierarchy.

As early as the summer of 1936 Hitler, in a secret memorandum on the tasks of the four-year plan, set the goal of making the army and the economy ready for war within four years. Without substantial interference with the legal forms of private ownership, the powers of the government were used to direct investment into the channels of a war economy—armaments, substitute raw materials, strategic roads. The control of the employers' organizations, the replacement of the trade unions by the Labor Front and of the peasant organizations by the Reich Food Estate, all of them coordinated under party discipline, served the same purpose. We know that in November 1937 Hitler explained to his inner council that war should not be postponed beyond 1943–45 at the latest. The change in the Army command followed within a few months of this announcement and was followed in turn almost immediately by the annexation of Austria—the first step on the road to territorial expansion.

But in the framework of the Nazi ideological vision war and territorial expansion were not conceived merely as means for increasing national power: it was the rule of the

Nordic racial elite that was ultimately to be established, with the German nation fighting in the service of this vision because it had had the good luck to come first under the rule of this elite. Being an instrument rather than the ultimate goal of this scheme, the German nation had itself to be transformed in the process—not only in its economic and social structure, but in its biological substance. Hence policy measures that were "rational" by the standards of classical power politics—rearmament, economic mobilization, conquest—were accompanied by equally systematic measures that by the same standards were "irrational" in their wanton brutality, and meaningful only in relation to the racialist ideology: the racial health measures at home, the systematic destruction of national elites among the Slav peoples, and the extermination of the Jews.

The first law for the prevention of biologically inferior offspring was passed as early as July 1933, the decree about the killing of the insane on the opening day of the Second World War, and long-term measures for further "improvement" of the biological substance of the nation were being prepared by the appropriate SS departments in the midst of war. The orders to destroy the leading strata of the Polish people were issued as soon as the Polish campaign was over. The anti-Jewish measures were first put on the basis of the principle of racial purity by the Nürnberg laws of 1935, and pursued to the "final solution" with unswerving energy, without regard to any political effects at home or abroad, or even to the strain on the war economy, from 1942 to the end of the regime.

German national-socialism may thus be said to have developed the possibilities of using the system of single-party dictatorship in the service of anti-egalitarian goals to their ultimate conclusion. Its unprecedented destructiveness, ending in what amounted to the self-destruction of the regime and indeed of the German national state, appears as the logical result of a utopia of racial domination that could in its nature not be approached, let alone achieved, without worldwide war and without measures of racial extermination.

CONCLUDING REMARKS

The experience of the deeds and collapse of the Third Reich makes it appear improbable that the model of the single-party regime will again be used for similar purposes in an advanced industrialized country. It is indeed remarkable that the model has not so far been applied to any such country in its original communist form either, except for the case of its imposition on Czechoslovakia in 1948, when the situation of that country within the Soviet sphere of control was decisive for the outcome. The only countries in which communist parties have established one-party states after coming to power by their own strength in independent revolutions have been underdeveloped countries—Yugoslavia and Albania, China and North Vietnam.

Taking a broad historical view, it thus appears that the chances of successful application of the one-party system are best in countries which share with the Russian model the basic unsolved problems of development, yet are not underdeveloped to such an extreme degree that the necessary cadres for such a regime cannot be found, as seems to be the case in some African states. Given the "proper" level of underdevelopment, the question whether a Communist or a nationalist single-party regime emerges victorious, or whether the task of development is left to a regime of an altogether different type, seems to depend primarily on historical factors within each particular country.

What seems remarkable, however, is the possibility of the transformation of a nationalist into a Communist one-party regime, that has reappeared in recent years. In a sense such a possibility was visible on the horizon in

China before 1927, but it then faded from public discussion for more than three decades. It was the decision of Fidel Castro to throw in his lot with the Communists, and to merge the remnant of his victorious but disorganized movement with their party, that reopened the question and, together with the radicalization of the Algerian and West African one-party regimes, caused the Soviets in 1963–64 to develop a political concept for achieving such transformations by means of a strategy of "licensed infiltration" of nationalist one-party regimes by Communists.

Yet while the pluralistic decay of the former organizational and ideological unity of the world Communist movement has made it easier for a revolutionary nationalist leader to welcome the cooperation of trained Communist cadres in his party, it may also have diminished the potential importance of such infiltration. If the Communists in question continue to be tied to Soviet leadership, to internationalist doctrine, or even to a precise programme for the road to the classless society, their influence on the Nationalist Party is likely to remain in most cases severely limited; to some extent this is even confirmed by the special case of Cuba, where it is still an open question how far Castro's regime has really become a Communist party regime in the classical sense, and how far it has remained a personal dictatorship using Communist slogans and cadres as exchangeable instruments. If, on the other hand, the communists adjust their outlook to the national needs and the nationalist emotions of the countries concerned, their influence may improve the systematic quality but will hardly change the direction of the nationalist regimes.

The future role of the Bolshevik model of the single-party state in developing countries is thus likely to be most effective where the leaders using the model are most successful in emancipating themselves from the specific ideological beliefs that were linked to the model in its country of origin.

III

BIG BROTHER'S TROUBLES, OR THE DILEMMAS OF COMMUNIST STRATEGY

3
From the Colonial
to the
Post-Colonial Revolution

In the famous "Theses on the National and Colonial Question" which Lenin presented at the Second World Congress of the Comintern in 1920,[1] he developed a two stage concept for the revolution in colonial and "semi-colonial" countries. On one side, he took it for granted that militant mass movements against foreign political rule and foreign economic privileges would develop among all the economically underdeveloped peoples who were kept in one or the other form of dependence by the imperialist powers, that these movements would also turn against the native traditional upper strata collaborating with the foreign exploiters, and that they would take revolutionary forms. He expected that those movements would at first result in national or "bourgeois-democratic" revolutions directed not against any native forms of capitalist ownership, which in most cases hardly existed as yet, but against precapitalist relations and ruling groups. At the same time, he predicted that these "bourgeois-democratic revolutions," arising in the age of proletarian revolutions and of Soviet power, would find their only allies for the struggle against imperialism in the Communist movement and the Soviet state and would thus become an integral part of the proletarian world revolution. Strategically, this meant for Lenin the vision of an alliance between the national, bourgeois-democratic revolutions of the colonial and semi-colonial countries and his own Communist world movement—creating a colonial "second front" for the worldwide struggle against imperialism.

On the other hand, Lenin expected that the colonial revolutions against imperialism and feudalism would in due course have to go farther than seemed tolerable to the bourgeois-capitalist strata of the countries concerned, chiefly because of the need for profound changes in the structure of agricultural property; this, he believed, would create favorable conditions for pushing these revolutions forward in a second phase, beyond their original "bourgeois-democratic" goals toward socialist goals. He asked explicitly whether it might be possible for such backward nations to "leap across" the capitalist stage of development altogether or bypass it, and he affirmed that in present international conditions, the support of the Soviet power and of the Western revolutionary proletariat would create such a possibility.[2] Pointing to the "non-capitalist road of development" taken by the Central Asian former "colonies of Tsarism" under Soviet rule as an example, he predicted that the revolutions of other colonial and semi-colonial countries might take a similar road, building state-owned industries under a Soviet type of government until the eventual achievement of socialism.

Looking back over half a century, it is possible to distinguish the shares of realistic foresight and of illusion in Lenin's vision. History has confirmed his prediction that the process of decolonization, once put on the agenda by the First World War, would proceed irresistibly and take revolutionary forms in many countries. Lenin was equally right in foreseeing that the struggle for independence of the colonial and semicolonial peoples would not only raise national problems in the narrow sense of the term, but also pose entirely new problems of economic development and of the restructuring of societies for which in many cases the classical methods familiar from Western capitalist development offered no solution. The combined revolutionary potential of these national and social transformations has indeed made possible Communist victories in several cases—including one case, that of China, that is of worldwide historical significance in itself, and cases like Cuba and Vietnam that have become the occasion for severe crises on the world scene.

At the same time, such confirmation of Lenin's revolutionary perspective for the colonial and semi-colonial countries has remained the exception rather than the norm. In the creation of dozens of new sovereign states in Asia and Africa, the Communists have nowhere been able to play a leading role—with the single exception of North Vietnam; nor has the contribution made by the external support of the Soviet Union and the international Communist movement to the overall success of decolonization been decisive. Many of the new states have gained independence by peaceful transition, without acute conflict or revolutionary struggle with the old colonial empires; in others, a militant "liberation struggle" has been conducted by nationalist movements that were in no way Communist. Again, the efforts of the new states to solve their problems of development show a wide spectrum of mixed systems combining private enterprise and the creation of industries by the state, market economy and planning, but no general tendency to follow the Communist model. In short, the expectation that the process of decolonization must in its very nature come to be directed by Communists and to issue into Communist revolutions has not been confirmed.

In what follows, we shall try to answer the questions which were the specific errors of Communist analysis that account for this relative disappointment of the hopes invested in the revolutions of colonial and semi-colonial countries, and how those errors and limitations of Communist theory have produced strategic dilemmas for Communist practice in successive phases of Soviet international policy.

THE PROBLEM OF LEADERSHIP IN THE LIBERATION STRUGGLE

Even when Lenin first developed his concept of the colonial revolution at the Second World Congress of Comintern, a significant disagreement arose on one of its basic problems: the nature of the nationalist movements arising in the countries concerned and the right way of dealing with them.[3] The leaders of those movements were in no case Communists—in Soviet language, they represented the "national bourgeoisie." Lenin, fully aware that in most of those countries not even embryonic Communist parties existed as yet, was in no way deterred from cooperating with those "bourgeois" movements and their leaders, but argued explicitly that it was the Communists' duty to support them in the first stage of the revolution: only in the course of a common struggle against imperialism and feudalism, begun under bourgeois leadership, would the Communists be able to gain sufficient strength to take over the leadership themselves in a later, second stage. The one condition for this was that the Communists should from the start build up their own organization and maintain their ideological independence.

That view, however, did not pass uncontested. One of the main congress participants from Asia, the Indian Communist Manabendra Nath Roy, put forward "countertheses" arguing that the bourgeoisie of the colonial countries was unable to mobilize the popular masses for revolutionary struggle because it was opposed to a thorough land reform; hence, even the first, national-revolutionary or "bourgeois-democratic" stage of the revolution could not be led by the parties of the "national bourgeoisie." As Roy's theses say:

> At first, the revolution in the colonies will not be a Communist revolution; but if the Communist vanguard takes the lead from the beginning, the revolutionary masses will be shown the right road on which the gradual accumulation of revolutionary experience will enable them to reach the goal. . . . During the first stage of its development, the revolution must carry out a program of petty bourgeois, reformist demands, such as land distribution, etc. But it does not follow from this that leadership in the colonies could be in the hands of the bourgeois democrats. On the contrary, the proletarian parties must carry on an intensive propaganda for Communist ideas and must form workers' and peasants' soviets at the first opportunity."[4]

The remarkable result was that, after prolonged commission debates, Roy's theses were adopted *together* with those of Lenin as a "supplement"—both in slightly amended form. Many participants were obviously not conscious of the remaining contradiction between both documents on the basic strategic question of who should lead in the first stage of the revolution; Lenin himself, who had to fight on many other issues at that congress, may have regarded the difference as without immediate practical significance—just because serious Communist parties hardly existed as yet in colonial or semi-colonial countries. But the practical significance of the unresolved contradiction was bound to become apparent as soon as the popular masses of a great semi-colonial country did in fact enter into a revolutionary movement, as happened in China in the 1920s.

The leading party of the Chinese revolution was then the

nationalist Kuomintang, which the Communists had joined
as individual members while maintaining their separate organization. In the official Soviet view, that party embodied
an alliance of four revolutionary classes-proletariat, peasantry, petty bourgeoisie, and national bourgeoisie—under
bourgeois leadership. Stalin justified the support of the
KMT with Soviet political and military advisers and the
instruction to the Chinese Communists to join it with
Lenin's thesis about the necessary leadership of bourgeois
elements in the first phase of the revolution; in fact, his
policy was above all determined by the interest of the Soviet Union in creating a strong, nationally united China as
a potential counterweight to Japan.[5] But as the revolutionary armies advanced northward from Canton while the
mass movement of the peasants grew (with the Communists
taking a large share in its organization), the problem anticipated by Roy became acute: the masses expected radical
land reforms which were not acceptable to the KMT leadership and to large parts of its officer corps. Now Stalin
wished to avoid, for reasons of foreign policy, a conflict
with the KMT's military-political leadership under Chiang
Kai-shek, and therefore sought to pull the brakes on the
agrarian revolution. Conversely, Trotsky and the other
leaders of the "Left Opposition," then in the final phase of
their power struggle against Stalin, demanded an open Communist bid for leadership of the revolution as laid down in
Roy's theses, including the creation of peasant soviets as
organs for land distribution, and preparation for the inevitable conflict with Chiang. There developed, both in Moscow
and among the Chinese Communists, a scholastic discussion
on whether one should break with Chiang Kai-shek at once
or only "after completion of the first stage"—meaning
presumably after the KMT had conquered the whole of
China. The outcome is known: Chiang preferred to determine
the timing of the break himself, destroyed his Communist
allies by a surprise attack, and sent home his Soviet advisers.

This outcome spelled equally severe defeats for Stalin's foreign policy and for the cause of Chinese communism. But "Stalin's failure in China" does not prove that Trotsky's alternative policy would have been more successful at the time: most probably, it would have produced a similar result at an earlier date. What had really proved wrong was the basic classification of the nationalist leaders as bourgeois democrats and the evaluation of their role in accordance with the classical model of European democratic revolutions. In fact, these leaders represented a type of grouping of intellectuals, officers and bureaucrats, variants of which have since become familiar at the head of nationalist movements in many developing countries; and such groupings, are, on the one hand, due to their different social origin and tradition, far less tied to specifically "bourgeois" interests than the Communist formula assumed, but on the other hand also far less democratic. They look to the modernization of their country by means of a strong state, and in that context are not afraid of assigning to that state a major economic role. But they are also determined to retain power for themselves and recognize no need to allow themselves to be superseded in a "second stage" by any foreign-directed party.

Now a recognition of these errors and a corresponding revision of strategy were not open to Stalin—not only because of the dogmatic limits of his vision, but also because that strategy had become an object of Trotsky's attacks in the factional struggle and had therefore to be defended as the only correct one—despite the catastrophic results. The official explanation of the Chinese defeat was henceforth the same as that for all Communist defeats in the European workers' movement: betrayal by some leaders. Chiang Kai-shek, it was now proclaimed, had betrayed the Chinese national revolution and gone over to the side of imperialism and feudalism; the Chinese revolution had to begin anew.[6]

In fact, however, such a new start of the revolution was only possible to the extent that Chiang failed in dealing with those tasks he had set himself—which was not at once; then, indeed, it could occur under Communist leadership. It was Mao Tse-tung who succeeded eventually, with his partisan armies and his shifting Soviet areas, in laying the foundations for this new revolution; and it fell to him also to accomplish the revision of Communist analysis and strategy which Stalin had evaded. He did so by coining, in late 1939, in the course of the war against Japan, the formula of a "new-democratic revolution," defined—just as with Roy and in sharp contrast to the Stalin of the twenties—by the need for the Communists to take the lead even in the first stage, in the revolution against imperialism and feudalism. But now he was speaking of a Communist Party that actually existed as a real force in Chinese society. Here is the core of Mao's definition:

> A new-democratic revolution is a revolution of the broad masses of the people led by the proletariat and directed against imperialism and feudalism. . . . This kind of new-democratic revolution differs greatly from the democratic revolutions in the history of European and American countries, in that it results not in the dictatorship of the bourgeoisie, but in the dictatorship of the united front of all revolutionary classes under the leadership of the proletariat. . . . This kind of new-democratic revolution differs also from a socialist revolution in that it aims only at overthrowing the rule of the imperialists, collaborators, and reactionaries in China, but not at injuring any capitalist sections which can still take part in the anti-imperialist, antifeudal struggles.[7]

In terms of the strategic task, Mao is thus still concerned with Lenin's first stage, yet with a movement under Communist leadership. Moreover, while Mao speaks like Stalin of a united front of four classes, this entire front is now *politically* represented by the Communist Party, which conceives itself as representing *all* revolutionary classes (with the aid of a few unimportant splinter groups). It follows that in Mao Tse-tung's view, once the "New Democracy" has been victoriously established by such an alliance of classes, the transition from the new-democratic to the socialist revolution may occur peacefully; for what will be required for that transition is not a change of political regime, not a transfer of power from one group to the other—only a shift in the content of the ruling Communist Party's policy.

This new concept of Mao Tse-tung's, which was to become decisive for the Chinese Communists' strategy, at first found no echo in the international Communist movement. But as in the post-war period the Chinese Communists were approaching final victory, they audibly raised the claim that Mao's strategy should become the model for the revolution in all colonial and semi-colonial countries. The formula inself was changed by Mao in June 1949, on the eve of the completion of his seizure of power: he now no longer described his regime as a "New Democracy" but as a "people's democratic dictatorship" (using a term coined in Soviet-controlled Eastern Europe), but he defined the new term exactly as he had previously defined the old one. In fact, his claim for international recognition of the Chinese model was accepted soon afterwards: when Liu Shao-chi proclaimed the model role of the Chinese revolution for all colonial and semi-colonial countries at a conference of Communist trade unionists from Asia, held at Peking in November 1949, his speech was reprinted both in *Pravda* and in the weekly bulletin of the Communist Information Bureau,[8] and subsequently the Cominform explicitly recommended the Chinese prescription to other Communist parties.[9]

Between the beginning in the twenties and Mao's victory in 1949, Communist strategy has thus veered along the entire curve from one to the other pole of the dilemma of leadership in the national revolution: from the view that

184 Big Brother's Troubles, or the Dilemmas of Communist Strategy

leadership in the first stage of the revolution necessarily belongs to bourgeois-nationalist forces whom the Communists must support, to the view that victory even in the first stage is possible only under Communist leadership. But once the latter thesis was adopted, it confronted Communist strategy with another type of dilemma—that of relations with those ex-colonial countries that had in fact obtained independence under non-Communist leadership, and in many cases by peaceful methods.

THE PROBLEM OF RELATIONS WITH THE EX-COLONIAL NATIONS

From Lenin's theory of the colonial revolution it was not to be expected that any imperialist power would give up her colonies by negotiated agreement, unless it was compelled by revolutionary struggle to yield them. From Mao's new version of the strategy of colonial revolution it was as little to be expected that any colonial peoples would obtain their independence under non-Communist leadership. Yet in fact, the era of de-colonization began in 1947 with the decision of the British Labour government to release the peoples of the Indian subcontinent, and with the emergence of India, Pakistan, Burma, and Ceylon as sovereign states under non-Communist governments. The first reaction of Stalin and the international Communist movement to this historic development was to deny it: events that were in such flagrant contradiction with their official theory could not possibly have happened. Soviet and international Communist publications stated unanimously that those countries had not become "really" independent: their new governments, under leaders like Nehru and U Nu, were mere puppets of British imperialism, sovereign in appearance only. It followed that the struggle for national independence had to be continued in those countries according to Mao's prescription—by national united fronts under Communist leadership—and that the same applied to other colonial countries which obtained their independence soon afterwards. Accordingly, we find the Asian Communists in the following years engaging in ruthless and whenever possible armed struggle against the new national governments in India and Burma, in the Philippines and Indonesia, using exactly the same slogans of a struggle for national liberation as they applied against the colonial regimes still ruling in Indochina and Malaya![10]

Yet the effect of that policy was naturally quite different in the two situations. In Vietnam, the Communists really became the leading force of the anti-colonial struggle; in Malaya they scored at least considerable initial successes among the Chinese element of the population; but in the new, ex-colonial states they were soon hopelessly isolated. Moreover, it soon became obvious that so unrealistic a policy was damaging not only for the Asian Communists themselves, but also for Soviet and particularly Chinese national interests. Nehru's India had recognized the Chinese People's Republic as soon as it was formally proclaimed, and during the Korean war Indian diplomacy proved to be the most important among the few channels then available to Peking for contact with the non-Communist world; indeed, India's tenacious efforts to mediate between China and the United Nations hardly fitted the Communist image of the role of "puppets of the imperialists." But a more realistic evaluation of the new ex-colonial states of Asia became really urgent only after Stalin's death, when both Moscow and Peking sought to end the fighting in Korea and Indochina in the context of a general policy of détente and consolidation: what mattered now was to prevent the formation, around the territory of the Communist powers in Asia, of a ring of hostile alliances and military bases as solid as had been forged, thanks to Stalin's post-war policy, around the European frontiers of the Soviet Union. To that end, Communist diplomacy must clearly endeavor to keep the new states neutral, rather than label them in advance as allies or puppets of the imperialists regardless of their real intentions.

Hence soon after Stalin's death, and with growing precision after the 1954 Geneva conference on Asia, the Communist governments and parties began radically to revise their attitude to the new, ex-colonial states of Asia: they not only recognized their independence from the imperialists in theory, but treated it as an asset worth defending in practice. Communist diplomacy now frankly pursued the aim of keeping the new states, under their existing, non-Communist governments, at least neutral, and if possible even winning them for a common front against the "imperialist camp." As instruments for this policy, it used the "five principles of peaceful coexistence," first formulated in Chou En-lai's 1954 agreement with Nehru, as well as visits of friendship by Chinese and Soviet leaders to the new countries, offers of economic aid without political, ideological, or military strings, and willingness to support these countries in any conflicts with the imperialists that might arise. Its propagandist climax was Chou En-lai's impressive performance at the conference of Afro-Asian governments in Bandung in 1955; its theoretical crystallization became Khrushchev's formula, proclaimed at the XX Congress of the CPSU in 1956, of a "Zone of Peace" to be formed by the "socialist camp" together with the ex-colonial neutrals; its practical culmination were the arms supplied to Nasser's Egypt on the eve of the Suez conflict, and the demonstrative support for him during it.

Now while this turn of the Communist powers toward diplomatic realism in their relations with the new states was remarkably successful in itself, it involved the Communists of the ex-colonial countries in serious difficulties. It was not only that they felt practically abandoned when, for instance, *Pravda* demonstratively praised Nehru's policy at the very moment the Indian Communists were bitterly attacking it during an election campaign in early 1955[11] : it was that they were suddenly left in a theoretical void and without clear strategic guidance. If it was now recognized that all these countries had achieved real and not only nominal independence, then Mao's thesis that the first stage of the colonial revolution could triumph only under Communist leadership had evidently been abandoned; but it had been abandoned silently, without theoretical discussion, and no alternative strategy had taken its place. In particular, the conditions for a transition to the second stage as originally conceived by Lenin—a socialist revolution under Communist leadership—were as absent in the new states as they had been in China after the break with Chiang: none of them were revolutionary democracies in continuing ferment, but the nationalist regimes were firmly in the saddle and the Communists far too weak to attempt a frontal attack on them with any chance of success.

The Soviet leaders seem not to have been worried by such questions at the time: apparently, they expected that new chances for the Communists of the new states would be gradually created by their diplomacy, as a long-term by-product of growing Soviet and Soviet bloc influence on the foreign and economic policy of the nationalist governments. The more effective support the Soviets would give to the urge of those states for independent development, the more they would get involved in conflicts with the foreign capitalist combines traditionally operating on their territory and with the imperialist powers backing them; and the more acute those conflicts, the more the ex-colonial or semi-colonial countries would inevitably come to depend on Soviet bloc support. The course of Egypt between 1955 and 1957, that had led from the acceptance of Soviet arms via the Suez crisis to a growing dependence of Egyptian foreign trade on the Soviet Block, seemed to indicate the road other developing countries would have to follow. In the circumstances, it might be sufficient in the Soviet view for the Communists of those countries loyally to support this course, so as eventually to profit from growing Soviet influence also by direct participation in the government and increasing influence on its policy.

For the Communists of the ex-colonial and semi-colonial countries, this concept amounted to a rather inglorious satellite role: instead of struggling for power on their own, they were to be introduced into the anterooms of bourgeois-nationalist power on the coattails of Soviet diplomats. But, while their dislike for this policy was clearly widespread,[12] they had at first no alternative—particularly as even the Chinese put forward no criticism of this policy and suggested no other road prior to 1958. Beginning in 1958–59, however, new developments in those countries began both to reveal a new kind of revolutionary potential and to cause diplomatic disappointments to the Soviets, thus forcing them once more to reconsider their strategy in this field.

On the one hand, the difficulties faced by a number of ex-colonial and semi-colonial countries in their economic development produced social tensions which caused their nationalist leaders to attempt further revolutionary changes beyond the winning of national sovereignty: they endeavored to reform land tenure and to liquidate feudal or tribal positions of power; they embarked on a planned development of industry and imposed state control of foreign trade; they took steps against Western capitalist firms and were prepared to face conflict with one or more of the major Western governments. The potential of a continuing anti-colonial revolution in legally sovereign countries, first demonstrated by Nasser's nationalization of the Suez Company, was confirmed by Kassem's revolution in Iraq in 1958 and by Castro's victory in Cuba at the turn of 1958–59, as well as by the continuing bitter conflict between newly independent Guinea and France and, far more important, between Sukarno's Indonesia and Dutch interests—all in accordance with Communist theory, but without benefit of Communist leadership (which was absent even in the early phase of the Castro regime).

On the other hand, though the Soviets were ready and eager to support the national-revolutionary leaders in their expected conflicts with the imperialists, it did not generally prove true that those leaders must therefore become increasingly dependent on the Soviets—not, at least, if they were determined and able to refuse any share of power to their native Communists. Thus Nasser had in 1958 begun to extricate himself, with American help, from excessively one-sided economic dependence on the Soviet bloc; moreover, he agreed to the proposal of the Syrian non-Communist Left to save their country from an impending Communist seizure of power by a surprise fusion with Egypt to form the "United Arab Republic," and followed this up by ruthlessly suppressing the Syrian Communists without regard to Soviet protests. Conversely, Kassem in Iraq had originally relied on Communist support against the pan-Arab followers of Nasser; but when the Communists came to demand a share of the government as a price for this support, he sharply turned against them in the summer of 1959 and permanently restricted their political activity. By contrast, President Sukarno's "guided democracy" led to a restriction of party life in general but to a steady growth of Communist influence on his government; and Fidel Castro was driven, by his growing conflict with the United States, to declare himself a "Marxist-Leninist" and to merge the loose organization of his original followers with the disciplined Communist Party.

Instead of the problem of dealing diplomatically with apparently stable nationalist regimes, the events of the late 1950s thus confronted the Soviets—and their increasingly independent Chinese allies—with new revolutionary developments in the ex-colonial and semi-colonial countries—but

also with the fact that these developments were not auto-
matically working to their advantage beyond a certain point.
Thus when the discussion on Soviet and Communist strategy for these countries revived early in 1959, it turned on a
new dilemma—that of the post-colonial national revolution.

THE PROBLEM OF THE POST-COLONIAL
REVOLUTION AND THE STRATEGY OF
'NATIONAL DEMOCRACY'

One of the first public signs of this revival of the strategy
discussion was an international debate on the role of the
"national bourgeoisie," held in May 1959 in Leipzig, ex-
tracts from which were subsequently printed in *Problems of
Peace and Socialism* (no. 8–9, 1959). The debate started
from the common recognition that the national and democratic revolution—the first stage according to the classical
theory—was not completed with the achievement of "formal independence" by the ex-colonies, and also remained
on the agenda of the "semi-colonies" of Latin America;
the struggle for real independence from imperialist economic control and for internal emancipation from the
rule of foreign monopolies and feudal landlords by democratic and agrarian reforms remained the immediate task
in all those countries. Accordingly, the classical four-class
alliance, including the "national bourgeoisie," was still
needed to fulfil that task. But as the contradictions inherent in the nature of that class were leading to more
pronounced waverings once independence was won and the
further the national and democratic revolution proceeded,
it followed that the completion of that revolution would
henceforth depend increasingly on the ability of the working class, led by the Communists, to rally the peasants to
its side and together with them exert effective pressure on
the national bourgeoisie in favor of a consistent revolu-

tionary policy. In other words, the Communists, while seeking to hold together a broad united front, including the national bourgeoisie, with a "national democratic" programme, must begin the struggle for leadership within that front—not necessarily and indeed not normally in the sense of seeking to overthrow the governments headed by popular nationalist leaders at that stage, but in the sense of seeking to force their own policy on them.[13]

Throughout the discussion, in which no Chinese Communist took part, the Soviet policy of economic aid for uncommitted governments of the "national bourgeoisie"—including those that suppressed thier own Communists—was not called in question; on the contrary, the importance of close economic relations with the Communist countries as a factor helping to keep the national bourgeoisie on the right path was stressed by several participants. But the new element in the discussion was not this endorsement of Soviet realism; the emphasis was rather on the point that Soviet diplomatic and economic support for the ex-colonial countries, however vital, was not in itself enough to ensure the completion of the national and democratic revolutions without the presence of skillfully led Communist parties within them. Egypt had shown the dangers of Communist weakness, Iraq the risks of rashness, Cuba and Indonesia seemed to indicate the gains that could be reaped with flexible tactics, while Guinea posed the problem of a revolutionary regime with a pronounced pro-Soviet orientation in a country where no Communist Party as yet existed.

It was only logical that this renewed concern with the Communist role in the emerging nations should soon afterward be reflected by the publication—in October, 1959—of the first issue of the *African Communist,* a magazine nominally issued on behalf of the South African Communist Party but clearly designed as a policy-making organ and a "collective organizer" for the whole of tropical Africa.

Right from the start, the new journal left no doubt that one of its principal purposes was to help overcome the backwardness of the dark continent in the formation of Communist parties and to stimulate their creation in all the new African states just then about to be born.

By June 1960, the new emphasis on the Communist task was clearly expressed in the resolution on the "struggle against colonialism" adopted by the Peking session of the General Council of the WFTU. It will be recalled that this session witnessed a major Chinese Communist attack on the Soviet concepts of peaceful coexistence and disarmament, and the rejection of the Chinese criticism by the large majority of delegates. No similar clash was, however, reported over the resolution that called on working class organizations in the colonial and ex-colonial countries to increase their activity in the movements for national liberation, and to "assume the leading role in forming and consolidating a united national front, based on the alliance of workers and peasants and rallying all other anti-colonial forces."[14]

In the declaration adopted by the Moscow conference of eighty-one Communist parties in December 1960, the new Communist strategy for the ex-colonial and semi-colonial countries finally found its official formulation. The Communists working in these countries were told to work for the creation of "an independent state of national democracy," and to rally the broadest possible national fronts for the achievement of that goal.

The declaration (*Pravda*, 6 December 1960) defined the new type of state as follows:

A state that consistently defends its political and economic independence, that struggles against imperialism and its military blocs, against military bases on its territory; a state that struggles against the new forms of colonialism and the penetration of imperialist capital; a state that rejects dictatorial and despotic methods of administration; a state in which the people enjoy the broadest democratic rights and liberties (freedom of speech, of the press, of assembly, of demonstrations, of forming political parties and social organizations), in which they have the possibility to strive for land reform and for the implementation of other demands for democratic and social transformations and for participation in shaping public policy. The rise and consolidation of national democratic states gives them a chance to advance quickly on the road of social progress and to play an active role in the struggle of the peoples for peace, against the aggressive policy of the imperialist camp, and for the complete liquidation of the colonial yoke.

A closely similar catalogue of "priority tasks for national rebirth" had been listed a few paragraphs before in the same declaration as capable of solution only if "all patriotic forces of the nation join in a national, democratic United Front." This section ran:

Strengthening of national independence, land reforms in the interest of the peasantry, abolition of the remnants of feudalism, extirpation of the economic roots of imperialist rule, limitation and ousting of foreign monopolies from the economy, foundation and development of a national industry, raising of the standard of living of the population, democratization of public life, an independent, peace-loving foreign policy, development of economic and cultural cooperation with the socialist countries and other friendly countries—these are the all-national, democratic tasks for the solution of which the progressive forces of the nation may and indeed do unite in the countries that have liberated themselves.

Finally, the relation of the new concept to classical Leninist doctrine was summed up in this formula:

The Communist parties struggle actively for the consistent com-

pletion of the anti-imperialist, anti-feudal, democratic revolution,
for the formation of a national democratic state, and for an effective raising of the standard of living of the masses of the people.

It will be seen that the Moscow declaration of the eighty-
one parties, while giving a more detailed analysis of the role
of the different classes in the "national, democratic united
front" than the resolution of the WFTU General Council
adopted in Peking six months earlier, is actually less explicitly emphatic on the "leading role" of the working class:
it paraphrases it by describing the working class as the most
consistent force demanding the full consummation of
the national, anti-imperialist, democratic revolution, and by
saying that the degree in which the national bourgeoisie
will join in the liberation struggle will depend largely on
the strength and solidity of the alliance between the working class and the peasants. But the more cautious language
used in this document intended for mass propaganda—
and also in the programme of the CPSU adopted in 1961—
does not express a less definite claim to leadership; that is
clearly shown by Khrushchev's report on the conference,
which states bluntly that "the correct application of Marxist-Leninist theory in the liberated countries consists
precisely in finding the forms which . . . will make it possible to unite all the healthy forces of the nation, and to assure the leading role of the working class within the national
front in the struggle to eradicate imperialism and the remnants of feudalism and to clear the way for a movement
that will ultimately lead to socialism."[15]
With this hint that the strategic meaning of the new slogan of "national democracy" was to open the road for the
transition to "socialism"—which in Communist language
is synonymous with the transition to Communist Party
rule—in the ex-colonial countries, Khrushchev had gone
beyond the text of the declaration of the 81 parties. Subsequent Soviet comment on the declaration was further to

elaborate that hint. In February 1961, Professor Arzumanyan concluded an outline of the conditions needed for
completing the democratic, anti-imperialist revolution in
those countries by asking: "But is that equivalent to socialism?" and replied, "It is not yet socialism, but a transitional stage on the road to socialism. It is the road of a state
of national democracy."[16]

A few months later, Boris Ponomarev, head of the department for relations with non-governing Communist parties
in the Central Committee of the CPSU (who has since
been promoted to membership of the Central Committee
Secretariat), explained that the transitional function of the
new type of state consisted in starting its country on the
"noncapitalist road of development."[17]

When the draft programme of the CPSU was published at
the end of July 1961, its section on "The National Liberation Movement" centered on the same tasks to be fulfilled
after the winning of political independence. Again, it was
laid down that "the political basis of national democracy
is a bloc of all the progressive, patriotic forces fighting to
win complete national independence and broad democracy,
and to consummate the anti-imperialist, antifeudal, democratic revolution," and the Communist parties were specifically instructed to struggle for this consummation and
for the establishment of a state of national democracy. But
now the goal of this struggle was officially equated with the
decision for a non-capitalist road of development, and thus
in effect with the choice between capitalism and socialism.
In introducing the draft at the 22nd congress, Khrushchev
was still more outspoken: "The seething underdeveloped
countries of Asia, Africa, and Latin America, pursuing to
the end the national-liberation, anti-imperialist revolution,
will be able to carry out the transition to socialism. In the
present era, practically every country, irrespective of the
level of its development, can take the path leading to
socialism." And, having repeated that "only the unifica-

tion of all democratic and patriotic forces in a broad national front can lead the peoples on to this path," he summed up: "Marxist theoretical thought, profoundly studying the objective course of development, has discovered the form in which the unification of all the healthy forces of a nation can be most successfully achieved. This form consists in the national democratic state" (*Pravda,* 19 October 1961).

We are now in a position to see the new concept of the "independent national democratic state" in its strategic context. First, it is the interim goal the Communists propose as a common objective for a united national democratic front in ex-colonial or semi-colonial countries. It is identical with the consummation of their classical first stage of the colonial revolution—the "national, bourgeois-democratic revolution" against imperialism and feudalism. In other words, *"national democracy" calls for a post-colonial extension of the first stage of the colonial revolution.*

Secondly, this post-colonial extension has become necessary because experience has shown that most former colonies are attaining independence without having passed through a first stage of the classical type, and therefore without having acquired the preconditions for the second, "socialist" stage of the revolution. The struggle for "national democracy" is to create these preconditions by breaking the new country's economic ties with the "world system of imperialism", and creating in their place economic links with the "socialist states," by destroying its pre-capitalist ruling class through agrarian reform, and by giving the Communists the chance to organize the working class and the peasants under their leadership which they may not have had under the colonial regime. *The demand for an "independent, national democratic state" is thus a*

*"transitional slogan" on the road to the second, "socialist"
stage of the revolution.*

Thirdly, because the demands summed up under this slogan still form part of the classical first stage, they call for a continuation of the classical four-class-coalition, of a broad national united front including the national bourgeoisie and the nationalist leaders representing it: "National Democracy" is *not* a "New Democracy" of the Chinese type, in which the Communists themselves claim to represent all four classes—it is only used as a slogan where independent nationalist political forces have to be taken into account. But because these demands are at the same time intended to put the country firmly on the "non-capitalist road of development," to create the conditions for the second, "socialist," phase, they can be clearly and consistently formulated only by the Communists. *The struggle for "national democracy" is a struggle for Communist leadership within the united national front,* for the extension of Communist influence on the nationalist government, and the Communist occupation of key positions in the political, military, and economic state machine, yet conducted wherever possible within the framework of the existing nationalist regimes—without aiming at this stage at the overthrow of popular nationalist leaders.

Finally, because in the struggle for "national democracy" the Communists are seeking to build up their influence and to win leadership of the united national front, it is accompanied by an open ideological attack on all native varieties of nationalist or populist socialism in the name of Marxism-Leninism. In campaigning for "national democracy," the Communists reject the description of the united front programme of planned industrialization and agrarian reform by their left-wing nationalist allies as socialist, calling such a term "demagogic" and "premature," and seeking to reserve it for their own second-stage programme of complete nationalization of industry and forced collectivization of agriculture. *Adoption of the slogan of national democracy for the united national front goes with the reassertion of the dogma that, contrary to the view of the Yugoslav "revisionists" and of many radical nationalists, the achievement of socialism in the ex-colonial countries (as in all other countries) will only be possible once state power is in the hands of a Communist party.*[18]

THE CHINESE CRITICISM

Because the document in which "national democracy" made its first appearance was the outcome of an international conference dominated by the dispute between the Soviet and Chinese Communists, some Western students tended at first to interpret the new formula merely in the context of that dispute, as a "semantic compromise" between Soviet and Chinese views on strategy toward the countries concerned. It should be clear from the foregoing that the new concept was in fact devised in response to real problems facing Soviet and Communist strategy in relation to those nations, and that some new formula of this kind would have had to be invented even if no dispute with Peking had existed. But because of the timing of its introduction, it was inevitable that the new strategy should eventually be involved in that dispute as well.

Inasmuch as the strategy of "national democracy" could be interpreted as a reassertion of Communist political and ideological independence from the "national bourgeoisie" and a more militant bid for Communist leadership of the new nations, the Chinese Communist critics of Soviet policy might have been expected to welcome it. In fact, however, the resolution of the Chinese Communist central committee approving the Moscow declaration of December 1960 (*Peking Review,* No. 4, 1961), made no mention of the new formula, and Chinese Communist propaganda has not used it since. While Peking has made no direct attacks on the new concept, an authoritative article published in mid-1961 on the corresponding phase of the Chinese experience[19] indicated its dissent by sticking to a different terminology throughout: where Soviet and international Communist documents spoke of a "national democratic front" completing the democratic phase of the revolution by means of an "independent state of national democracy," the Chinese attributed that function to a "people's democratic united front" and a "people's democratic dictatorship." Nor is the difference purely verbal: the Chinese concept, taken from Mao's theory of the "new democratic revolution," requires the conquest of full power by the Communists (though in the name of a four-class coalition) as a condition for completing even the "democratic" phase of the revolution; the new Soviet concept, as we have seen, implies a real if transitional sharing of power between the Communists and their "bourgeois nationalist" partners in the "national democratic" regime.

What made the change unacceptable to the Chinese was above all the Soviet view that in favorable conditions, both the "national democratic" transition from bourgeois-nationalist to Communist leadership of the united front and finally of the government, and the later transition from a Communist-directed "democratic" to a "socialist" revolution, may be peaceful. In the words of Ponomarev, "there can be no doubt that the state of national democracy offers prospects for a transition to a higher type of social order, according as the objective and subjective conditions for it are brought to maturity by the struggle of the peoples of those countries. For achieving a socialist order, revolutionary changes in one or another form are necessary. But it is not excluded that the road to a non-capitalist development will lead in some countries through the state of national democracy." The Chinese were willing enough to admit the peacefulness of the change from the "democratic" to the "socialist" phase of the revolution once Communist power is complete, but they denied that the original achievement of full Communist power in the course of the democratic revolution—the wresting of power from the hands of the nationalists—can be peaceful: they clung to their recently restated dogma that no transition from a bourgeois-led government to a Communist-led government is possible without the violent destruction of the old state machine.[20]

Closely linked to this is a second major difference which concerns the usefulness of extending the economic power of "national democratic" governments, even when still led by Bourgeois Nationalists, by nationalization measures and the development of state-owned industries. In the Soviet view as expounded by Ponomarev, these are important steps along the non-capitalist road: "The experience of the development of states that have recently liberated themselves from the imperialist yoke shows that, as a result of the nationalization of foreign banks and monopolies and of the creation of state-owned factories, banks, etc. on this basis, there arises a more progressive form of ownership than private ownership—the state ownership of the means of production." He also argues that the growth of the public sector in a state of national democracy offers the "progressive forces" an opportunity to occupy important economic positions and thus to increase their political influence. But in the Chinese view, the growth of this sector under a bourgeois government may only pave the way for "bureaucratic capitalism which is an ally of imperialism and feudalism";[21] by this they understand the use of the economic power of the state for the accumulation of private fortunes and privileged economic positions by political officeholders and their families, as happened under the Kuomintang regime—a phenomenon not unknown in other underdeveloped countries today.

But the main Chinese disagreement with the new—as with the old—Soviet policy for the ex-colonial countries is bound to concern the link between Communist strategy within them and Soviet diplomacy toward them—the co-ordination between the diplomatic and the revolutionary planes on which Soviet relations with the non-Communist world have always proceeded.

Between their turn in 1954 to the diplomatic courting of newly independent countries and the end of 1958, the Soviets had given the impression of relying for influence on them almost entirely on goodwill between governments—on the importance of their backing for the new states in all conflicts with the imperialists, the attraction of their anti-colonialist policy, the value of their offers of credit and trade, and the prestige of their own example of successful forced development without Western help. In discussing the future of the ex-colonial nations, they had presented it in terms of completing political independence by the achievement of economic independence from the "imperialist world system" with its lop-sided division of labor, and had never tired of pointing out that the existence of their own "socialist world system" would enable the new nations to cut their economic ties with the West and rely increasingly and in the end exclusively on Communist aid and trade. The chance for the former colonies to follow a "non-capitalist road" of development thus appeared to be due to the growing political and economic strength of the "socialist camp," and it would improve as the relation of forces between this camp and its imperialist opponents improved.

In the discussion of Communist strategy within the new nations by Soviet writers from 1959 onwards, it was increasingly emphasized that the use of these international chances, the choice of one or the other road of development by the former colonies, depended on the internal decisions of the peoples concerned. While solemnly disclaiming any intention of interfering with the free choice of the ex-colonial peoples, Soviet writers began to show an undisguised interest in the outcome of that choice. States that were, in the Soviet view, showing by their anti-imperialist orientation and their nationalization of foreign capital assets that they were moving towards "national democracy"—notably Cuba, Guinea, Ghana, Mali, and Indonesia—were freely praised and promised generous support. More and more frequently, the examples of the once backward republics of Soviet Central Asia and even of the Mongolian People's Republic were cited[22] as proof that even fairly primitive peoples could now avoid capitalism and "take the path leading to socialism"—provided they cut all ties to the capitalist world market and relied exclusively on Soviet bloc aid and guidance. There were indeed indications that the Soviets looked on the pre-socialist Soviet Republics of Khorezm and Bokhara, founded in 1920, and on the Mongolian People's Republic, as the classical models of a "national democratic" development carried to its logical conclusion.

At the same time, nationalist governments that showed by measures against their native Communists that their internal development was tending in an "anti-democratic" direction—notably Nasser's Egypt and later also Kassem's Iraq—were now as frankly criticized by authoritative spokesmen from Khrushchev downwards, and were warned that such "despotic" methods, by undermining the unity of their nations, might ultimately even jeopardize their hard-won independence from imperialism. But to the new sharpness of the ideological distinction between "progressive" and "reactionary" regimes in the new states, there corresponds no similarly clearcut contrast between the promise of Soviet aid to the incipient "national democracies" and its refusal to emergent "nationalist despotisms." On the contrary, substantial amounts of Soviet aid have continued to be granted to the latter as well—to the evident dismay of Peking.

In fact, the Soviets clearly consider that their diplomatic and economic practice towards the new countries must continue to be governed by their *actual*, diplomatic independence from the "imperialists"—not by internal developments that might, according to Communist theory, *potentially* endanger that independence. They have decided against making their loans conditional on the increase of Communist influence in the recipient countries, not because they are opposed in principle to interference in their internal affairs, but because they cannot afford to impose such conditions owing to the intense competition between themselves and the West for the goodwill of these countries—just as the Western countries cannot afford to make their own aid conditional on the abandonment of military neutrality. In reply to Chinese criticism, the Soviets have defended their policy by saying that they are "granting economic and technical assistance to the former colonies on an intergovernmental basis, rendering it to nations and not to some classes within them," claiming that the struggle there was "not solely or chiefly" an internal class struggle, but a joint struggle against imperialism.[23]

Although this statement antedates the adoption of the formula of "national democracy"—it was published in June 1960—the latter has made no difference to the policy it expresses. The promises of Soviet aid for all countries striving to consolidate their newly won independence from imperialism remain unqualified by any reference to the internal development of those countries both in the 1960 Moscow declaration and in the new programme of the CPSU. The reason is hinted at once again in Ponomarev's authoritative comment on the concept of national democracy: "What matters here is not to classify all liberated countries and to say: these belong to one category, those to another. Such an approach would be schematic and harmful." In other words, the Soviets are aware that the development of most of the new countries is still in flux, and while they seek to analyze its direction in each case, they bear in mind that it may still change. The concept of national democracy is intended as a signpost for Communist strategy within the ex-colonial nations, not as a classification for the disbursement or refusal of Soviet credits.

A EUROPEAN MODEL?

As a strategic concept for Communist parties in the ex-colonial countries, "national democracy" has a significant European model in the concept of "people's democracy" as used between 1945 and 1947. Today, the word is used only for the Communist states of Eastern Europe, and the programme of the CPSU describes it as "a variety of the dictatorship of the proletariat." But it was originally intended both as a slogan for the West European democracies freshly emerging from the war and from occupation by Nazi Germany, and as a description of a state of affairs in some East European countries which, while clearly brought about by Communist initiative, still seemed to fall short in important respects of a full-fledged Communist Party dictatorship.

"People's Democracy" as then described, mainly with pre-1948 Czechoslovakia as an example, was the rule of a coalition of progressive, democratic forces—basically the same forces that had united in the liberation struggle against fascism. Out of this struggle, according to the Communists, a democratic revolution had developed which was not completed with the expulsion of the defeated German armies: to complete it, the Fascists and their collaborators must be eliminated from the political and economic life of the nation, their parties suppressed and their property nationalized, while radical land reforms had to create the basis for a lasting democratization of public life. In the Communist view, those were democratic and not specifically socialist demands, and it was premature and demagogic to talk of socialism at that stage; but since implementation of such a program required a growth of the state sector at the expense of some forms of private property, the patriotic sections of the bourgeoisie were beginning to waver at this point, so that completion of the democratic revolution must increasingly depend on the leading role of the working class and its close alliance with the peasants. Hence the Communists, while still striving to maintain the unity of a broad anti-Fascist front, had to put forward an independent program with which to fight for its leadership: the slogan of "people's democracy" summed up that program. Wherever they succeeded, they would establish close cooperation with the Soviet Union, and by completing the democratic revolution would create a political and economic basis on which the later construction of a socialist order with Soviet help would be possible without violent upheaval.

When this concept of "people's democracy" was first put forward by Communist leaders in both Eastern and Western Europe, strong Communist parties were sharing in the governments of France, Italy, and Czechoslovakia in formally quite similar coalitions, though the crucial facts of ultimate military power and of control over police and communications differed fundamentally on both sides of the postwar demarcation line between the Russian and Western armies. Even so, as late as the spring of 1947 it was neither a foregone conclusion that Czechoslovakia must become a Communist dictatorship nor that no West European country would turn Communist: only with the break-up of the French and Italian coalitions, the announcement of the Marshall Plan and its rejection by the Soviets, and the formation of the Cominform in the course of that year did the transitional era of European post-war fluidity come to an end, and only with the success of the Prague coup in February 1948 and the failure of the Communist bid for power in Italy in April did "people's democracy" finally lose its value as a transitional slogan. In the West, the anti-Fascist democratic revolution had failed to achieve its pre-ordained consummation, and the bourgeois state, backed by U.S. imperialism, was once more in control; in the East, the consummation of "people's democracy" had been attained, and it turned out to be "a variety of proletarian dictatorship"—formally distinct from the Soviet system by its retention of the trappings of parliamentary government and of a sham coalition with satellite parties deprived of the last vestiges of independence, but substantially identical with it in the exercise of total control by the Communist Party.

From what has been said, the similarity of the two strategic concepts appears too striking to be unconscious. The attempt to extend a broad movement of national liberation beyond the fact of liberation, to inspire it with more far-reaching revolutionary aims without proclaiming straight communist demands, to maintain a common front with bourgeois elements but struggle to assume its leadership, even to use examples from inside the Soviet orbit as models for countries in apparently similar situations outside it—all this the present use of "national democracy" has in common with the original use of "people's democracy." But it does not follow that the prospects of the new slogan can be deduced from the results of the old—for the situation and problems of the ex-colonial nations are quite different from those of post-war Europe. On one side, the situation in most of these countries appears rather more truly "revolutionary," in the sense of requiring radical changes in the economic and social structure, than in most of post-war Western Europe; on the other, the Communist parties in most of them are far weaker, and the prospects of indigenous and undoctrinaire movements combining nationalism with a passion for radical social change correspondingly stronger.

THE PROSPECTS

Much of the Communist immediate economic and social programme for the under-developed countries—whether ex-colonial or not—reflects their genuine problems, even if in a doctrinaire and one-sided form. It is true, for instance, that in many of these countries a radical reform of land tenure is urgently needed, that none of them can achieve a harmonious and all-round economic growth without state planning of investment and a more or less pronounced growth of the public sector, and that in many cases these measures cannot be achieved without hurting the interests and therefore provoking the resistance not only of the traditional native oligarchy or upper crust, but also of some major Western business firms enjoying a privileged position inherited from the colonial or semi-colonial past. The road of national independence and development for these countries must indeed be to some extent a "non-capitalist road," not in the sense that it would be incompatible with an important contribution by capitalist private enterprise, both domestic and foreign, but in the sense that in those countries such a contribution can be fruitful only in the framework of a national plan —that they cannot follow the road of classical *liberal* capitalism once travelled by the old industrial countries of the West.

But it is not true, as experience increasingly shows, that the developing countries have only the choice between the roads of doctrinaire liberal capitalism and doctrinaire communism—that a "non-capitalist" road in the above, realistic sense must be a "socialist" road in the Communist sense of complete nationalization of industry and forced collectivization of agriculture. Nor is it true that a policy of state-controlled national development which conflicts with the interests of some important Western firms will necessarily be resisted by the Western powers, or that "capitalist" countries like the United States are bound to refuse aid for such a policy of planned development, leaving the nationalist planners with no option but one-sided dependence on the Soviet bloc. In general, the best chance for these countries lies in choosing a road of economic development which is neither the classical capitalist nor the Communist road, and a foreign policy which does not lead to one-sided dependence either on the Western or on the Soviet bloc.

Here is the fundamental flaw of the strategy of "national democracy." The true interests of the developing countries do not require a policy that calls for Communist leadership and exclusive reliance on Soviet support, but are served best by a policy of nationalist planning and bloc-free independence. Where the nationalist leaders adopt such a policy, which they frequently describe as their own homegrown variety of socialism, the Communist chances of gaining mass influence and ultimately achieving the transition to their "second stage" revolution are correspondingly reduced: hence the growing irritation in the ideological attacks on such eclectic socialist doctrines,[24] not only in the case of Nasser but even of such erstwhile candidates for the "national democratic" label as Sekou Touré. Whenever a non-Communist leader uses the term "socialist" to describe his own policy, he is indicating his confidence in his ability to find his own road of development and his refusal to see his regime as a mere transition to Communist rule.

To this increasingly typical situation, the strategy of "national democracy" provides no answer. It tells the Communists to seek nationalist allies and to press for influence on the nationalist governments while striving to avoid premature conflict with them; but it leaves them at a loss what to do if the intended allies refuse to accept them as partners, as in Morocco and Algeria, and if the nationalist rulers will not permit Communist Parties, as in Egypt or even in Guinea. They may attack Nasser as a despot, but they

hesitate to go to the same length in the case of Touré—
and Soviet credits continue to reach both. In fact, by continuing to support uncommitted countries even if their
governments show no willingness to accept Communist
guidance for their road of development, the Soviets tacitly
admit that a third road between classical capitalism and
communism is possible for those countries. But, as we
have seen, the doctrine of "National Democracy" presupposes the denial of that possibility. Soviet diplomacy
towards the new countries and Communist strategy within
them thus appear to be based on premises that stand in flat
contradiction with one another.

4

Transformation by Infiltration?

A NEW APPROACH TO NON-COMMUNIST
ONE-PARTY REGIMES

In the summer of 1963, a marked favorable revision occurred in the official Soviet view of the role which certain
non-Communist one-party regimes, particularly in Africa
and the Arab world, could play in assuring the choice of
a "non-capitalist road of development" for their countries,
producing important consequences for the practical policy
of both the Soviets and the local pro-Soviet Communists
toward these regimes. Previously, the Soviets, though ready
to give development aid and diplomatic—and indirect military—support against the "imperialists" to these as to other
nationalist regimes of ex-colonial countries, had insisted
on combining such support with outspoken criticism of
their political system and ideology, and had propagated
the replacement of one-party rule by "national-democratic"
coalitions with legal Communist parties as partners. Now,

such criticism was gradually abandoned with regard to a number of "progressive" single-party regimes, and the demand for Communist partnership in coalitions was replaced by the deliberate renunciation of any visible, independent Communist Party activity in the countries concerned—a step without precedent in Soviet policy and international Communist history.

The problem of Soviet relations with non-Communist one-party regimes is almost as old as the Soviet Union itself. For (as has been discussed more fully in Chap. 2 above) the institutions of the Bolshevik single-party state .had been barely consolidated when it began to be regarded as a possible model for other countries and parties—including nationalist parties in underdeveloped countries whose leaders in no way shared the ideological goals of the Communists, but were impressed by the potentialities of this form of government as an engine of modernization. With its monopoly of organization and information, the one-party regime permits both the mobilization of backward peoples for their own re-education and the maintenance of national unity during a period of enforced sacrifice. The use of the model for such purposes was first attempted in the twenties by nationalist leaders who looked to the Soviets as an ally against Western imperialism—by Kemal Ataturk in setting up the regime of his Republican People's Party, and by Dr. Sun Yat-sen and his successors in reorganizing the Kuomintang with Soviet aid and advice.

In both cases, the wish of these nationalist leaders to ensure the monopoly of political activity for their own parties naturally created an obstacle for the work of Communist parties which their Soviet allies wished to promote at the same time. In the Turkish case, the Soviets soon resigned themselves to the suppression of the Turkish Communists by Kemal, registering some verbal protests but maintaining an unchanged friendship with Ankara. In China, they compromised by the expedient of the "bloc within," under which the Communists individually entered the KMT while the Communist Party retained the right to conduct independent propaganda outside it. This first form of licensed infiltration proved a sham solution: it was to lead to severe disappointments for both sides, from Chiang Kai-shek's suppression of the Communists in 1927 to his final overthrow by them after two decades of civil war.

After this catastrophic experience, a long time elapsed before any new attempt was made to establish a one-party non-Communist state. Only in the later 1950s did decolonization in Africa lead to the rise of a number of such regimes, the first being the Convention People's Party in Ghana, the Parti Démocratique de Guinée, and the Union Soudanaise in Mali. These parties were not Communist, but were markedly pro-Soviet. In particular, the two in former French West Africa had grown up before decolonization under the influence of the French Communist Party and the Communist-dominated French trade unions; their leaders had gained a good grounding in Marxism before they freed themselves from that influence—largely because of the French CP's habit of sacrificing a consistent anti-colonial policy to the passing tactical needs of Soviet foreign policy or French domestic politics.[1] The official ideology of these parties was therefore much closer to Communist doctrine than was the case with the national-revolutionary parties of the twenties; it showed a mixture of revolutionary Marxism with nationalist and pan-African elements, to which observers gave the telling name of Afro-Marxism.[2] Yet in the very nature of the case, this ideology was bound to be different from the orthodox Marxism-Leninism of the USSR, since the undeveloped social structure of these countries offered no possibility of applying the idea of class struggle to their internal problems; nor did the need to concentrate all national energies on safeguarding independence and tackling the tasks of development make a class struggle within the country appear in any way desirable. Because of this immense difference in the real problems facing them (reflected in the eclecticism of the official ideology), these new ruling parties, while feeling a sense of broad kinship and solidarity with the Soviets and other Communist parties, were not in the least inclined to accept Moscow's ideological authority, much less its organizational discipline. They found this steadfast adherence to their own mixture of national communism and classless African socialism the more easy to maintain as Moscow's ideological authority was visibly shaken even within the Communist movement after 1956, and as the Yugoslav Communists, after their second excommunication in 1958, deliberately encouraged the tendency of national-revolutionary regimes to assert their ideological independence and to keep clear of blocs in foreign policy, offering them for this purpose not only Marxist arguments but tactical advice and technical assistance.

For the Soviet Union, the rise of non-Communist, or even semi-Communist one-party regimes in Africa presented serious diplomatic and tactical difficulties, the more so as it largely coincided with a change in Soviet policy in the direction of greater Communist Party activity in the non-aligned countries. Between 1954 and 1958 Soviet policy towards these countries consisted primarily in support from outside—giving economic and diplomatic aid to the existing non-Communist regimes, and supplying arms when they were engaged in disputes with "imperialism." The Communist parties within these countries were also instructed to give "critical support" to the policy of the national bourgeoisie, whether their rule was democratic or dictatorial. But in 1959, influenced on the one hand by the revolutions in Cuba and Iraq, and on the other by the anti-Communist measures taken by Nasser in Syria and Nehru in Kerala, Moscow came to the conclusion that external aid was not enough to influence developments among the non-aligned, and that greater internal Communist pressure had to be exercised to reinforce external aid from the Soviet bloc in order to push these countries on to the "non-capitalist road of development."[3]

THE ONE-PARTY STATES FOIL "NATIONAL DEMOCRACY"

The new line took explicit shape in 1960–61 in the formula of the "national democratic front" and the "national democratic state," used for the first time in the declaration of the conference of Communist parties held in Moscow at the end of 1960, and repeated in the CPSU programme adopted the following year. It meant that Communists in ex-colonial and semi-colonial countries were to fight to complete the revolution against imperialism and feudalism in alliance with the national-revolutionary forces, to accept initially the leadership of Bourgeois Nationalists, but at the same time to advocate their own immediate programme of radical land reform and of industrialization by the state and to go ahead in building up mass organizations; they were thus to direct the national-democratic front toward the non-capitalist road, and to prepare themselves to take over the role of leader. As applied to the new states of tropical Africa, this policy required an intensive effort to create Communist parties, which did not exist in the majority of the countries in question. *The African Communist,* a periodical which began publication in the autumn of 1959, was designed primarily to serve this purpose.

In practice, however, the policy proved difficult to carry out, particularly in the growing number of non-Communist one-party states. The first Soviet list of countries which were said to be on the national-democratic road consisted of Indonesia, Cuba, Ghana, Guinea, and Mali. Of these only Indonesia had a national-democratic front in the Soviet sense, that is a coalition of Nationalists and Communists led by the Nationalists but with increasing Communist influence. Under Castro, Cuba jumped the national-democratic stage more quickly than the Soviets expected (or perhaps desired) and proclaimed itself a "socialist state ruled by a Marxist-Leninist party." The three West African one-party states, though willing to maintain the friendliest relations with Moscow and to send fraternal delegates to the XXII CPSU Congress, were not prepared to tolerate the creation of competitive Communist parties in their countries, not to speak of bringing them into a coalition. In Guinea, suspicion of Soviet participation in establishing Communist cells in the teachers and youth organizations of the ruling party led at the end of 1961 to a diplomatic crisis and to the recall of the Soviet ambassador at Sekou Touré's request.

Similar difficulties soon arose with the development of one-party states in North Africa—in the first place with the consolidation of the Algerian revolutionary regime. The Algerian National Liberation Front (FLN) had been supported politically and materially by the Soviets and the entire eastern bloc once it had shown itself to be a serious factor in the situation; Soviet support was not so wholehearted and consistent as Peking's, since Moscow had to consider French susceptibilities, but it made a substantial contribution to the success of the revolt which the FLN recognized. The Algerian Communist Party, on the other hand, which took no part in the early stages of the revolt, tried later to gain recognition as an ally of the FLN, but in vain: the FLN advised Communists to join its organizations as individuals, but rejected a pact between the two organizations. When the war for independence ended in 1962 and a sovereign Algerian state was established, the FLN promptly proclaimed itself the sole party and, after some hesitation, explicitly banned the Communist Party. This blow to Soviet hopes was the heavier as it was not a case of preventing the foundation of a Communist Party, as in West Africa, but of suppressing a party which had been in existence for many years. The CPSU Central Committee took the unusual step of expressing its "deep regret and alarm" in a statement published in *Pravda* (4 December 1962). By early 1963, the Communist parties throughout Arab North Africa, from Morocco to Egypt, had been banned, while in tropical Africa the formation of new parties encountered as many difficulties as it had under the old colonial regimes.

The failure of Soviet strategy in the growing number of new one-party states might have been accepted with resignation as a temporary triumph of reaction had the suppression of Communists been accompanied by concessions to capital, domestic and foreign, as Communist theory would suggest. What compelled Moscow to reconsider its theory and practice was the fact that some of the regimes which banned independent Communist activity put through unexpectedly radical measures of expropriation of both domestic and foreign capital and were ready to rely on the support of the Soviet bloc in any ensuing conflict with the Western powers.

This was true even of the UAR, not exactly a one-party regime but rather a national-revolutionary military dictatorship that was trying *après coup* to transform itself into a one-party state. Nasser's Arab Union, and the later Arab Socialist Union, had been created more than once on paper, but remained stillborn. But this regime, which put its Communists in prison, extended the state sector of the economy far beyond the scope of large-scale industry by the nationalization decrees of summer 1961, which covered medium and parts of small-scale industry as well—a victory for nationalist anti-capitalist ideology over economic rationality which stood in sharp contradiction to the expectations of Nasser's Soviet critics. And while Nasser thus followed the path of non-capitalist development, Syria, whose separation from the UAR had been enthusiastically welcomed by Arab Communists, took up a much less militant anti-Western attitude, but soon proceeded no less severely against the Communists.[4]

In Algeria, the FLN had on the eve of independence in its Tripoli programme proclaimed its goal of achieving social-ism under the leadership of peasants and workers and had warned the bourgeois and petty-bourgeois elements that their role in the new state would depend on their loyal co-operation on this road. In the spring of 1963, this socialist outlook found expression in Ben Bella's land seizure decrees under which the estates of the former French colonists were nationalized and their collective management entrusted to elected committees of the laborers—a measure of distinctly revolutionary character, as the Soviet and Communist press recognized a few months later.

If the Soviet leaders and theoreticians still hesitated to admit the contradiction between the "reactionary" anti-Communist and the "progressive" anti-capitalist measures of one and the same regime, there was no lack of good friends to bring it to their attention. In 1962 friendly rela-tions between the Soviet Union and Yugoslavia had again been resumed, not the least important reason on the Rus-sian side being the desire to use Belgrade's influence in a number of non-aligned countries. The Yugoslav concept of "different roads to socialism" had always implied that in ex-colonial countries the road to socialism could be taken without seizure of power by the Communists or even the existence of a Communist party; the lead could be taken by forces which managed to combine the nationalist tradition with socialist goals. Moreover, intellectual contact between the Yugoslavs and the Italian Communists had never been interrupted by the second excommunication of the former, and the discussions of the Italian Central Committee in November 1961, following the XXII Congress of the CPSU with its "second destalinization," showed a marked influ-ence of the Yugoslav heresy concerning the developing countries; this was all the more important as the Italian party had long been in charge of liaison with the Communists of Arab North Africa. Thus the Yugoslav and Italian revisionists could throw the joint weight of their practical experience into the scales on the side of a reconsideration of policy. Finally, the impression created by the unexpected events in Africa and the Middle East was reinforced by the case most obviously in conflict with the theory, that of Cuba, which had become a "socialist" state under the leadership of a man who had never belonged to the Communist Party before the capture of power and did not owe his power to that party, but only merged his own political organization with it years after victory.

THE REVISION OF THEORY

The discussion which preceded the change in Soviet policy towards non-Communist one-party regimes in the underdeveloped countries turned on four inter-related questions:

The first, raised by a few Soviet experts in 1962, concerned the class character of these regimes. Was it still possible to describe Nasser, who had taken radical expropriation measures against the big bourgeoisie and substantial sections of the middle bourgeoisie, as representative of the "national bourgeoisie"? Had not the undifferentiated application of this label to the nationalist leaders of the non-aligned countries, irrespective of their actual policy, become a serious obstacle to Communist activity? Should it not be admitted that the mass basis of many of the ruling national-revolutionary parties was essentially peasant, and in part proletarian, and that in many cases their leaders also were not bourgeois in the classical sense, but intellectuals and officers of petty-bourgeois or peasant origin? In the West the peculiar characterisitics of the typical leaders of national-revolutionary movements—their origin in the intelligentsia, or the "intelligentsia in uniform," their transformation into a "state bourgeoisie," that is, a bureaucracy wielding political power—had long been a subject for analysis. Now the Russians began to turn their minds in this direction.

The second question concerned the possible role of these leaders and their regimes in the decision whether their countries would pursue a capitalist or non-capitalist road of development. If they represented the "national bourgeoisie," they were bound to promote capitalist development and so become an obstacle to the further advance of the revolution once national sovereignty was achieved. Intellectuals and officers of petty-bourgeois or peasant origin, on the other hand, were in principle free to choose between the two roads according to the domestic and international situation, but also to· their own personal history and ideological convictions. Was this not the explanation of the radical measures taken by some of these regimes? According to the national-democracy theory, the choice of the non-capitalist road depended on growing Communist influence in a coalition with the national-revolutionaries; but had not the actual course of events shown that some of the national-revolutionary regimes could take this road in the absence or after deliberate suppression of a Communist party, though admittedly with the help of "the socialist world system," that is, the Soviet bloc? In the words of a protagonist of revision: "Where the conditions for the leading role of the proletariat have not yet matured, the historical task of breaking with capitalism can be accomplished by elements close to the working class. Nature abhors a vacuum."[5] These "elements" were the same nationalist-socialist leaders that had only yesterday been described as representing the national bourgeoisie, and the vacuum they filled existed partly because of the natural weakness of the Communists in their countries, and partly because of their own anti-Communist measures.

From this analysis a third question arose—that of a new evaluation of the various eclectic ideologies going by the name of "African socialism," "Arab socialism," etc. In their mixture of nationalist and socialist elements they resembled the ideas of the Russian *narodniki,* and they had been combated in Soviet and Communist propaganda as an attempt by the national bourgeoisie to mislead the masses with sham socialist slogans; the Communists alone stood for *scientific* socialism, and all those who preached "socialism of the national type" were so many frauds.[6] This dogmatic attitude was in keeping with the idea that only the Communists could show their allies the non-capitalist road; but if a few of these national-revolutionary regimes had actually taken that road without Communist guidance, should not their professions in favor of "socialism of the national type" be recognized as expressing their choice of this road, and be encouraged accordingly? Soviet theoreticians now began to take the actual policy of the leaders and movements in these countries as the basis for distinguishing between the misuse of socialist slogans by reactionary regimes and the honest if still confused efforts of genuine national-revolutionary forces to provide an independent rationale for their anti-capitalist decision.

It was only when these three questions were cleared up that the Soviets could seek a new approach to the strategically decisive question of the appropriate attitude to be adopted toward the claim of non-Communist revolutionary one-party regimes in the ex-colonial countries to a monopoly of political power. The question now presented itself in the following form: Was it really necessary to challenge this claim by promoting Communist parties in competition with national-revolutionary parties which had chosen the non-capitalist road and were honestly anxious to pursue socialist goals? What was the point of the slogan of an alliance of equals, a "national-democratic coalition" of Communists and nationalists, in countries whose national-revolutionary leaders were prepared in large measure to carry out the policy desired by the Communists, but considered the very existence of independent Communist parties a threat to national unity? Was the pressure of competing Communist parties really necessary in order to eliminate the ideological confusion of these leaders, to lead them on from "petty-bourgeois" African or Arab socialism to a "scientifically-based proletarian socialism" that is, to Marxism-Leninism? Or could this not be achieved more effectively by the co-operation of Communist cadres within the framework of the ruling parties?

The question was the more timely as a number of new one-party regimes were showing signs of a lack of political stability and ideological unity. Imitation of the external features of the bolshevik model was no guarantee that in all these regimes, some of them hastily improvised, the leaders would in fact have the authority to control effectively the mass organizations grouped round the one and only party, or that the latter, as spokesmen of separate interests and groups, would not rather exert pressure on the party leaders. Even where the leader's authority was uncontested, as in Egypt, his performance in the realm of ideology was often too poor to imbue the state party he had created with a convincing and concrete conception of its tasks. In one case the pluralism flourishing behind a sham-totalitarian façade, in another the weakness of the official ideology might open wide opportunities to Communist influence inside these parties.

Apart from a few isolated instances, the systematic discussion of these questions became public only in the spring of 1964, that is, at a time when the decision in favor of revision had already been made;[7] that had happened in mid-1963.

THE TURN TO LICENSED INFILTRATION

The first outward sign of a change in Soviet policy toward non-Communist one-party regimes was an article by Mikhail Kremnyov in the August 1963 issue of *World Marxist Re-*

view, in which the conclusion was for the first time reached that "one can envisage the possibility of the influence of the growing working class increasing in these parties and turning them into mass parties of the Marxist-Leninist type." This implied the recognition that these parties were by no means monolithic, but offered opportunities for influence to the "working class," that is, to Communist-trained leaders of affiliated trade unions, students' associations, etc. Many of these countries had government-controlled trade unions which had for some years been affiliated to the Communist World Federation of Trade Unions and whose leaders had been trained in Communist-run schools even earlier. A similar state of affairs prevailed in the mass organizations for students, teachers, journalists, women, etc., so that even in countries where there was no Communist party a considerable number of Communist-trained cadres held important positions. The idea of concentrating Communist activity in these countries on the use of these opportunities was not proclaimed by Kremnyov as a new general line, but rather mentioned in passing, but the very publication of the article in that particular journal showed that it was no mere contribution to a debate, but a directive.

The immediate occasion for the underlying decision was the situation in Algeria, and the application of the directive to the FLN regime was made manifest in the subsequent comments of the Soviet press and in the reports it published of statements by Algerian Communist leaders when the new Algerian constitution was introduced in September 1963. These showed that an understanding was being reached, if not already in operation, between Algerian Communist leaders and the FLN on recognition of the one-party regime and Communist collaboration within it. In *Pravda,* on September 9, Bachir Hadj Ali stated that the revolutionary-socialist orientation of the FLN programme had laid the basis for a "fruitful dialogue" between the two, and shortly thereafter an authoritative article in *Kommunist* (16, 1963) declared that Algerian Communists were "not oppressed" and were free to propagate their views. The authors admitted that in 1962 the Communists had opposed the one-party system, for which the country was not then ripe. Since then, however, the FLN, by its revolutionary land decree of March 1963, had set the country firmly on the non-capitalist road and proclaimed its goal of a socialist society; this justified the one-party regime and Communist collaboration within its framework.

Final confirmation that the turn of the Algerian Communists to a new form of "licensed infiltration," approved both by the FLN and the Soviets, had been completed, came early in 1964. In January Luigi Longo gave a report on the visit of an Italian CP delegation to Algeria; not only was the general policy of the FLN socialist and increasingly based on class struggle, but Communist representatives of affiliated mass organizations were exercising considerable influence on that policy and particularly on the drafting of the new FLN programme.[8] In contrast to the Tripoli programme, which made a conditional offer to the bourgeoisie to collaborate in the leadership, the new charter of Algiers, adopted by the first party congress of the FLN in April, asserted that the bourgeoisie had shown itself unwilling to work with the regime toward socialism, and that it was therefore necessary to base the state exclusively on the co-operation of the toiling classes—workers, peasants, and revolutionary intelligentsia. The same congress which adopted the programme imposed a new structure on the FLN, designed to make it both "vanguard" and "mass party"—a small core of selected cadres and a large outer ring of members. These changes were explicitly welcomed in the Soviet and international Communist press.[9] Immediately after the congress *Alger Républicain* (19–20 April 1964), the Communist paper which had continued publication even after the suppression of the Communist Party, announced that it would in future appear as an organ of the FLN, with no change in the editorial board.

Clearly, a far-reaching understanding of this kind on the

"bloc within" was bound to bear fruit in closer and more friendly relations not only between the two governments, but also between the ruling parties in the Soviet Union and Algeria. When, immediately after the congress, an Algerian government and party delegation visited the USSR, "Comrade Ben Bella" was given the title "Hero of the Soviet Union" (*Pravda,* 2 May 1964), and the final communiqué on the visit emphasized the satisfaction of both sides with the development of party relations between the two, the commitment of the FLN to the "socialist road of development," and its recognition by the CPSU as "the unifying center of all the contemporary patriotic and democratic forces of the Algerian nation in the fight for the socialist reconstruction of their state" (*Pravda,* 7 May 1964). Without abandoning non-alignment or proclaiming allegiance to the Moscow version of Marxism-Leninism (which would have given the Soviets the right to intervene ideologically in their affairs), the Algerian leaders nevertheless avowed their faith in "socialist construction" in the Soviet sense of the term, no doubt in exchange for the recognition by the CPSU of their party monopoly. Henceforth this solution was to serve as a model for Soviet policy toward other non-Communist one-party states in the ex-colonial world.

That the policy would be so extended was indicated by Khrushchev at the end of 1963 when, in an interview with editors from Algeria, Ghana, and Burma, he said that the road of "national democracy", that is, a Nationalist-Communist coalition, was not the only possible road for the further progress towards socialism of national revolutions in the underdeveloped countries. While again condemning the use of socialist phrases by certain "objectively" reactionary regimes, he now also welcomed the declarations of "revolutionary democratic statesmen who sincerely strive to solve their national problems by non-capitalist methods and proclaim their determination to build socialism"; such regimes, he pledged, would get the support of the USSR (*Pravda*, 22 December 1963).

The interview was immediately greeted throughout the Soviet press as "a document of creative Marxism," and interpreted as the signal of a general turn. Potekhin, the leading Soviet Africanist and prominent critic of the ideology of "African socialism," now wrote (*Kommunist*, 1, 1964) that the term was ambiguous and was misused by reactionaries, which was why the "scientific socialism" avowed by the ruling parties of Guinea and Mali was preferable; what must be decisive for judging other parties, however, was not the confusion of their ideology, but their action in choosing the non-capitalist road. The discussion which had until then scarcely reached the ear of the public, was now brought to a conclusion in a debate arranged by the Institute for World Economics and International Relations, in which the triumphant revisionists warmly welcomed the evolution of a number of leaders in the ex-colonial countries "from the ideology of nationalism to the ideology of socialism of a national type," and expressed the hope that soon "petty-bourgeois and even bourgeois leaders of the national liberation movements would come over to the working-class position."[10] This hope implied nothing less than that the new strategy of renouncing competitive Communist parties would facilitate the evolution of a number of non-Communist one-party regimes into "socialist" regimes—an evolution to be accomplished under the same leaders, whose legitimacy derived from their nationalism, more or less on the model of Castro's Cuba.

The countries encompassed by this hope were, in addition to Algeria, Ghana, Guinea, and Mali once again, moreover Burma and the United Arab Republic. In Burma General Ne Win who, after his 1958 coup "to restore order," had returned constitutional power to the civilian government in 1960, had during his second and "definitive" seizure of power in March 1962 installed a "Revolutionary Council" that had prepared a Marxist program of social transformation with the help of the so-called "White Flag," that is, Moscow-oriented, Communists, and was now engaged in creating from above a single state party, called the "Burma Socialist People's Party," around this program. Nasser's Egypt, because of its international weight, was indeed the main target of the new line, but it also presented the greatest obstacles because of the strength of Nasser's personal dictatorship, the low degree of political vitality in the official Arab Socialist Union, and the intensity with which Communists had been persecuted.

The first Soviet-Egyptian feelers about turning the Egyptian Communists into "loyal collaborators" in the country's internal affairs, were probably put out in the autumn of 1963, about the time when Nasser released a number of political prisoners, including many Communists. On 26 November *Pravda* advanced the view, until then held only by a few Soviet experts, that Nasser's "state-capitalist reforms from above" had dealt a severe blow to the Egyptian bourgeoisie, thus beginning to create the conditions for entering the non-capitalist road. To make these achievements secure, political life would have to become more "democratic"; in particular, Communists would have to be brought into it. And in his December interview Khrushchev emphasized once more that a country could not both build socialism and persecute its Communists.

When, in May 1964, shortly after receiving Ben Bella in Moscow, Khrushchev made a state visit to Egypt, the pro-Soviet Communists there were no longer in prison, but they were still forbidden to form a party. During the visit Khrushchev seems to have proposed to Nasser to allow them to work as individuals in the Arab Socialist Union and in the press, provided they renounced independent party activity. In any case, at the end of the visit, *Pravda* (24 May 1964) said it was "logical to raise the question of enabling all those to collaborate who were interested in the victory of a socialist UAR." The official commentary in *Kommunist* (8, 1964) bore the title: "Unity of the forces of socialism and the national liberation movement." Yet the aftermath of the visit revealed differences among the Soviet leaders as to the degree to which an optimistic appraisal of the possibilities of the development of the Nasser regime in a socialist direction was justified. While Khrushchev himself took an affirmative view in the many speeches he made during the visit, and not only designated Nasser, like Ben Bella, a Hero of the Soviet Union, but also addressed him on that occasion as "Comrade," the official statement of the Supreme Soviet bestowing the order avoided the term. The final communiqué on the visit, in the introductory paragraph, said the UAR had "taken the road of socialist development," but in a later section attributed this formula to the Egyptian side, and quoted the Soviet side only as praising Nasser's policy of "fundamental economic and social reforms" (*Pravda*, 15 and 24 May 1964).[11]

In the following months it became apparent that the Soviet leaders had decided on the more cautious appraisal of Egyptian developments but approved Khrushchev's policy of seeking to influence them by rapprochement in practice. A leading article in *New Times* in June (23, 1964) referred to continuing ideological differences with the UAR, but suggested that closer relations with the Soviet Union would help its people to tread the non-capitalist, and eventually the socialist road. In July Kremnyov wrote with greater precision in the *World Marxist Review*: in the economic sphere, the big and even the medium bourgeoisie had been practically eliminated in Egypt, but the old bureaucratic state apparatus was still in existence; ideological development was lagging behind economic and social progress, and official propaganda was often reactionary in tone; the cure lay in drawing the masses into political activity; if the Communists were really free, they could help in this.

This semi-official qualification of Khrushchev's optimism

did not imply either a retreat from the new line or from its application to Egypt, but only a more skeptical appraisal of what was already achieved there, in contrast to the rapid progress of Soviet and Communist influence in the Algerian FLN. Real opposition to the application of the new line to the UAR came however from a number of Arab Communists, above all from one figure of international standing, the Syrian Communist Party leader Khalid Bagdash. The Syrian Communist Party had always been the strongest of the Arab Communist parties, and had suffered severely under Nasser during the time when the two countries were amalgamated. In a series of contributions in *World Marxist Review* (7, 8, 11, 1964) Bagdash contested the idea that Nasser's anti-communism could be overcome by a change in Communist tactics and the renunciation of open criticism of his policy; nationalist intellectuals and officers, he argued, could in the absence of a strong proletarian party successfully lead the struggle for national independence and make real progress along the road to socialism by economic and social reforms, but they could never build socialism itself; for that the "leading role of the working class," that is, a Communist party acting independently, remained indispensable.

This criticism could hardly be suppressed by the Soviets, the less so as the Syrian Communist Party was one of the 26 parties then invited to Moscow for the preparatory conference that was to discuss the Sino-Soviet conflict. Nevertheless, preparations for applying the new line to Egypt apparently continued during the Moscow visits of Nasser's Prime Minister Ali Sabri in September and of the Egyptian Communist Khaled Mohi ed-Din, who had been a member of Nasser's "Revolutionary Command Council" from its formation to the fall of Naguib in 1954, in November 1964. In December, at any rate, after Khruschev's fall and the postponement of the international conference to the following March, *Pravda's* publication of the communiqué put out by a conference of "representatives of Communists of

Arab countries," showed that, despite the objections of Nasser's opponents, the new line was definitely to be applied to Egypt as well. The communiqué spoke consistently of "Arab Communists," not of Communist parties; it did not once mention the Syrian CP, and throughout it concentrated on the parallel, if differentiating discussion of experiences in Algeria and Egypt. It was acknowledged that the FLN "unites all revolutionary and socialist forces, including the Communists," and that Algeria had taken the socialist road. In more cautious tones the communiqué welcomed the great economic and social transformations in the UAR, which had "entered the non-capitalist road of development"; these would enable that country to make its way to socialism if growing activity of the masses was encouraged, democracy was broadened and the Arab Socialist Union transformed into an organization fully representative of the interests and ideology of the working people (*Pravda*, Dec. 11, 1964).

The application of the new line to Egypt was finally accepted by the Egyptian Communists themselves, following discussions in which only a small Maoist group refused to submit, in a proclamation of April 25, 1965.[12] It announced "the termination of the existence of the Egyptian CP as an independent body" and instructed all members to apply individually for membership in the Arab Socialist Union, so that "a single revolutionary vanguard party" could be formed. The aim was to support Nasser in following the road of non-capitalist development toward socialism, to democratize the party and gradually win a majority for true scientific socialism within it.

PURPOSE AND LIMITS OF THE NEW APPROACH

Despite its obvious outward similarity to the "bloc within" practised in the twenties by the Chinese CP on Soviet urging, the new policy of licensed infiltration differs from it

in three respects: in the stage of revolutionary development at which it is introduced, in the limits it imposes on
Communist party activity, and in the aims which it pursues.

First, the "bloc within" was negotiated at an early stage
of the national revolution, before the Kuomintang had become the government, whereas the policy of licensed infiltration is directed at ruling parties which have achieved
national independence and is designed to move them on
from the national to the socialist phase of the revolution.

Second, during the "bloc within" period the Chinese
Communists insisted on their freedom to conduct their
independent party propaganda outside the KMT, which
they regarded—following Lenin and the theses of the Second Comintern Congress—as an indispensable condition
for taking the lead in the second phase of the revolution.
After 1963–64, the Communist cadres in the countries concerned were advised by Moscow to renounce such independent propaganda and to present themselves as advisers and
assistants of the nationalist leaders, but on no account to
appear as their potential rivals.

The difference in tactics is explained by the difference in
aim. The aim of the Communists in the "bloc within" in
China, as in the "bloc without" normally used in united-
front tactics, was to increase their own strength at the expense of their allies in order eventually to *eliminate* them,
take over their power, and destroy their organization. The
object of the new policy of licensed infiltration is to *win* the
national-revolutionary leaders step by step for a "socialist"
policy, in the Soviet sense of the word, to occupy positions
of power under them, and to transform their ruling parties
into parties of a Communist type. As a model for the new
strategy, Castro's Cuba is more relevant than the China of
the twenties.

We are thus faced with a completely new departure in the
history of communism, which at first sight appears extremely bold. It is true that the first non-Russian Commun-

ist parties were formed by the deliberate "bolshevization" of parties or groups of the democratic-socialist Left, but these were not parties in power, and the ideological authority of the Soviet Union among all revolutionary socialists was then unchallenged. Castro's "conversion" to Marxism-Leninism, on the other hand, was not the result of conscious Soviet strategy, but came as a surprise to Moscow; and the fusion of the Cuban Communists with Castro's own 26 July Movement was not the cause but the consequence of that conversion. It may indeed be argued that Cuba's development into a "socialist state" was the result of the coincidence of three weaknesses—the ideological and organizational weakness of Castro's own movement, which was totally unprepared for the seizure of power; the weak political standing of the Cuban Communists, who had no prospects of competing with the prestige of the victorious revolutionary leader; and the weakness of Moscow's international authority, which could no longer enforce the subordination of a revolutionary regime that was geographically remote and independent in origin, even though that regime depended economically and militarily on its help and professed allegiance to "Marxism-Leninism."

Yet it is just in this combination of weaknesses that the Cuban model is relevant for non-Communist one-party regimes in the ex-colonial countries; for the ideological and organizational defects of Castro's movement which caused him to sponsor its fusion with the disciplined Communist Party and its relatively well-trained cadres are typical for many, if not for all the younger single-party regimes. True, many of the monopoly parties in these countries are better organized than was Castro's, but ideologically most of them are just as confused, and all of them suffer from a far more marked shortage of trained personnel than comparatively developed Cuba, where Castro's movement was recruited largely from intellectuals. For all these parties, therefore, there is a strong temptation to accept the offer of loyal cooperation of even a small number of Communist-trained functionaries who have clear, if often rigid ideas about economic policy, are accustomed to a measure of discipline of rational thought and systematic work, and have proved their devotion to the cause.

The poor standing of the Communist Party, due in Cuba to the lateness of its support for Castro's revolution, has very similar reasons in Algeria; more generally, the Communists did not lead the struggle for independence in any of the former colonies now ruled by nationalist parties, and thus are nowhere in a position to compete with the prestige of their victorious leaders. Their chances of coming to power as rivals of the ruling party are minimal for at least another generation; on the other hand, their opportunities of gaining influence in these parties as functionaries and experts are considerable, and the attractions of licensed infiltration are consequently as great for them as for the nationalist leaders.

Finally, the weakening of Moscow's ideological authority not only diminishes the reluctance of the non-Communist one-party regimes to cooperate with thier local Communists, but is also a consideration affecting Soviet policy itself. So long as the rule of a Communist party guaranteed the subordination of the state concerned to Soviet interests, or at least seemed to promise an effective coordination of its policy with that of Moscow, any extension of Communist rule meant the extension of the Soviet sphere of power. Today it means to the Soviets at best a weakening of the West and a *chance* to increase their influence, at worst an obligation to give aid and protection without corresponding control, and the danger of ideological attack if Soviet aid does not come up to expectations. On the other hand, a non-aligned national revolutionary regime with an anti-imperialist and broadly pro-Soviet outlook offers Moscow no fewer possibilities of exerting infuence and far fewer burdens and dangers: in 1964, it seemed by no means certain that relations with "Communist" Cuba were more advantageous or freer of complexities for the Soviet Union than its relations with non-Communist Algeria. The establishment of "party relations" between the CPSU and national-revolutionary ruling single parties thus has come to appear to Moscow as a natural device for converting its loss of doctrinal authority and the progressive dissolution of Marxist-Leninist orthodoxy into a means to extend its political influence in the world on a more flexible basis.

This last consideration, however, reveals the inherent limits of the new strategy. Its immediate advantages for the Soviets depend on its negative features—on the renunciation of independent activity by the Communist parties in national-revolutionary one-party states, and the consequent reduction of the grounds for possible diplomatic friction with them. But the long-term effect of licensed infiltration on the development of these countries depends on the cohesion and credibility of the very Marxist-Leninist doctrine whose disintegration is being accelerated not only by the pluralistic decay of the world Communist movement but also by the new revisionist strategy in these countries. How long will the Communist cadres, having accepted Moscow's advice to work loyally within the National-Revolutionary State Party, retain their belief in an internationalist doctrine which each Communist state interprets differently, or preserve a higher loyalty to a Soviet Union which has visibly ceased to be the recognized center of world communism?

The second inherent limitation lies as with all previous strategies in the national interests of the new states themselves. Some "non-capitalist" measures against landlords and privileged foreign firms or in favor of the planned promotion of industry by the state may correspond to the genuine development needs of these countries; others, whether due to bureaucratic dilettantism or to Communist influence, may have a harmful effect on economic growth.

But their actual foreign policy will in most cases be determined less by anti-imperialist resentment or ideology than by the attitude of the rival power groups to their interests—the amount and form of their development aid, their intervention in regional conflicts, and so on. Hence any infiltrated Communists who would try to induce their government to foreign-political actions which its leaders consider incompatible with the national interest would soon find themselves isolated. The strategy of licensed infiltration may overcome the specifically organizational barriers which a non-Communist one-party system opposes to Communist influence. But no organizational stratagem can overcome the basic political barrier of nationalism—least of all in the age of the disintegration of the world Communist movement into its national elements.

POSTSCRIPT

In the decade that has passed since the policy of "licensed infiltration" was adopted, the high hopes of its initiators have not been fulfilled.

At first, indeed, conditions looked favorable not only in Algeria, Egypt, and Burma, but in a number of African countries. In Kwame Nkrumah's Ghana, an openly Marxist weekly, called "Spark" after Lenin's "Iskra," was published since 1962 within the framework of the ruling Convention People's Party and with the encouragement of its leader. In Guinea, the 1961 conflict with the Soviets, which had led to a temporary rapprochement with the West, was largely overcome by 1964–65; in November 1964, Sekou Touré ordered a purge of his *Parti Démocratique de Guinée* to rid it of "petty-bourgeois factions" and turn it more nearly into a cadre party, and when this led to an attempt at founding an opposition party during the following year, he crushed it and denounced it as a French plot. In the Congo-Brazzaville, a radical leftist "Revolutionary Council" took power by a coup in 1963 and subsequently declared the country a "People's Republic," consciously adopting Communist terminology and seeking close relations with the Communist powers. In Tanzania, the ethical type of "African socialism" first proclaimed by Julius Nyerere in 1962 was gradually transformed, following the merger of his "Tanganyika African National Union" with the more anti-Western Afro-Shirazi Party of Zanzibar on one side and some conflicts with Britain and West Germany on the other, into the more concrete and institutional socialism of the "Arusha Declaration" of early 1967, followed by the nationaliza-tion of all banks and other key enterprises, while the originally loosely all-inclusive TANU itself after the abortive military revolt of 1964 became properly organized to con-trol both the army and all mass organizations.

Yet no "second Cuba" has developed in any of these countries, and no tendency toward one has become visible. On the contrary, some of the first non-Communist one-party regimes to be recognized as "revolutionary democracies" have been overthrown, like the rule of Nkrumah in Ghana in February 1966 and that of Modibo Keita in Mali in November 1968. Even more significant, in Algeria, the first model country of the experiment, the Communists' license to infiltrate the ruling FLN was withdrawn in June 1965, immediately after "Comrade Ben Bella" had been replaced as its head by the military coup of Boumedienne, and their leaders were thrown into prison for several years. As for Egypt, the principal target of the new policy, the license for Communist work within the Arab Socialist Union was long formally maintained, but their actual influence on policy and organization soon severely circumscribed by the holders of real power, using methods ranging from counter-propaganda in the name of Islam and Arab national-ism to a tight grip on all executive key positions and to a cat-and-mouse game of arrests and releases.[13] If in other states of the type there have been no similar anti-Communist measures, it remains true that in none of them have Communists obtained operational influence remotely corresponding to the appearance given by some of their programmatic ideological documents, and that all the leaders have continued to play a balancing game at least between the Soviet Union and China, and frequently also with Western countries.

Among the causes of these disappointments, next to the weight of nationalist ideology and of religious, particularly Islamic, tradition, the predominant institutional strength of the Army, its will to power and its view of itself as the guardian of national unity and independence must be assigned a crucial role in all the cases of major importance. In Egypt, the victorious officers' junta had founded, and repeatedly refounded, the official state party after its seizure of power, and Army and security services continued to be the core of the state machine to which the party remained at best an annex. In Burma, the state party was formed by the Army's Revolutionary Council with a "Marxist" program approved in advance by the General Staff, and all economic key positions seem to be held by officers while the workers' and peasants' councils provided in the party blueprint could hardly play a more than consultative role.[14] In Algeria, it now seems clear that Ben Bella owed his position as head of the government and the FLN to the Army, which constituted the real power from the moment it entered Algiers in the summer of 1962; his willingness to cooperate with the Communists and other Leftists was linked to a plan to reduce his dependence on the army by creating a "people's militia" under party control—an attempt that led to his overthrow by the Army, the arrest of the Communist leaders, and the definite transformation of the FLN into a mere annex to the Army's Revolutionary Council. While in these three countries Army predominance was due to the fact that a revolutionary war or an officers' coup had been the origin of the regime (as later in the Sudan, Somalia, and Libya), in Ghana and Mali, where a ruling party under civilian leaders had gained power peacefully, it came later to be overthrown by the Army on grounds of incompetence and corruption—much as has happened to a number of multi-party governments in developing countries.

Soviet experts and policy-makers began to discuss the lessons of these experiences as early as 1966, chiefly on the basis of events in Algeria and Ghana. The general tendency to a growing role of the Army in the new states was belatedly recognized and explained by their weak degree of class differentiation and their frequent ethnic diversity: the Army appeared as the main factor of national cohesion, as well as the most technically modern and rational organization in these countries.[15] In some, though by no means all, developing countries Army rule under leaders of petty-bourgeois origin could therefore play a progressive role, particularly in the Arab world and in Burma; specifically, it was attested to the Algerian regime that it had not lost its "revolutionary-democratic" character under Boumedienne— despite the purge and arrest of the Communists![16]

On the other hand, Soviet and international Communist writers pointed out that this type of military rule was dangerous in that the leaders could not be *relied* upon to *remain* progressive in the Soviet sense, unless there was strong Communist political influence built into their system. The aim must therefore be to "demilitarize" these revolutions by strengthening the civilian party institutions in countries like Burma, Egypt, and Algeria, by transforming the shapeless, all-inclusive mass parties that were nominally governing some African countries but in fact only providing acclamation into cadre parties able to play the role of a true vanguard, and by eventually "politicizing" the Army itself in the sense of submitting it to the control of the vanguard party.[17] These ideas, discussed theoretically in Soviet periodicals at the time, were outlined as practical tasks in late October 1966 in a seminar for African "Revolutionary Democrats" in Cairo, organized jointly by the Egyptian Marxist periodical *At-Taliah* and the international Communist monthly *Problems of Peace and Socialism,* by At-Taliah's editor, the Communist Lotfi El-Kholy.[18] Yet it was a wry comment on the chances of implementing this program that, though At-Taliah was an organ of the official Arab Socialist Union and El-Kholy a member of its Central Committee and chairman of its External Relations Committee, he and three other Egyptian organizers of the seminar had been arrested on the eve of its opening and only been released after a last minute intervention by Nasser himself.

A serious chance for strengthening Communist influence decisively seemed to have come after the Arab defeat in the Six-Days-War of June 1967.[19] The fall of Marshal Amer in Egypt gave rise to open charges that, with the help of the secret services, he had constituted a "parallel center" of power which had also blocked Communist progress, and to demands for opening the Army to the work of the Arab Socialist Union which had hitherto been kept outside it. In January 1968, Vice-President Zakharya Mohi ed-Din came forward as leader of the government's Right wing with a program for "restoring economic health" by slowing down industrialization, closing unprofitable state enterprises and reducing economic dependence on the Soviet bloc—but the program was rejected and he lost all his posts. Now the Communists announced their own proposals for creating a true vanguard party of determined socialist cadres within the ASU, which would take control of the latter as well as of the state's administrative, economic, and military machines and of all mass organizations, and in which there would be no barriers against Communist influence.[20] In fact, Nasser agreed to a reorganization of the ASU, starting from the reconstitution of its basic units in May and culminating, after the election of committees and delegates, in a National Congress in September 1968, at which 68 out of 75 Communist candidates were elected to office. During the same period, Nasser appeared to accept the Communist demand for measures not only against the "new bourgeoisie" of subcontractors and the growth of bureaucratic corruption, but also against "kulak domination" in the villages: his program of further social transformation announced in March 1968, and particularly a decree redefining the concept of peasant so as to limit it to holders of no more than 10 feddan (4.2 ha) against 25 feddan (10.5 ha) previously, were hailed by Soviet commentators as the beginning of a "new revolution"—the third after the seizure of power in 1952–54 and the nationalization measures of 1961.[21]

It was also in 1968 that patient diplomacy achieved at last an accommodation between the Algerian Communists and Boumedienne's regime. Their arrested leaders were released early in the year; in July, they were allowed not indeed to resume work within the FLN, but to form their own *Parti de l'Avantgarde Socialiste* outside it. They nevertheless concluded that this was a sign that Boumedienne and the Left wing of the FLN needed their support against the bourgeois and bureaucratic Right wing that had been effectively delaying the promised land reform and limiting the effectiveness of "workers' self-management" in industry, and that they might be allowed to return into the fold after a possibly impending split in the ruling party.[22] Altogether, 1968 marked a new high tide of Communist hopes in the Arab world, with rather less emphasis on winning influence within the ruling parties as a long-term task than in 1964, and more urgent pressure to promote the "class differences" between their moderate and radical wings. That seems also to have been the keynote of a new conference of Arab Communist and Workers' Parties held in July 1968.

Once again, the Communist hopes turned out to have been premature. In Egypt, the really effective adversary of

Communist penetration into positions of executive power had been none of the purged Right-wingers, but the "radical" Ali Sabri, who had been General Secretary of the ASU since October 1965 and maintained close links with the security services—and it was he who remained in charge of the party's reorganization and kept control of it with his own "secret apparatus"; for this, the small band of 800–1000 Egyptian Communists were no match, all the less since some of their main exponents, by seeking the patronage of rival regime leaders, came to be played by the latter against each other.[23] As for the "third revolution," it seems to have fizzled out without major results even before Nasser's death in September 1970. His successor Anwar Sadat has from the start rejected the renewed demand of the Communists for more positions of influence and engaged on what is in the Communist view a "right-wing economic policy" of moderate liberalization. It was only the fall of the Left—and pro-Soviet—Sabri and of his successor as head of the ASU, Guuma, in May 1971, and the purge of the security services linked with them that paradoxically gave the Communists a respite from harassment for several years—but it took place in the context of a general political evolution that, because of the popular relief at the more liberal climate, offered them little chance to extend their influence. Thus both during the expulsion of part of the Soviet military advisers in the summer of 1972 and during Sadat's rapprochement with the United States following the October war of 1973, the Communist opposition has been of little account. When Sadat, in August 1974, announced his intention to permit greater pluralistic freedom for organized interest groups within the framework of his one-party system, he was no doubt aware that the Communists, like other critics, would try to exploit the new opportunities for getting a hold on trade unions or student organizations—but he seems to have discounted this risk because of their political isolation.

In different conditions in Algeria since 1968, it was

apparently just these "mass organizations" on which the Communist "Vanguard Party" concentrated in its effort to organize support for the Left wing; and the widespread disappointment not only at the delay of agrarian reform, but at the privileges granted to Army veterans in every field of economic activity and at the general economic situation of the country, may have provided a fertile soil for its agitation. The Boumedienne regime reacted quickly: in October 1968, it deposed the entire trade union leadership "in order to remove subversive purveyors of foreign ideology," and appointed an Army officer, who is also a large landowner, as new trade union chief.[24] At the beginning of 1971, the National Student Union was simply dissolved and the houses of student activists searched for Marxist books.[25] Thus in practice, the presumed Left wing of the Algerian military regime, for all its formal commitment to "Islamic Socialism," has proved no more of an ally for the Communists than did the Left wing of the Chinese Kuomintang in 1927.

No attempt had ever been made to apply the policy of "licensed infiltration" to successive regimes of the Baath Party in Syria or Iraq, due both to the solid resistance of the Syrian Communists under Khalid Bakdash to the concept and to the negative attitude of the Baath leaders of every faction which offered no opportunity for it. After the return of the Algerian Communists to the formation of a separate party in 1968, application of the formula in the Arab world was thus in practice confined to Egypt and could no longer be regarded as a "general line" for that area. This proved important when a Sudanese military junta led by Numeiry took power with a "revolutionary democratic" program in May 1969, with the active support of the well-organized Communist Party despite the initial dissent of its General Secretary, Abd-al-Khalik Mahjub. Both the new Revolutionary Command Council of officers and the government formed under its control contained several Communists; yet at the same time, all existing parties including the Communists were declared dissolved, and by January 1970 Numeiry announced his plan to form a "Sudanese Socialist Union" as a monopolistic state party on the model of the Egyptian ASU.[26]

It quickly transpired that the Communist leaders inside and outside the government were divided on this project: Mahjub and some of the Communists in the Command Council and government opposed the project and wished to maintain an independent party as a coalition partner, while others were willing to renounce independence and be integrated in Numeiry's Egyptian-style organization. After an arrest of Mahjub followed by exile, he was allowed to return in July, and at a Communist Party congress in August was able to win a majority against self-dissolution. As the danger of conflict with Numeiry mounted, a Soviet delegation headed by Poliansky visited Khartoum, but no compromise was reached: soon after its departure Numeiry struck in November, removing three pro-Mahjub officers from the Command Council and arresting Mahjub and other members of the Central Committee. While the anti-Communist campaign was gathering momentum, another Soviet delegation arrived in March 1971, on the eve of the XXIV Congress of the CPSU; its mediating intention may be guessed from the fact that at that congress, a representative of the Revolutionary Command Council delivered fraternal greetings, but a delegate of the Sudanese CP was listed as present and Brezhnev stressed in his report that the cooperation of revolutionary-democratic parties with Communist parties, "including the Communist parties of their own country," served the interests of the anti-imperialist movement.[27]

Yet it was all to no avail: in the Sudan the anti-Communist campaign and the preparations for a monopoly party continued, and during April and May, the Youth, Women's, and Students' Unions, all strongholds of the Communists, were dissolved. Then, following Mahjub's escape from prison at the end of June, came the crisis in July: a coup by the dismissed Communist members of the Revolutionary Council, seizing power in the name of an opening of the regime to democratic participation, and the arrest of Numeiri and the leading pro-integration Communists. Only three days later, a countercoup, supported by Egypt and Libya, restored Numeiri's rule and led to the execution of Mahjub, the three leaders of the coup and other prominent Communists.

Experience has thus confirmed that while "licensed infiltration" may be futile, resistance to integration into a non-Communist single-party regime may be dangerous if its leaders refuse to accept the Communists as an independent partner. Even in the original model country of such a "national-democratic" partnership, Indonesia, it had ended in catastrophe when the Communist Party—then the strongest outside the countries under Communist rule—had allowed itself, in September 1965, to get involved in a putsch of radical officers against the more conservative military leadership, and had suffered a frightful massacre after its defeat; only the fact that the victim of this ghastly mistake had been a pro-Chinese party had limited its repercussions in Moscow at the time. Within the Arab world, the Iraqi Communists had first experienced the limits of cooperation under Kassim and then suffered cruel mass persecution after his overthrow by an extremist regime of the Baath in 1963; subsequently they had continued to be treated as enemies, though in a more moderate way, under the military rule of the Aref brothers even while these pursued a pro-Nasserite foreign policy and took some measures of nationalization, which caused the Communist leaders to limit their underground action and thus led to the breakoff of a more militant section that after 1967 engaged in a rural guerrilla revolt.[28] The new regime under General Bakr, which ruled from July 1968 once again in the name of the Baath, was the first to offer to the official Communists a chance of cooperation, but no agreement proved then possible on its terms; what developed can at best be described as an uneasy relationship of limited and insecure toleration by the regime and limited, non-violent opposition by the Communists.

As the real new model for cooperation of an independent Communist party with a "revolutionary-democratic" regime, the rule of the Baath in Syria since February 1966 has become recognized. Ever since the Baath had ended the post-Nasser interregnum there by a military coup in March 1963, most of its leading officers had been more favorable to radical nationalization measures at home and a pro-Soviet orientation abroad than the party's veteran ideologues Aflak and Bitar; February 1966 marked the moment when this radical wing, led by General Jadid as deputy Secretary-General of the party, finally took power and expelled its "rightist" founding fathers. The new government, strongly supported by the Soviets, co-opted one Communist, gave many economic posts to party members, and allowed Khaled Bakdash to return from exile; it formally established party relations with the CPSU; but it stopped short of concluding a "National Front" agreement with the Syrian Communists, as these demanded, and allowed them no say in the selection of the Communists appointed to official positions.

New differences arose on the eve of the Six-Days-War and immediately afterwards over the determination of Defense Minister Assad to put all armed volunteer forces under the Army's control, and also over nationalist criticisms of Soviet Middle Eastern policy as too moderate. By the fall of 1967, a "nationalist" wing of the regime, led by Assad and supported by most of the officers corps, which gave priority to the struggle against Israel in cooperation with all Arab states, began to confront a "socialist" wing, led by Jadid and supported by most of the party machine, which gave priority to social transformation and favored a "people's war" and reliance on Soviet backing. In November an article by Bakdash in the Moscow *Kommunist* criticized the regime and pledged support to its Left wing only—a clear parallel to the efforts of the Egyptian and Algerian Communists in 1967–68. By early 1968, Assad had reacted with an anti-Communist campaign, while the CP was openly calling for a purge of the Right, free elections, and a coalition government.

The tug-of-war between the two wings lasted through more than two years, several "extraordinary congresses" of the Baath, and repeated threats of military action: the comparative deadlock was due to the fact that while Assad's Right wing, in increasingly complete and independent control of the Army, was stronger, it had to recognize its dependence on Soviet political support and military supplies. But before the end of 1968, Jadid's Left wing had felt the need not only to concede a change in the leadership of the government but to announce a purge of any "concealed Marxists" that had entered the Baath—a clear testimony to the effectiveness of the anti-Communist argument with Baath opinion. In April 1969, the Communists drew the conclusion: aligning themselves with the repeated Soviet efforts to mediate between the embattled factions of the Baath so as to preserve its power, they came out no longer as partisans of the Left, but as supporters of unity at any price. Thus ended their attempt at an offensive campaign for a recognized partnership. When in the fall of 1970, Soviet attempts at mediation finally failed and Assad took power by a bloodless coup, the Communists reaped the modest reward of their neutrality during the final stages of the struggle: the victorious Right wing has continued to tolerate them.

Since then, it has been Assad's victorious Right wing that has ironically fulfilled the Communists' old demand to be recognized as partners: in March 1972, it offered them an opportunity to join a National Front with the Baath and some other nationalist groups—on condition that the Baath should have a permanent majority in all the institutions of the front and a monopoly of propaganda in the armed forces and among the students. The conditions were so tough that for a time, the Syrian Communist leadership split over the issue. The dilemma was underlined when by April, the Iraqi Baath government, then looking for Soviet support in its conflict with Iran, also offered its Communists two minor government positions. By the fall of 1972, following the dismissal of Soviet advisers by Sadat in July, the Soviet leaders had come to the decision that even Communist participation in a clearly subordinate posture in such coalitions was better than no government influence at all: R. Ulyanovsky, the CPSU Secretariat specialist for party relations with the developing countries, came out publicly supporting Communist subordination to the leading role of the Baath as the price for participation in National Fronts. On a more general level, at a joint conference of Communists and Middle Eastern nationalists on "problems of anti-imperialist unity," called by the international Communist journal, its editor K. Zarodov exhorted the Communist parties in the presence of representatives from the ASU, the Syrian and the Iraqi Baath, to continue to struggle for an alliance with such parties even where it proved difficult. By the spring of 1973, National Front governments formed on the terms of the Baath leaders were in power in both Syria and Iraq.[30]

THE BALANCE SHEET

If Syria and Iraq are, on present showing, the relatively most successful cases of the Communist attempt to be recognized as partners of the ruling nationalist leaders, and Egypt perhaps the last surviving case of the attempt to acquire influence by "licensed infiltration," the balance sheet of Communist activity in the developing countries must be regarded as disappointing indeed. But the same is by no means true for the balance sheet of Soviet foreign policy towards these countries. True, no developing country since Cuba and Vietnam has clearly entered the road to the Soviet type of socialism. But the number of developing countries who show an "anti-imperialist" preference for the Communist powers over the West, and who are following a "non-capitalist road" in the minimum sense of making selective loans from the Soviet arsenal of methods for the control of economic development, is large and may still increase—despite such dramatic reverses as Indonesia and Ghana. In fact, however, the successes of Soviet policy in these countries, such as they are, have largely depended on the Soviet leaders' willingness to give aid and support to their regimes independent of their behavior toward their own Communists—not only to those who admitted Communists to positions of influence, but also to those who kept them strictly on the sidelines and even to those who persecuted them.

The theoretical debate in the Soviet Union has in recent years increasingly reflected these facts, without, of course, fully admitting the extent of the Communist failure or of the emancipation of Soviet diplomacy from Communist solidarity. The sanguine hopes of 1964 have given place to more sober estimates: in particular, no Soviet writer would now describe one of the new "revolutionary democratic" regimes as "building socialism"—it is clearly stated that both the economic and the political preconditions for that are lacking in them so far, and that the period of transition will be long and hazardous. The true achievement of these regimes is seen in that they have turned against imperialism, broken the monopoly of power of the national bourgeoisie and entered the non-capitalist road of development; and the Soviets congratulate themselves that the number of states in this category is increasing despite some setbacks—Somalia, Sambia, South Yemen, at times the Sudan and even Libya were listed as new recruits in recent years, and there is now some tendency to shift India into that category. The leaders of these regimes are viewed as people coming from the large intermediate strata of these countries with a radical turn of mind, but no ultimate reliability of outlook; the risk of backsliding to the capitalist road, owing to their overthrow because of mistakes—such as "premature" nationalization of small producers—or to their own waverings, will continue so long as leadership has not passed to the—so far often embryonic—working class and its Marxist-Leninist vanguard, and that may take a long time yet.[31]

Another consequence of the sobering experiences of the past decade is that Soviet writers now show no definite preference for one form of those regimes—non-Communist single party rule, military rule or loose national front governments—over others; there is still a general directive for Communists to support such regimes, but no longer a "general line" for the form of their cooperation. Correspondingly, the term of "national democratic state" is now used for all such governments, not only for those that accept Communists as independent coalition partners, and the term "revolutionary democrats" for all the non-Communist political or military leaders in them.[32] At the same time it is admitted implicitly, and sometimes explicitly, that they may continue to pursue the "non-capitalist road" and play a progressive overall role even though they "temporarily" reject Communist cooperation or even suppress the Communists. Similarly, the acceptance of Marxist or even Marxist-Leninist formulations in programmatic ideological statements, while still appreciated, is no longer regarded as either a necessary or sufficient criterion for their progressive character.

The new attitude clearly shows a gain in realism in that it dispenses with the expectation of the quick making of new converts to Soviet-style "socialism" in the Third World, and with the effort to make the expectation come true. It also frees Soviet diplomacy in its dealings with the national revolutionary states from any consideration for the active role or passive suffering of the local Communists, or rather it justifies in theory the large degree of indifference to their fate already long apparent in Soviet practice. But it maintains, with the concept of the "non-capitalist road," a special category of developing countries that are still regarded at least as long-run candidates for membership in the "Socialist Commonwealth," and with it the existence of a special group of problems for Soviet and Communist policy. For the Communists, the problem of the acceptance of regimes that persecute them as "objectively progressive" has become if anything even harsher than it was in the middle fifties, before the turn toward "National Democracy." For Soviet current practice, there remains the problem that it cannot grant the ideologically preferred "national democratic states" a monopoly of Soviet bloc economic aid, or even a preferential treatment in this field, but must be guided in its apportionment by the importance of the country concerned for the objectives of global Soviet policy at a given moment: thus India remains the most important single recipient without belonging to the special category. Finally from a long-term point of view, the likelihood of the eventual growing over of these states from the pursuit of the non-capitalist road to true "socialism" remains highly doubtful: the advantages of the selective use of Soviet-type economic controls seem much more apparent at an early than at a later stage of modernization, and the seduction of a market economy and of at least a substantial share of private investment may consequently grow with its progress—as the case of Egypt seems to show.

5

Development vs. Anti-Westernism— Soviet and Chinese Roads for the New States

One of the major factors of instability in the world of the late 1960s was the uncertainty over the political orientation and long-term objectives of the large number of new states that have emerged from colonial status since the end of the Second World War. All of these states look back on a longer or shorter history of Western rule and a more or less bitter struggle by their political and intellectual elites to win independence from the West. All of them owe to the West the ideal of modernization—which to them means chiefly the achievement of material prosperity and power through the help of modern technology—as well as the more or less limited beginnings of the actual process of modernization. All of them are also striving to continue, and to accelerate, this process in a spirit of rivalry with the West; they seek to throw off the alien and cramping influence of the West in order to catch up with it or, to put it the other way around, to take over its techniques of production and organization in order to become independent of it. This underlying ambivalence toward the West, inevitable under the circumstances, is cultural as well as political: for, while the process of technological modernization requires the acceptance of habits of rational thought and attitudes that were first developed in the West, the conscious purpose of the modernizing drive is to preserve, though in a modernized form, the cultural identity of the peoples concerned— the specific character of their traditional values as distinct from those of the West.

The subject of the present essay is the influence that the Soviet Union and China have exercised on the unfolding of the dilemma posed by this underlying ambivalence for the development policy of the new states, and the repercussions that the dilemma has had on the evolution of Soviet and Chinese thinking on the problem of development. Our discussion is intended to show that the dilemma faced by the new states between the imperatives of economic development and the ideological passions of anti-Westernism has not only been a major issue in their own political evolution, but has also been an important element in the divergence between Soviet and Chinese policies.

THE EARLY OUTLOOK OF THE NEW STATES

In trying to follow the unfolding of the dilemma, we may take as our starting point the Bandung Conference of 1955. It was at this conference that the governments of Asia, together with a few independent governments of Africa, made their first attempt to define a common attitude in world affairs. If we leave aside the early illusion that the new states, having been born free from the taint of power politics, could place themselves above the conflicts of the Old World and try to arbitrate them from a higher moral plane, and concentrate instead on the hard core of common interests expressed in the debates and resolutions, we find that they revolved around two principal concerns. The first was to protect the newly won independence of the participants against any return of colonialism and to continue—and accelerate—the process of decolonization until the last dependent peoples had shaken off alien tutelage. The second was to make use of this independence in order to achieve what could not be achieved under colonial rule: planned, all-round economic development, with the aim of bridging the gulf between the industrially advanced minority and the poor, underdeveloped majority of mankind.[1]

In the minds of most, if not all, of the Bandung participants, the relation between these two main concerns was one of interdependence rather than of conflict; imperialist control appeared to them as the principal obstacle to all-round development. Despite the warnings of a few pro-Western governments, the political atmosphere at Bandung was dominated by the view, shared by the neutralist majority and the Communist states present, that the old colonial powers, together with their American allies, constituted the only possible threat to the independence of the new nations; moreover, the privileged positions held by Western business firms in many of the newly independent states were seen as a continuing roadblock to development. Thus anticolonialism and planned development were considered as aspects of a single forward movement by the underprivileged nations, which could achieve their goals of modernization only through repeated conflicts with the Western "imperialists." Yet, to most leaders of the new nations, this concept appeared to be perfectly compatible both with selective imitation of Western models and with reliance on large amounts of Western development aid. In short, while inclined to emphasize the anti-Western aspects of their orientation, the neutralists at Bandung were not yet conscious of a possible dilemma between anti-Westernism and the requirements of economic development; certainly they were not inclined to make a clear choice between the two.

The Communist participants, led by China, were of course much more aware of the implications of anti-Westernism and were correspondingly more willing to advocate a firm commitment to it; but in so doing, they explicitly denied that any dilemma existed. In the years following Bandung, both Soviet and Chinese Communists advanced a coherent doctrine according to which the Western imperialists were not only the persistent and insidious enemies of the political independence of colonial and ex-colonial peoples, but also the natural opponents of their economic development. The imperialist powers, by backing the establishment of privileged capitalist combines in those countries, had created the lopsided structure of many of their economies, with their concentration on raw material production and export crops, in order to keep them dependent and exploited; and the imperialist powers would seek to maintain that structure and to prevent all-round development in order to continue to draw profits from these countries, even after the granting of political independence. They would invest capital only to maintain this structure and would grant development aid only to protect the investments of the private capitalists. Hence, all-round development could only be achieved by breaking with the capitalist world market and thus escaping its pressure to preserve the lopsided structure of the underdeveloped countries. Accordingly, the new states would find their only political support for resisting imperialist pressures in the "socialist camp," and their only economic alternative to capitalist exploitation in the "socialist world market" and in development aid from the Communist states. In short, the only road to independent development was the "noncapitalist road," which required a break with the West and economic and political reliance on the Soviet bloc.[2]

To understand the early impact of that doctrine on

many of the new states, it is important to remember that there was no lack of illustrations from the actual behavior of Western governments and firms to confirm the Communist theory. During the Dulles era, the government of the United States tended to use development aid as a means of obtaining alliances and military bases from Asian governments, at a time when the Soviets had demonstratively accepted the right of those governments to remain militarily neutral. The Suez adventure of 1956, organized by the French and British governments in defense of the privileges of a capitalist corporation, would be cited for years afterward as proof that the danger of colonial reconquest was not a figment of Leninist imagination; the conflicts arising from time to time over the rights of oil companies in Iran and Iraq, or of mining interests in Katanga, illustrated the same tendency. Yet, while these events served as fuel for Communist propaganda against the imperialist powers and as confirmation of its thesis that anti-Westernism and independent economic development were simply two sides of the same coin, other facts were gradually undermining that thesis.

THE DILEMMA APPEARS

In the first place, experience showed that both Soviet bloc aid and the socialist world market were too limited in extent to make an economic break with the West practicable for the bulk of the underdeveloped countries; there was simply no alternative to Western aid and investment or to Western markets.[3] Secondly, despite the cases of nationalization of Western assets and frequent political conflicts, Western investments in the ex-colonial countries showed a steady tendency to increase. Indeed, the steady growth of Western investments after decolonization is one of the few points about which economic experts on all sides—in advanced and underdeveloped countries, in Russia, China, and the West—are today in full agreement.[4] Thirdly, it turned out that Western governments were not as rigidly committed either to the use of aid as a means of obtaining military advantages or to the protection of the vested interests of capitalist combines as had appeared during the early period of the "aid competition" between the Western powers and the Soviet bloc. The West, and the United States in particular, soon abandoned the Dulles view that nonalignment in world affairs was immoral and reprehensible; the West has come to accept the neutrality of the majority of the new states just as the Russians have accepted it, and to offer them development aid from public funds without pressing for military alliances or bases. Similarly, Western policy-makers have come to recognize that they cannot make the granting of such aid dependent on the internal political or economic systems of the new states— that they will have to aid not only Western-style parliamentary democracies and traditional autocracies but also revolutionary nationalist dictatorships, not only free-enterprise economies but also governments describing themselves as socialist and engaged in a planned policy of development centered on a strong, publicly owned sector. In a number of cases, though not always, Western governments have also continued to offer aid to governments of developing countries that had nationalized the assets of large Western companies, and have even advised these companies to negotiate with the governments concerned in order to smooth the transition. In other words, while there have been repeated cases in which the Western "imperialists" behaved according to the Communist textbook, they have not done so consistently and, indeed, less and less frequently. From the point of view of the developing countries, this has meant that Western aid has not only turned out to be irreplaceable, but that its acceptance has also proved, in the majority of cases, to be compatible with the preservation of real independence in both foreign policy and the choice of their road of economic development.

At the same time, the over-all problems of development were found to be far more difficult than anyone—and the governments of the new states in particular—had expected. It was not only that the total amount of capital aid from all sources, East and West, proved insufficient for the combined needs of industrialization, agricultural modernization, and the creation of a modern infrastructure in countries with rapidly increasing populations; a shortage of capital was by no means the only limiting factor. The obstacles to a concentration on rational economic effort that derived from the inherited social structure and traditional cultural attitudes proved in many cases immensely strong, and the struggle against them difficult and time-consuming at best. The shortage of administrative, managerial, and technical cadres with the necessary skill and integrity turned out to be nearly catastrophic in many new states, and the problem of training sufficient numbers of them quickly well-nigh insoluble, while many new states were threatened with disruption by the separatism of communities based on religion, language, tribe, or caste.[5]

But while the difficulties of development proved unexpectedly serious in all the new states, they manifested themselves with the most devastating effect in those countries that concentrated their main effort on waging an ideological struggle against the West and on exporting their particular type of nationalist revolution. This latter activity, which Professor Hugh Seton-Watson has aptly termed "revolution-mongering," was not, after all, confined to the Communists; for a time it was the favorite occupation of those nationalist leaders who were least willing and able to make the change-over from the struggle for national liberation to the problems of constructive modernization. Inevitably, the countries governed by such revolution-mongering regimes as Ghana under Nkrumah, Indonesia under Sukarno, and, to a lesser extent, Egypt under Nasser had to pay for the glory of playing a role on the world stage with failures of development, because their governments did not have sufficient attention and energy, or sufficient capital and technicians, to spare for a serious effort to deal with the problems of economic development.

In short, it turned out that consistent anti-Westernism, of the kind the Communists had advised and in which some of the revolutionary nationalist regimes had indulged, was incompatible with successful economic construction, which appeared difficult enough in itself. The principle that Sukarno formulated in the classic words "To hell with your aid!" meant, in effect, "To hell with economic development!" The need for a choice between priority for economic development or for anti-Western politics proved to be a real dilemma, and eventually it forced itself on the attention of all concerned. In due course, this dilemma also forced itself on the attention of the Soviet and Chinese leaders, and, once they recognized it, they responded to it in sharply divergent ways and it became one of the major issues dividing them.

SOVIET AND CHINESE STRATEGIES

In order to understand these divergent responses, it is first necessary to look at the different political objectives that the Soviet Union and Communist China were pursuing during the sixties in the new states and in the underdeveloped world. The Soviet Union appeared to be following, in the main, a "strategy of denial" in those areas. Its principal objective, in the short run at least, was not to create more Communist states or more direct power bases for the Soviet Union but to transform regions that formerly constituted secure power bases for the West into contested areas. The consequences of the withdrawal of the former colonial powers from Asia and Africa, together with the growth of anti-Yankee nationalism in Latin America, were to be exploited so as to deny to the Western powers not only the use of these regions as military bases but also the more or less exclusive use of their material resources and their more or less automatic political support. While in most cases the Soviet Union had little hope at that time of drawing these countries into its own sphere of influence, it would regard its policy as successful if as many of them as possible adopted an attitude of "positive neutrality"—in other words, if they could be prevailed upon to support Soviet policies on a number of international issues.

In concentrating on this strategy of denial, or on winning over the largest number of underdeveloped countries to positive neutrality, the Soviets normally preferred to deal with the existing governments of those countries, many of which offered good prospects for being influenced to the limited extent required. After all, in order to obtain a situation in which an underdeveloped country avoids aligning itself formally with the West and allows itself occasionally to be manipulated, through economic aid and diplomacy, into supporting Soviet policies, it is not necessary for that country to be ruled by a Communist, or even a militant revolutionary, government. This Soviet preference for working whenever possible with the existing regimes in the new Afro-Asian states led to an increasing Soviet concern with helping those regimes to deal effectively with their problems of development—with promoting their political stability and economic growth. This in turn led to an increasing sophistication in Soviet expert discussion of the economics of development and to a gradual transformation of the Soviet outlook in this field from a purely doctrinaire and ideological attitude toward a more pragmatic and constructive one. In short, in order to pursue its conflict with the West by means of a realistic strategy, the Soviet Union began to influence its friends in the "third world" in the direction of giving priority to economic development over emotional anti-Westernism.

Meanwhile, the Chinese Communist objectives and strategies in the underdeveloped world evolved in a radically different direction. The central Chinese interest in the developing countries until at least 1965 was not simply to limit the secure spheres of the Western powers by a strategy of denial, but to promote immediate, active conflicts with the West; it is only for the purpose of promoting such conflicts that the Chinese were prepared to offer economic aid to non-Communist countries. Once conflict with the West, or with a pro-Western neighboring country, was present, the Chinese were willing to aid any regime, regardless of its internal character, even if it was a traditional autocracy; in the absence of such conflict, they were not interested in aiding even a revolutionary nationalist regime with "socialist" aspirations. In practice, this meant that for a number of years the Chinese were primarily concerned with fomenting outbreaks of anti-imperialist violence in the form of armed risings and "wars of liberation"; Chinese propaganda stressed this need for violence even in countries that, once having achieved their own liberation, were clearly no longer interested in it. Thus Chou En-lai, during his first journey to Africa, made a major speech about the need for revolutionary violence in Algiers, the capital of a new country that had just emerged from a victorious war of liberation; he was surprised at the lack of response by the Algerians, who were by that time concerned with different problems.[6]

In the course of time, the Chinese naturally discovered that one major reason why many of these countries refused to commit themselves to a consistent anti-Western policy was their interest in receiving a continuing flow of Western aid. Accordingly, the emphasis of Chinese propaganda shifted. Direct appeals for violence against the West were supplemented and in part replaced by denunciations of all Western aid and indeed of all economic ties with the West, which Peking represented as mere means to enslave the under-developed nations and keep them at a backward level. Thus, the early Communist thesis of the need for a radical choice between Western and Communist economic ties received increasingly urgent priority in Chinese Communist propaganda in the underdeveloped world.

When the Chinese found that most of the governments in the underdeveloped world were not prepared to make a radical break with the United States—an insight which their failure to turn the projected "Second Bandung Conference" of 1965 into an anti-American demonstration must have driven home to them—their interest became increasingly concentrated on winning the support of the new revolutionary movements directed against those governments, and also, of course, on aiding and influencing the small number of non-Communist governments that were themselves involved in revolution-mongering. The Chinese were looking not for means to promote economic progress in these countries but for means to promote further revolutions—and they did it not out of any illusions about the short-term chances of Communist victories in those areas, but because of the absolute priority they gave to a break with the West.

THE REVISION OF SOVIET DOCTRINES
OF DEVELOPMENT

Let us now look at the manner in which the different strategic objectives of the Soviet Union and China have been translated into different doctrines of economic development.

The basic fact is that, since about 1962, a considerable revision of the Soviet theoretical concentration on development "along the non-capitalist road," as well as of the practical orientation of Soviet economic aid, has taken place.

This revision affects the Soviet estimate of the relative importance and success of development along the non-capitalist and the capitalist road; the attitude toward Western development aid, to links between the developing countries and the "capitalist world market," and even to private capitalist investments; the view of the universal validity of the Soviet model, particularly with regard to the priority given to the growth of heavy industry and to the pace and manner of diversification; and the extent and direction of Soviet aid to various types of developing countries.

To begin with, Soviet experts have increasingly noted that poor developmental results in a number of "revolutionary democracies" have both been major causes of the political instability of those regimes and severe limits on the attraction of the "non-capitalist road." They have been critical of unrealistic planning based on insufficient study of concrete national conditions, and particular of a neglect of the interests of the small producers who constitute the large majority of the population in those countries, and have recommended to the overeager pupils of Soviet methods the example of Lenin's New Economic Policy.[7] They have stressed the difficulty and slowness of the struggle for economic independence in such countries, which was likely to last longer than the earlier struggle for political independence from colonialism, and have even bluntly stated that the soil in the underdeveloped countries was more favorable for capitalist than for non-capitalist development.[8] Conversely, they have shown themselves impressed by the *relative* economic success of such countries on the "capitalist road" as India, Iran, Turkey, the Philippines, Argentina, Brazil, and Mexico, and particularly by the "progressive" role of "state capitalism" in some of these countries, which they see as a unifying force in the national bourgeoisie's struggle for independence from the imperialist monopolies:[9] one author explicitly speaks of "anti-imperialist etatism" as a characteristic of such regimes.[10]

They recognize that in such countries a transition to the "non-capitalist road," though technically facilitated by the existence of a strong state sector, is unlikely while successful development continues and will only occur at a later stage when "conditions are ripe."[11]

Next, the Soviet leaders have realized that even together with their bloc countries, they cannot possibly replace Western aid and investments, and that the economic success of the governments they wish to back therefore depends on their receiving aid from the West as well as from the East. Accordingly, talk about the inevitable harm caused by Western aid was stopped or at least soft-pedalled in the later sixties; occasionally, it was even admitted that the developing countries might need Western aid more than the West needed their profits. On the other hand, it was stated that those countries might now be able to demand and use Western aid on *their* terms thanks·to Soviet backing, at any rate if a "progressive" regime integrated the aid in its own plan and prevented it from making an impact on its internal structure—as Lenin under the New Economic Policy had offered concessions to foreign capital but kept the "commanding heights" of the economy under firm control. The Soviets thus came to argue that the victims of imperialist exploitation had a "right" to obtain aid from their former masters as a kind of reparation, and to demand that this aid be given on their own terms.[12]

A few individual Soviet writers have gone even further in this kind of revisionism. Some have argued that in view of the insufficient amount of aid available from public funds, both Western and Eastern, the developing countries cannot be asked to do without private capitalist investments, and that in certain cases a more cautious attitude toward the expropriation of foreign companies may be part of the price to be paid for economic development. Similarly, some have recognized that in countries where technical and managerial skills are very scarce, a limited number of not-too-powerful capitalist enterprises may be helpful in stimulating development and in increasing the supply of trained manpower. It would appear that these Soviet writers have taken the pragmatic view that a little capitalism is needed to move forward along the non-capitalist road, or to vary an old song, "a little of what you don't fancy does you good."[13]

At the same time, the former doctrinaire emphasis on giving priority to the creation of heavy industry everywhere, regardless of the specific conditions in each country, has been abandoned. Originally, priority for heavy industry had been urged, as in Russia itself, as a means to ensure full independence from the imperialists as fast as possible, regardless of the sacrifices involved. With the recognition that Western aid will be needed in any case, Soviet spokesmen have increasingly argued that protection against imperialist blackmail can be assured by the strength of the "socialist camp." Accordingly, the arguments for a policy of balanced growth which, when first put forward by Western economists, were rejected as devices for keeping the underdeveloped countries in a state of dependency, have increasingly been taken over by Soviet experts as well.[14] In particular, it is now recognized that the forced development of heavy industry may not be feasible for very small countries; that for agricultural countries with a large visible or disguised surplus population it may be more urgent to create labor-absorbing light industries than capital-intensive heavy industries; and that in countries with an acute deficiency of food production an improvement of agricultural productivity may be the most urgent requirement of political stability. Lately, the view that the Soviet Union favors priority for heavy industry in all underdeveloped countries has even been attacked by Soviet writers as a Western slander!

The difficulties of financing rapid economic diversification in countries with a lopsided economy have also come to be appreciated by Soviet experts, particularly in the light of their experience with Castro's Cuba. That experience has shown, on one hand, that a program of diversification may lead, over and above the heavy initial capital investment (which in the Cuban case was financed by Soviet loans), to a permanent increase in production costs, because the import of raw materials for the new industries may prove almost as expensive as the import of the finished products; on the other hand, it has proved that the continuing heavy import budget cannot possibly be met by the developing country if production of the traditional export crop is reduced at the same time (as Cuban sugar production was for some years), because these countries have no other source of foreign exchange. Unless the Soviet bloc were to assume permanent financial burdens quite incommensurate with its economic strength, diversification had thus to be accomplished slowly and without an early reduction in traditional exports.[15]

A final revision of Soviet policy that began in the second half of the sixties concerns the distribution of Soviet aid. In the years 1967–70, total new Soviet credits dropped drastically below the peak reached in 1966, while the Soviet government tried to catch up on some of its delivery commitments under earlier agreements.[16] At the same time it began a policy of increasing concentration on certain priority zones in its geographic neighborhood, notably in South Asia, the CENTO states and the Arab Middle East, which was to be maintained when total aid expanded again from 1971 onward. The basic idea underlying this regional concentration was an increasingly clear orientation of development aid according to specific political and economic interests of the Soviet Union, rather than a general and unspecific competition with the West for influence in the Third World.

The new attitude was also reflected in the Soviet government's initial reluctance to accept the demands of the underdeveloped countries for a price policy that would in fact subsidize their exports. The complaint of those countries that the secular decline in the prices of raw materials relative to manufactured goods puts them at a disadvantage in the world's markets, and that this form of "non-equivalent exchange" tends to undo many of the benefits they would otherwise reap from development aid, is recognized as justified, in principle, by both Soviet and Western economists, and the Soviets never fail to point out that this handicap of the underdeveloped countries is due to the lopsided structure and low productivity of their economies, which are the result of past imperialist control. But when, at the 1964 United Nations Conference on Trade and Development, the victims of imperialism first put forward proposals for a compensatory price policy, the Soviets refused to consider such "leveling" at the expense of their own consumers; the disadvantage of countries with low productivity was an "economic law," and they would not tamper with it.[17]

The basic argument for orienting Soviet aid to specific regional interests, as well as for limiting Soviet support for revolutionary movements in the underdeveloped areas, was clearly stated in a *Pravda* editorial published a year after the fall of Khrushchev.[18] Its starting point was the standard formula, coined by Suslov in the course of the polemics with Peking, that the principal international duty of the Soviet Communists consists in building communism at home—in raising domestic productivity and living standards to serve as an example to others.[19] From that doctrine that "internationalism begins at home," the editorial went on to say that the Soviet Union would, of course, always help its weaker brethren, but only at a limited sacrifice or risk; the basic problems of development, like the basic problems of the struggle for liberation, must be solved by the new nations themselves. But it follows that if the Soviet Union cannot take responsibility for solving the development problems of others, it cannot urge detailed prescriptions for their solution on them either. Limitation of aid implies limitation of influence, and the Soviets have recognized this to some extent. The pluralistic formula that the Soviet Communist Party has come to accept in its relations with non-ruling Communist parties— that "each detachment of the world movement must make its own decisions about strategy"—has now come by analogy to be applied to the friendly governments of developing countries as well.

Of course, the Soviets have not given up the hope of influencing the future course of development in those countries, any more than they have given up the hope of influencing other Communist parties. But they realize that there are limits to the means they can use; they cannot attempt to exercise a doctrinaire control over the development policy of countries that receive Soviet aid, nor to insist on presenting the details of Russian experience as the only "correct" model. Actually, Soviet ideologues appear now to disagree about the extent to which the early experience of the Central Asian Soviet republics, and particularly of the Mongolian People's Republic, should be put forward as a model for countries wishing to take the non-capitalist road of development. While some Soviet experts have stressed the different starting conditions in the new countries of Asia and Africa, others still emphasize, as the crucial point of comparison, that those republics could not have succeeded without the protection and guidance of the Soviet Union.[20]

On the whole, however, it now seems to be accepted Soviet policy that each developing country will have to discover the measures that will prove most effective in its particular circumstances. This process of adjustment must, to some extent, be seen as a parallel to the increasing flexibility and undoctrinaire outlook on the Western side. In fact, the adjustment is prompted in both cases by the requirements of a competitive situation. Just as the West has come, in the course of its competition against the Soviet Union, to accept the need for aiding nonaligned, national-revolutionary dictatorships—even if they nationalize Western firms—so the Soviet Union is coming to accept the need for aiding not only nonaligned and non-revolutionary countries, but even countries that depend primarily on Western aid and do not follow the Soviet example in their development policy. The demand of the nationalist leaders of many of the new countries that they be allowed to follow their own road of development—a "third road" between Western capitalism and Soviet communism—while rejected by Soviet ideologists in theory, has come in fact to be accepted by the Soviet Union as well as by the West.

THE CHINESE COUNTERDOCTRINE

The Chinese, on the other hand, in the sixties not only stuck to the original Communist doctrine that the underdeveloped countries must cut their ties with the Western economies as a condition of development, but elaborated it and made it more rigid in the process. The basic Chinese arguments were summed up in two articles by Kuo Wen, published in June, 1965, in the *Peking Review*.[21] The articles started from the uncontested and striking fact of the steady growth of Western capital investment in the decolonized countries, but only in order to denounce this investment as the biggest obstacle to development. According to the Chinese, Western investments do not only maintain the underdeveloped countries in a state of economic and political dependence on the imperialist powers by conserving their lopsided economic structure; the Western investors are also accused—with the help of some rather odd statistical calculations—of currently taking out of those countries a larger amount in profits than the sum total of aid and investments being put in. This continuing massive exploitation by Western capital is then offered as the principal reason for the widespread failure of development. If the standard of living in the poorer countries is not improving (or at least not improving rapidly), if the gap between the real per capita income of many poor countries and that of the rich countries is still growing, this is due, in the Chinese view, not to the inherent problems of population pressure or to the difficulties of changing the social structure and traditions in these countries, nor is it to be explained by the fact that total aid from all sources is insufficient to cope with the magnitude of the problem: on the contrary, the increase of Western investments is denounced as the principal *cause* of the widespread failure of development, because it allegedly means an increase of exploitation.

The corollary of this view is, of course, that if the underdeveloped countries were to nationalize all Western investments and to retain all the profits for themselves, they would be able to develop successfully without benefit of any Western aid at all. Thus, while for Moscow increasing economic independence from the West is now merely a desirable *result* of successful economic development, Peking declared the immediate and complete elimination of all dependence on Western capital to be a *condition* of successful development. The Chinese advice to the underdeveloped countries was to expropriate all foreign capital and to accept no more—not, of course, because the Chinese would be able or willing to replace the West as a supplier of aid, but because the poor countries must rely on their own efforts and mutual cooperation and shun like poison any so-called aid from the rich.

In view of the obvious difficulties that most of the poor countries of the world are bound to experience in achieving economic growth under *any* kind of policy, this Chinese advice amounted in effect to telling them that they should renounce their hopes of material improvement for an indefinite period rather than try to speed it with the help of Western aid. The Chinese were thus coming to be seen in many of these countries as offering not so much an alternative model for economic development as a startling model for "nondevelopment"—for giving absolute priority to the politics of anti-Westernism over the imperatives of economic growth. The course of the Cultural Revolution in China itself naturally strengthened that impression.

ROOTS AND PROSPECTS

The first conclusion from our analysis, then, is that, underlying the differences between the Russian and Chinese responses to the dilemma of the new states, there was a basically different trend in the evolution of the Soviet and Chinese Communist regimes themselves. In the Soviet Union, the adoption of the new program by the CPSU at its Twenty-second Congress, in 1961, may be said to have marked a triumph of the logic of economic rationality over the logic of ideological dogma—at least in principle. Since then, and particularly since Khrushchev's attempt at a worldwide breakthrough came to grief in the Cuban missile crisis, the Soviet leaders have tended fairly consistently to give priority to the needs of their country's economic growth over the revolutionary demands of "classical" Communist doctrine.[22]

Conversely, the policy pursued by Mao Tse-tung, at least up to the end of the cultural revolution, must be seen as a desperate attempt to prevent a similar triumph of economic rationality over ideological doctrine in China; for it was precisely this triumph that Mao regards as leading to the restoration of capitalism, and against which he warned when calling for the elimination of all "people in authority who are walking the capitalist road." In other words, Mao had decided in favor of a consistent rejection of Western values, which logically includes the refusal to promote in his own country the rise of that Western-invented human type, "economic man," even though in the long run this refusal must prove incompatible with successful economic development.[23] Whether a policy giving such consistent priority to ideology over economic requirements can be continued for any length of time, even in China, is of course an open question. But so long as it determines Peking's official outlook, China risks to continue to serve as a model for nondevelopment.

Our second conclusion concerns the impact that this divergent evolution of Russian and Chinese policies has had on the new states of Afro-Asia. On one side, the growth of a revisionist theory and practice of development in the Soviet Union has produced a considerable convergence of Soviet and Western policies of development. This convergence is one of means rather than ends—that is, it takes place in a framework of competition and rivalry rather than of cooperation between the Soviet Union and the West; nevertheless, this degree of convergence enables those governments of underdeveloped countries that wish to concentrate on solving their economic problems to obtain aid from both sides on their own terms and to choose their own road between the blocs with a considerable degree of independence.

On the other hand, the more rigidly ideological orientation of China coincided with the collapse of those revolution-mongering regimes in the underdeveloped world that seemed most willing to join China in giving priority to anti-Westernism over development, and hence with a low point in the isolation of China. While the fall of Nkrumah was only of symptomatic importance, the failure of the pro-Communist coup in Indonesia and the subsequent loss of power by Sukarno was a major blow to Chinese plans, not only for a regional bloc in Southeast Asia but for a rallying of the largest possible number of new states in an anti-imperialist front (possibly in the form of a counter-United Nations) under Peking's leadership; Peking's decision, in the fall of 1965, to press for the indefinite adjournment of the "Second Bandung Conference," of which it had been one of the main sponsors, was an acknowledgment of its inability to give such a conference the character it had intended.

POSTSCRIPT: AFTER THE
CULTURAL REVOLUTION

During the years of the Cultural Revolution, from 1966 up to and including 1969, Chinese activity in the developing countries and Chinese economic aid to them declined as steeply as did all the international activity of the CPR in that period of total absorption in domestic problems.[24] But in 1970 Chinese development aid suddenly jumped to an all-time record, thereafter to be maintained on a higher level than before the Cultural Revolution[25] —and this sudden increase went with a radical change in its orientation.

Gone was the preference for revolutionary regimes in conflict with the West, gone also the concentration on regional allies in South and Southeast Asia, of which only the keen competition with the Soviets for influence on Pakistan remained important. Instead, there was suddenly a wide distribution of "goodwill credits," given primarily for the purpose of winning sympathies for the Chinese position in the United Nations, and beyond that for the general campaign against the hegemony of the super-powers. In Africa in particular, the number of states receiving Chinese aid increased from 13 to 27 in those years, and the amount granted in the single year 1970 was greater than the sum total hitherto invested in the dark continent.[26] While this special jump was due to the granting of $ 400 million to Tanzania and

Zambia for the spectacular project of the Tanzam railway, intended to rival the prestige the Soviets had gained by the Aswan dam, that effort was exceptional in size but not in character: the Chinese were now willing to aid any government, including some of the most conservative governments of the former French Communauté, that was prepared to establish diplomatic relations with them. Their propaganda for "self-reliance" continued, as did their willingness to distinguish themselves from their "imperialist" and "social-imperialist" competitors by giving their credits free of interest and allowing their technical experts to be rewarded at local rates. But there was now no hint of making an anti-Western or anti-Soviet attitude of the receivers, let alone a renunciation of Western and Soviet aid, a condition for their support.

This new Chinese effort in the field of development aid has clearly been conceived in the framework of China's return to the international scene following the IX Congress of the Chinese Communist Party, held in the spring of 1969, in general and of the People's Republic's campaign for winning the right to China's exclusive representation in the U.N. in particular. But it has outlasted the success of that campaign: though the total of Chinese credits granted in 1973 fell somewhat below the high level reached in the preceding three years,[27] the principle of their distribution according to diplomatic rather than ideological criteria has been maintained. The Chinese, whose aid policy had once been based on a militant anti-Western strategy, thus have at last renounced the priority they long gave to "anti-Westernism" in their relations with the Third World—not so much in favor of a priority for successful development, but for a flexible diplomacy. They have thus turned to a "non-discriminating" broad competition for goodwill at the very moment when the Soviets decided to concentrate their aid according to specific objectives of political and economic strategy.

THE PUPIL
TURNS TEACHER,
OR THE
IDEOLOGICAL
BOOMERANG

6

Soviet and Chinese
Communist World Views

The foreign policies of any sovereign power are shaped, to a considerable extent, by the view its rulers take of the outside world—by their ideas about the strength of other powers and the motivating forces of their policies, about the compatibility of the objectives of those other powers with their own or among each other, and about the tendencies toward a change in these factors and the power constellations determined by them. One reason why the concept of the "national interest" is so often liable to widely differing interpretations is precisely that the requirements of the military security and the economic and political stability of a given state can never be determined by looking at the geographic situation, the resources and needs of that state alone—that the evaluation of those requirements must always depend on an estimate of the strength and an interpretation of the objectives of other powers. The classic formula according to which foreign policy is dictated by national interest is thus strictly true only in the tautological sense that it depends on the view of that interest taken by the government in power, and therefore in a large part on its views of the outside world.

Any attempt to understand, predict, and possibly modify the policies of a foreign power therefore presupposes an effort to understand the "world view" of its government in the sense defined above. In the case of Communist powers, the specific character of their ideological regime both provides an easier approach for such an effort and besets it with certain pitfalls. The Communist parties legitimate their rule by a coherent system of doctrinal beliefs, including explicit public statements of their views about the forces at work in world politics and the inherent "laws" shaping the development of world affairs; those doctrinal statements thus offer a ready-made starting point for the student investigating the world views of a Communist power. The pitfalls lie, of course, in the fact that the doctrinaire statements are unlikely to be identical with the actual operative views of the rulers of Communist states, and that for at least two main reasons. One is that, precisely owing to the legitimating function of the ideology in Communist regimes, their spokesmen seek to create an exaggerated image of their doctrinal consistency, to minimize the practical importance of adjustment to unforeseen events, to describe as the pursuit of principle what may in fact have been the outcome of contingent necessity. The other is that no fixed political doctrine can provide in advance for all the dilemmas with which its ruling practitioners may one day be faced; hence situations are bound to arise in which different aspects of the doctrine may serve as arguments for different decisions, while the actual decision is determined by preferences that were not explicit in the doctrine—which is subsequently "reinterpreted" accordingly. In either case, the explicit satements and their claim to doctrinal consistency have to be critically evaluated in the light of the actual conduct of policy over time in order to arrive at the really operative world views of Communist powers.

Because of the pitfalls inherent in an uncritical acceptance of the Communist claim to doctrinal consistency in foreign policy, it is often suggested that the student of international affairs should confine himself to observing the practical behavior of Communist governments, ignoring their ideological verbiage as a mere cloak used to cover the nakedness of their power politics, or as the pious Sunday talk of statesmen who in their workaday practice have long settled down to the agnostic pursuit of the national interest. Yet we have pointed out that a statesman's concept of the national interest depends on his view of the outside world; and in the case of a Communist government, it would be absurd to deny that Communist ideology is at any rate *one* major factor determining that view—indispensable, even though not by itself sufficient, for its understanding. Moreover, even when Communist doctrinal statements reflect a policy decision rather than motivate it, they frequently furnish, once properly decoded, early and important clues for perceiving the decision and its causes. To deprive ourselves of this kind of clue in the name of the exclusive observation of Communists' behavior from the outside would mean that we should gratuitously renounce the advantage of the fact that we are not dealing with the incomprehensible actions of some sort of Martians but with articulate human beings whose language and thought processes, however strange, are intelligible to us in principle.

In seeking to derive the operative world views of the Soviet and Chinese Communists from their official formulations on world affairs, we have above all to watch out for three major sources of distortion. First, we must expect that until the emergence of major conflict between the two Communist powers, both sides would have tended to use common formulas even where their views actually differed on important specific issues, and that the Chinese in particular would have clung to the Soviet model more closely in their public statements than in their actual thinking. Second, after the emergence of open differences, each side had an interest in presenting its own views as a continuation or at least a logical development of the former common orthodoxy, and in minimizing the departure from that orthodoxy implied in the innovations it had adopted in response to new conditions. Third, each side had a corresponding interest in magnifying the deviation from orthodoxy committed by the other and in distorting its views accordingly, so that once the conflict had passed a certain point, the formal statements were likely to give an exaggerated picture of the gulf between the actual views of the Soviet and Chinese Communist leaders. In attempting to trace, in the following pages, the divergent development of Soviet and Chinese Communist world views from their common roots in Stalinist orthodoxy, and to analyze the factors that have caused this divergence, we shall seek to bear these reservations in mind.[1]

THE COMMON FRAMEWORK

For a long time, both Soviet and Chinese Communist world views developed within the framework of the official "Marxist-Leninist" doctrine laid down by Stalin. While it is true that this doctrine grew out of Lenin's thought and action with a high degree of continuity, it was only Stalin who created a fixed and frozen system out of the flux of that thought and action, eliminating some of the contradictions in Lenin's thinking and putting one-sided emphasis on those of its elements that could serve as the official ideology of a totalitarian state.

This Stalinist version of "Marxism-Leninism" became for many years the basis of the political education not only of Soviet Communists but of all "orthodox" foreign Communists, including the leading cadres of the Chinese Communist Party. That applies without reservation for the period of total Soviet control of the Chinese party leadership, roughly from the fall of Ch'en Tu-hsiu in August 1927 to the takeover of Mao Tse-tung in January 1935. Even after Mao's assumption of the leadership had led—not without several years of underhand struggle—to the growing emancipation of the Chinese Communist Party from Soviet control in matters of their own strategy, tactics, and organization, Mao and his team remained sincerely loyal to Stalin's general doctrine and more particularly to his interpretation of world affairs. During the Yenan period, the same campaign for the retraining of the party cadres which served to consolidate Mao's independence in Chinese affairs was used for the intensive study of Stalin's writings, and massive efforts to popularize these writings continued after the creation of the Chinese People's Republic and even beyond Stalin's death. The effect of these writings on the world view of the Chinese Communists must have been all the more profound because they lived and fought in practically complete isolation from the outside world between 1935 and 1945, and to a large extent right up to 1949; and it was reflected in their unquestioning acceptance of such crucial Soviet actions as Stalin's pact with Hitler and—more important to them—Soviet wartime diplomacy toward Japan.

It will be sufficient for our purpose merely to sketch the broad outline of this common standard version of "Marxist-Leninist" doctrine. Its core is the view of the world as divided into two irreconcilable "camps," representing respectively the capitalist and proletarian classes or the capitalist and socialist systems and their allies. The capitalist world is viewed as inevitably declining in political cohesion and material power as well as in productive growth potential and ideological creativity and attractiveness, owing to the progressive unfolding of its internal contradictions—the conflicts among the imperialist powers, between those powers and the oppressed colonial peoples, and between the capitalist exploiters and the productive classes led by the proletariat within the imperialist countries. The socialist world is seen as rising and expanding with equal inevitability thanks to the superiority of its economic and social system, the scientific leadership of its ruling Communist parties, their international solidarity, and their alliance with the struggling proletarian classes and colonial peoples. The conflict of the two camps can only end with the final victory of socialism on a world scale, but according to the Stalinist version of Marxist-Leninist orthodoxy, this will not come about by a single blow and need not, and preferably should not, be the result of a final world war: by exploiting the conflicts among the imperialists and mobilizing the desire of the peoples for peace, the socialist powers may prevent a united imperialist attack on them again and again until the declining enemy has become to weak to risk it. Since the laws of History work in any case in favor of the socialist camp, steadily shifting the relation of forces to the disadvantage of its opponents and offering ever new chances for exploiting the crises of the capitalist system by successful revolutions, the Communists have no interest in precipitating a general showdown and may content themselves with seizing these revolutionary opportunities as they arise. In that sense, "peaceful coexistence," or the strategy of protracted worldwide conflict with controlled risk, is good traditional Stalinist doctrine.

As far as we can judge, the concrete application of this common framework of analysis to the interpretation of the world situation by Soviet and Chinese Communists also developed on roughly parallel lines until 1957. For instance, both had by 1946 come to the conclusion that after the defeat of Germany and Japan, the United States with its atomic monopoly was seeking to unify the capitalist camp under its leadership and had become their main enemy; but both Stalin and Mao argued at the time in authoritative interviews[2] that an American-led all-out attack on the Soviet Union was unlikely, despite the temptation offered by that atomic monopoly, owing to American preoccupation with inter-imperialist conflicts. There are some indications that around 1948, at the height of the East-West conflict in Europe, the Chinese leaders may have come to believe in the imminence of major war,[3] as some other Communist leaders did and even some Soviet leaders may have done, but Stalin certainly did not. But by the time of the Korean War, both Soviet and Chinese actions were clearly based on a rejection of the "war perspective." Again, both Soviet and Chinese Communists were prevented by doctrinaire blinkers from grasping the authenticity and significance of the beginning of decolonization when Britain started the process by granting independence to India, Pakistan, Burma, and Ceylon in 1947–48—though Peking, being geographically and psychologically closer to the phenomenon, gave earlier indications than Moscow of recognizing the fact of Indian independence and its possible diplomatic usefulness.

Even after the death of Stalin, Soviet and Chinese Communists at first proceeded more or less in step in adjusting the common doctrine to new realities. Both now turned eagerly to an effort to keep the new, ex-colonial nations at least neutral and thus incorporate them in a "zone of peace" around their borders, a policy that presupposed acceptance of the independence of the new nations from the "imperialist camp" and understanding of the strategic value of their anti-imperialist outlook. Both also came to agree on the need to transform the Soviet bloc into a "Socialist Commonwealth," based on continued Soviet leadership in foreign policy and in the interpretation of the doctrine but allowing considerable domestic autonomy for all member governments; here again, Peking was somewhat ahead in its "revisionism" in the Polish case, but full harmony was preserved during all phases of the Hungarian crisis, and the two parties presented a common formula on the issue at the Moscow conference of November 1957.

Finally, both interpreted the development of a thermo-nuclear stalemate and particularly the growing vulnerability of the United States after the invention of intercontinental missiles as a major shift in the world balance of power offering increased chances for new advances of the socialist camp. It was only at this point that serious differences arose about the extent of the shift and the best strategy for exploiting the new opportunities.

THE DIFFERENT BACKGROUND

Yet while Soviet and Chinese Communists for many years professed a common world view, they had long been conscious of the differences in their own role in the world; and that awareness inevitably led to less conscious differences of emphasis in the use of the common doctrine. In the light of the later open disagreements, we may discern three major interconnected differences in the historic background of the two parties: they concern the importance of anti-colonial nationalism as a revolutionary factor, the role of armed force in the struggle for power, and the relative weight of the "subjective" and "objective" elements of strength—of revolutionary determination against economic and technological maturity—in the class struggle.

Anti-colonial nationalism was recognized as one of the major revolutionary forces of our time by Lenin. It was he who first conceived the strategic idea of a grand alliance uniting the oppressed colonial and semi-colonial peoples with the proletariat of the advanced industrial countries and with the young Soviet state in a common struggle to overthrow the imperialist order. But in the view of Lenin and his successors, the anti-colonial nationalist movements (the "bourgeois-democratic revolutions" of the East) were ultimately auxiliaries; the Communist movements of the industrial working class (the "proletarian revolutions" of the West) would have to provide the hard core, even though the auxiliaries might conceivably decide the final battle by their sheer bulk.

This was not simply a matter of strategic doctrine but of identity and experience. The Russian revolutionaries in general, and the Bolsheviks in particular, did not regard themselves as members of an oppressed, but of an oppressing, nation; desperately impatient as they were with Russian backwardness, it did not occur to them to blame the Western imperialists for causing it. Though the Bolsheviks eventually came to inherit the Narodniks' dream of leading Russia to socialism along a new road that would spare her the evils of Western capitalist society, they were never consciously anti-Western before the conquest of power. It was only after that victory had been followed by the futile intervention of the Western imperialists and the defeat of the Western Communists that the Bolsheviks reluctantly settled down to fulfill the Narodnik's testament in isolated Russia. When Lenin talked about former colonial peoples taking the "non-capitalist road of development" with the help of the proletarians of the advanced countries, he saw the young republics of Central Asia as examples of such former colonial peoples, but Soviet Russia as representing the advanced proletarians.

In Russia, in short, anti-Western nationalism arose only as a by-product of the victory of the Bolshevik revolution—it had not been among its motivating forces. Chinese communism, by contrast, may be said to have arisen as a by-product of anti-colonial nationalism. It had its immediate origin in the atmosphere of the May Fourth Movement of national protest against the Versailles transfer of Chinese territory from one imperialist power to the other, and in the consequent desperate search for means to overcome national weakness and humiliation. In a longer perspective, it has been described as the final outcome of the quest for identity pursued by an intelligentsia that had to break with its cultural tradition to achieve modernization, yet had first set out to achieve modernization in order to recover its national dignity.[4] Though the founding fathers of Chinese communism were by no means anti-Western in a cultural sense and had turned to Marxism as an advanced Western message that seemed relevant to their problems,[5] the influence of those Westernizing intellectuals from the coastal cities has been increasingly replaced by that of profoundly anti-Western backwoodsmen like Mao Tse-tung and his Hunan clan, until China's spiritual climate today has become much closer to that of Mao's youthful tract about the patriotic value of physical jerks[6] than to that of the early writings of Li Ta-chao or Ch'en Tu-hsiu. Before its final postwar bid for power, the two periods that saw the greatest expansion of Chinese Communist influence were that of the struggle for national unification up to 1927, and that of the national resistance against Japan after 1937; while the decisive struggle after 1945 was accompanied by unceasing denunciations of American imperialist intervention.

The Chinese Communists' view of themselves and of the world has been profoundly marked by this history. Lenin believed that he had creatively applied Marxism to Russian conditions; but if he had been told that he had "Russified" it, he would have rejected the phrase as an insult. Mao began to boast of his "Sinification" of Marxism in 1938, in his address to the first plenary session of the Central Committee after the coup that had given him leadership of the party[7]—the session that marked the final legitimation of that leadership and its acceptance by the Comintern; and within a year, he formally claimed that the "New Democracy" he was creating must become a model for the revolutions in all colonial and semi-colonial countries.[8] Subsequently, "Sinification" became an essential part of the Cheng Feng movement for the retraining of party cadres, while the claim for a model role of the Chinese revolution for all revolutions in colonial and semi-colonial countries was repeated on the morrow of Communist victory on the whole Chinese mainland by Liu Shao-ch'i from the international platform of the Peking conference of Asian and Australasian trade unions.[9]

Against this different background, it appears natural that the two parties should have reacted differently to one of the basic experiences of the international Communist movement in the past half century: I mean the decline in revolutionary tensions in the advanced industrial countries, and the mounting evidence of the revolutionary potential, or at any rate the social and political instability, of the underdeveloped countries both before and after decolonization. To the Soviet Communists, whose own successful industrialization increased their sense of community with the advanced nations, this experience posed the problem of whether there might not be other roads to Communist power than violent revolution; to the Chinese Communists it suggested that the underdeveloped continents were becoming the main "storm centers" of the world revolution, and that they themselves, being the model and guide for these national liberation movements, were destined to become the leaders of world communism.

A second difference of background concerns the role of armed force in revolutionary strategy. Lenin taught his followers that the true revolutionary must in principle be ready to use all means of struggle—legal and illegal, violent and peaceful—according to criteria of political expediency. He believed that final victory could be won only by an armed insurrection, started on a signal from the political leadership once conditions were ripe for it, and that any truly revolutionary party must therefore maintain at least the nucleus of a military organization in being at all times, in order to study the techniques of insurrection and train its cadres for rapid expansion as the revolutionary crisis approached; and he imposed those principles on all parties that wished to join the Communist International. But while he regarded the use of armed force for revolutionary purposes as legitimate at all times and as crucial in the hour of decision, he never viewed it as a means of gaining mass influence or of *bringing about* the revolutionary crisis. In his experience, a revolutionary military organization could go into effective action only when the masses were ready to follow it, and when the cohesion and loyalty of the army and police of the bourgeois state had been undermined by other factors, such as defeat in war. In the fifteeen years of revolutionary struggle that preceded the Bolsheviks' seizure of power, their military organization saw only two brief phases of armed insurrection—in December 1905 and in November 1917—and a comparatively short period of minor violent actions of the "expropriation" type; major civil war came only *after* political victory, and not until then was a revolutionary Army created to defeat the uprisings of the "Whites" and to consolidate the new power.

This pattern of a small, secret military organization "in being" that is quickly expanded for overt action at a time of (real or supposed) revolutionary crisis was also followed, on Bolshevik advice, by the European Communist parties: it may be studied in detail, for example, in the history of the abortive Communist risings of 1921 and 1923 in Germany.[10] In China in the twenties, the Bolsheviks were helping the Kuomintang to build up a political army and instructing the Chinese Communists to occupy positions of influence in that army as well as in the Nationalist Party and government machines; but when the Chinese Communists proposed to set up independent military units of their own, Stalin repeatedly turned down their suggestion.[11] To many of those Chinese Communists who survived the debacle of 1927, when Chiang Kai-shek turned on their party and crushed it, and to Mao Tse-tung in particular, this failure to build up an independent military force during the period of the "bloc within" appeared as one of the decisive causes of their defeat, as the subsequent creation of such independent forces, on however small and shifting a territory, became the decisive precondition of their political survival.[12] From this experience starts the development of Mao's new, radically different view of the role of armed force in revolutionary struggle—the view that "political power grows out of the barrel of a gun."[13]

Mao's own power certainly did. It was as the political leader most trusted by the Red Army commanders that he first gained control of the party in 1935. It was as the exponent of a policy of maintaining that army's *de facto* independence within the framework of the anti-Japanese united front with Chiang that he defeated Stalin's emissary Wang Ming and finally legitimated his leadership of the party in 1938.[14] It was for the sake of preserving this military independence that he was prepared to let the coalition talks fail after the defeat of Japan. Altogether, the Chinese Communists' experience has been victory after a quarter century of continuous armed struggle, of civil war interrupted only by war; and Mao's interpretation of that experience is not only that military independence is the key to survival, but that unceasing armed struggle, even if begun by small minorities on severely limited territory, is the sure way to undermine the stability of an apparently strong hostile regime and to *bring about* a revolutionary crisis. [15] Not, of course, that Mao would regard armed terrorism as sufficient to achieve this *by itself;* he has never tired of pointing out that to be successful, armed struggle must always be combined with policies designed to secure popular support for the guerrillas and prevent their isolation. But given such policies, the struggle may be begun locally, without waiting for a nationwide revolutionary situation, and be protracted indefinitely. It may be started with vastly inferior forces opposing a strong enemy, and may gradually weaken his manpower, resources, and morale until the relation of strength is finally reversed. Armed struggle is thus the highest form of revolutionary struggle, because it is the most effective way of increasing the "contradictions," that is, the difficulties and divisions, of the hostile regime, and thus turning a dangerous, real tiger into a "paper tiger."[16]

In the view of the Chinese Communists, based on the experience of their own victory after decades of fighting against originally overwhelming odds, the crucial importance of armed struggle is thus linked with their belief in the fundamental instability of all "reactionary" regimes. Their successful resistance against the Japanese until their final participation in the Allied victory over them, and their postwar victory over Chiang Kai-shek despite initial American support for him, has enabled them to persuade themselves that foreign imperialist powers are as basically unstable as the Kuomintang regime was in its later phase, and may likewise be brought down by the appropriate, that is, tactically cautious but unceasing, use of armed violence. Their tendency to see the defeat of Japan as primarily their own work and the defeat of Chiang as a victory over the military might of the United States has probably been reinforced by the experience that their massive intervention in the Korean war resulted in a quick growth of their military prestige without damage on their own territory.

By contrast, the Soviet experience of international affairs has been as different from the Chinese as that of the two parties' rise to power. In the half century since the October revolution, the comparative stability of the "capitalist" order in the advanced industrial nations, despite war, economic upheavals, and decolonization, has been the source of repeated major disappointments to the Russian leaders; and it is the advanced industrial nations which have been their main concern—as potential threats to their own security no less than as revolutionary targets. The risk of war with one or more of these powers has always appeared serious to the Soviets, and its avoidance—by exploitation of their mutual conflicts but also, if necessary, by appropriate compromises—has been a major goal of their diplomacy under Lenin and Stalin as well as later. The one major war they were unable to avoid, Hitler's attack, came close indeed to destroying the Soviet Union, and its human and material cost certainly prolonged the period of deprivation and sacrifice by which the present military and economic strength of the Soviet Union was built. In Soviet experience, then, major war has been a terrible risk to be avoided if possible, even before the nuclear age, and its revolutionary effects have been uncertain at best.

A third historic difference between Soviet and Chinese Communists arises from the different degree to which they have been willing to give priority to political and ideological over economic considerations. All Communists do this to some extent: Lenin broke with the Marxian tradition in establishing the dictatorship of his party in the name of the proletariat, even though Russia lacked the economic preconditions of an advanced industrial society, and its industrial working class was very much a minority; and Stalin even defined the need *first* to seize political power and *then* to use it to create the missing economic basis for a new social order as the characteristic distinguishing the proletarian revolution from the bourgeois-democratic one.[17] But the Russian Bolsheviks, at any rate, found their main support in the struggle for power among the industrial workers, and once in control they took it for granted that both the strength of their country and its approach towards socialism would depend on rapid industrialization and technological progress. However many errors of economic policy they may have committed, however many setbacks they suffered, at no time after the end of the civil war have they been willing consciously to sacrifice economic efficiency to ideological principle. On the contrary, when Stalin became convinced that increased income differentials and privileges

for scarce leading personnel and good foremen were a condition for quick economic results, he strained ideology to
prove that egalitarianism was not a socialist principle. During his five-year-plans, statistics of industrial production
with special emphasis on heavy industry became the official
yardstick for socialist progress, a view still reflected in the
formulation of the "basic economic law of socialism" in
his final pamphlet; while the great purges of the thirties resulted in the massive replacement of revolutionary veterans
by bureaucrats and technicians who had won their entrance
into the party by their merits in the management of "socialist industry." In the view of this new ruling elite, it was
largely the degree of industrialization achieved by 1941 that
accounted for the Soviet Union's ability to survive and
finally defeat Hitler's assault, and to fill so large a part of
the resulting power vacuum. The same kind of thinking has
continued under Stalin's heirs, with the difference that they
have felt the need to grant improved economic incentives
not only to managers and foremen but to the masses of
workers and kolkhoz peasants, thus increasingly replacing
a climate of enforced sacrifice by a climate of recognized
consumer claims, and that the discussion has moved from
the characteristics of socialism to those of the "higher
stage" of communism—defined in (Marxist) terms of the
most highly productive technology and of abundance for all
to be achieved on this basis.

The Chinese Communists did indeed, like their Russian
teachers, start with a largely urban composition and with a
similar admiration for economic progress. But after their
urban strongholds had been destroyed, the surviving intellectual and working-class cadres had to recruit a new following in the rural fastnesses to which they had been driven,
and to fall back on the economic resources of these isolated
regions; the result was a type of "war communism" based
on a near-subsistence agriculture and primitive craftsman-
ship organized under military discipline. The experience

that prolonged survival and gradual expansion of an armed community inspired by an ideological faith is possible under such conditions is deeply imprinted on the thought and emotions of an entire generation of Chinese Communist militants—all the more so since the ideologically formative period of emancipation from exclusive dependence on the Soviet model, the Yenan "thought reform," took place in these conditions, and since the final outcome was total victory; and in contrast to Russia, this veteran generation, so far from being purged in later years, was actively encouraged by Mao to reassert its control and transfer its spirit to the very young in the course of the Cultural Revolution.

True, the Chinese Communists, too, after the end of the civil war endeavored first of all to rebuild economic life, and indeed did so with remarkable flexibility and success in the early years; but they never concentrated so one-sidedly on industry as Russia had, and their own criterion of success was at least as much the remolding of the consciousness of the various petty-bourgeois strata as the production figures achieved. Hence when the inevitable difficulties of development arose in China by 1957/58, the true underlying priorities turned out to be different from Russia's: the Chinese Communists' first choice was not all-out industrialization but a new version of their "war-Communist" methods in the People's Communes, not material advantages for the privileged few but equality, moral enthusiasm, and military discipline. Though the grave economic crisis produced by this experiment soon forced the Chinese Communists to correct some of the specific policies of the communes and the Great Leap Forward, the attempt to change the fundamentals was rejected in 1959.[18] Equality was still preferred to income differentials, moral incentives to material ones, political reliability to expert training, military discipline with "politics in command" to economic rationality, which was suspected as a tool of the class enemy.

Up to and right through the Cultural Revolution, political stability and ideological consistency remained more important than general industrial progress; apart from specific war industries, the Chinese leaders seem convinced that maintenance and even expansion of their power may be assured for as long as necessary even on the basis of a comparatively low level of economic performance.

THE ROAD OF DIVERGENCE

The differences noted above between the Soviet and Chinese Communist views of their own role, and the resulting differences of emphasis in their views of the contemporary world, did not lead to explicit ideological disputes between the two parties so long as there was no practical conflict between their policies. But since the late fifties, such conflict has been brought about by the divergent development both of their national interests and of the requirements of their internal self-preservation; and at the same time, the decline of Soviet doctrinal authority in the post-Stalin era has made it possible for the Chinese leaders to express their disagreement with Soviet policies in the form of an open ideological challenge. As a result, the original common world view has been explicitly "reinterpreted" in two opposite ways, with each side naturally developing its new interpretation out of its earlier specific emphasis.

The divergence of national interest between the two leading Communist powers may be viewed as having arisen from their different levels of economic development, of military strength, and of freedom for diplomatic maneuver. The Soviets have long had a capacity for steady and all-sided economic advance, for deterring any deliberate attack on their territory, and for influencing the behavior of their opponents by graduated moves in a world-wide field of diplomatic action which was until recently denied to the Chinese. As long as the alliance functioned, this situation led to a one-sided material dependence of Communist

China on Soviet economic, military, and diplomatic support: and one-sided dependence within an alliance inevitably leads to disagreement about the degree of priority to be granted by the stronger ally to the needs of the weaker, and about the burdens and risks to be assumed on his behalf. Moreover, the different capacities for international action of the Soviet and Chinese Communists combined with their different traditions and experiences to inspire different concepts of the strategies to be followed in fighting the imperialist enemy, and particularly the United States, in dealing with uncommitted, ex-colonial countries and their nationalist governments, and in supporting and guiding the revolutionary movements of the underdeveloped world and the Communist parties of the advanced capitalist countries respectively. As the point was reached where Moscow was no longer willing to appease the Chinese demands by compromise and Peking was no longer willing to submit to Soviet leadership in silence, the Chinese Communists began to argue publicly for the adoption of their own strategy and to develop in justification their view of the decisive forces and tendencies of the contemporary world. The Soviets had to respond to this challenge to their ideological authority by making their own divergent view more explicit.

The core of the strategic dispute concerned the relative importance of violent revolution, including in particular the "wars of liberation" in the underdeveloped, colonial or ex-colonial countries, on one side, and of diplomacy, economic competition, and other methods aimed at directly influencing the policies of the advanced imperialist countries on the other, for ensuring the survival of the Communist states and shifting the world balance of power in their favor. Around this core a series of in part real, in part pretended differences of analysis has been built up, dealing with the "chief contradiction" of the present epoch; the existing relation of forces between the two "camps"; the character of imperialist and particularly United States policy in the nuclear age, the possibility of avoiding wars before the disappearance of imperialism, and the consequences of not avoiding them; the chances of further consolidating and increasing the power of the "socialist camp" without further revolutionary advances abroad; the degree of economic and political instability in the advanced imperialist states and the consequent chances of violent revolution there; the chances of Communist parties in these states of winning a share of power by non-violent means and of influencing their foreign policies even before transforming their social structure; the role of economic progress in the "socialist camp" in improving the attraction of those parties in the West and their chances of success; the possibilities of influencing the foreign policies of the imperialist powers by the pressure of neutral opinion and the mechanism of the United Nations; the role of revolutions in the underdeveloped continents, including wars of national liberation, in increasing or diminishing the risk of world war and in shifting the balance of world power in favor of the "socialist camp."

Parallel with the growth of the dispute on strategy caused by the divergence of national interest between the two leading Communist states, their different stages of economic development have also led them to adopt sharply divergent internal policies and to justify them by conflicting views on the nature of socialist construction after the elimination of the exploiting classes. The nationwide outburst of criticism of the regime that occurred in China when controls were tentatively relaxed in the later part of 1956 and the first half of 1957—the period when a hundred flowers were supposed to bloom and contradictions among the people to find legitimate expression within the framework of the socialist order—has convinced the Chinese Communist leaders that the efforts and sacrifices they must demand from their people during the long and difficult period of industrialization that lies ahead of them are incompatible with such relaxation. As a result, they have returned to a concept of "uninterrupted revolution" and unceasing vigilance in the class struggle on the home front; and this concept has survived the partial retreat from the policies of the Great Leap Forward with which it was originally connected, and has even been given a more extreme doctrinaire form in the context of later polemics with the Soviets.

Conversely, the Soviet experience under Khrushchev has not only generally confirmed the need for a more relaxed internal climate, based on the renunciation of mass terror and the increasing use of material incentives at the stage of industrial maturity reached by Russia; it has also shown that the attempt to bring about further upheavals in the social structure even by non-terrorist means, as initiated by Khrushchev at the XXI Congress in 1959, must at this stage lead to setbacks in economic performance which are incompatible with the power competition against the advanced Western countries, and must therefore be abandoned. In the new party program adopted at the XXII Congress in 1961, recognition of this fact has found expression in formulations that, in announcing the end of the internal class struggle and of the "dictatorship of the proletariat," are diametrically opposed to the Chinese Communists' concept of their own regime. As a result, rival interpretations of the process of socialist and communist construction and of the role of the ruling Communist Party in this process have also led to different views about the relations between such ruling parties and between them and the revolutionary movements in the non-Communist world; and this difference has greatly contributed to the elaboration of the divergent world views of the two sides into complete rival systems.[19]

THE RIVAL WORLD VIEWS AS SYSTEMS

Both these systems are presented by their authors as orthodox applications of the common framework to the present world situation; each is attacked by its opponents as totally heretical and incompatible with the essence of the common tradition. What matters to the outsider is that they are incompatible with each other because their interpretations of the contemporary world have developed the tradition in opposite directions. For our purposes, it will be convenient to summarize these rival views under three main headings. The first concerns the forces shaping the policy of the imperialist powers in the nuclear age, the impact on them of the various "contradictions," the relation of strength between the two camps, and the consequences for the danger of world war. The second concerns the problems of construction within the socialist states and the relation between their solution and the victory of revolutionary movements elsewhere. The third concerns the prospects and forms of such revolutionary victories in the advanced imperialist countries and the underdeveloped world respectively.

The Imperialist Camp and Its Contradictions

Both in the Soviet and Chinese views, the basic nature of imperialism has not changed: it continues to depend on exploitation and oppression at home and abroad and to seek to expand its basis by all means including aggressive war. The Chinese polemical charge that the Soviets have abandoned this view is demonstrably untrue; the Soviet statements that "general and complete disarmament" was possible, used by the Chinese to substantiate that charge, were of a propagandist character and not part of serious Soviet analysis. But Soviet and Chinese views differ in their estimate of the factors that may modify this inherent aggressive and warlike tendency of imperialism, and of the manner of their operation.

In the Soviet view, the most important modifying factor is the military strength of the "socialist camp" and above all of the Soviet Union. The socialist camp is said to have become the decisive factor in the development of mankind, with the conflict between it and the imperialist camp constituting the "main contradiction" of our epoch. The strength of the Soviet Union is viewed as sufficient to deter any deliberate imperialist attack on its territory and that of its immediate sphere of influence, and to act as a major limiting factor on the scope and forms of imperialist aggression elsewhere, because it is now on the same scale as the power of the United States and historically bound to grow faster than the latter. But it is not yet regarded as by itself sufficient to prevent every imperialist aggression or decide every conflict in its favor, let alone to win offensive objectives at will,[20] because the use of Soviet socialist strength is limited by the same nuclear balance as that of United States imperialist strength.

A second factor modifying the aggressive tendencies of imperialism is seen in the continuing contradictions among the imperialist powers. This factor was far less stressed in Soviet analysis during the Khrushchev era than it had been under Stalin (and continued to be in China), but it was never entirely written off and has again received more emphasis under Khrushchev's successors.

A third modifying factor of great importance both in Soviet thinking and Soviet practice is the impact of "peace-loving" neutral opinion, as embodied chiefly in the uncommitted new states and exercised in part through the United Nations, on the policies of the imperialist powers. While many of the states in question are ruled by governments of the "national bourgeoisie" and not by representatives of revolutionary movements, their interests in the preservation of peace and national independence are seen as conflicting with the plans of the imperialist aggressors, and their role in the balance of power as capable of hampering these plans.

A fourth modifying factor is constituted by the class conflicts and other conflicts of interest within the advanced imperialist countries. This is seen as underlying not only the activity of working-class movements but also all kinds of opposition to "the aggressive plans of the monopoly capitalists" which the various Peace Councils are striving to mobilize, and indeed as effectively dividing the capitalist classes themselves. The modifying factors from outside the imperialist countries, including Soviet diplomacy and propaganda, are indeed viewed as influencing the policies of those countries through their impact on such "reasonable" elements within them and on their political spokesmen even among the ruling class.

Last not least, the fifth modifying factor is, of course, the resistance of the semi-colonial and ex-colonial peoples to "neo-colonialist" imperialist aggression, which makes such aggression more costly and, owing to the support of that resistance by the socialist camp, more risky and uncertain in its outcome than it would otherwise be.

According to the Soviet view, then, imperialist aggression may be "checked" by the operation of all these factors, of which the strength of the "socialist camp" under Soviet leadership is by far the most important one. The means for checking it, that is, for influencing the policy of the imperialists and foiling their aggressive plans, range all the way from violent revolutionary action and nuclear blackmail to peace propaganda and diplomatic compromise. Again, the Chinese charge that the Soviets have come to reject the use of violent means in principle, and that this is the meaning of their "general line" of "peaceful coexistence," is demonstrably untrue; but it is true that in the Soviet view the scope of such violent conflicts must be kept under strict control so as to avoid at all cost their escalation into nuclear world war, in which the Soviet Union itself might be destroyed along with its imperialist opponents. Because of the common realization by both sides of the risk of nuclear destruction, the avoidance of world war and the reduction of its risk by mutual agreements, for example, on the limitation of the arms race, are definitely possible in the Soviet view. But this implies that the danger of escalation sets limits not only to imperialist but also to Soviet action: rather than risk the destruction of the main stronghold of socialism, the Soviet leaders may have to accept the occasional success of peripheral imperialist aggression whenever the latter cannot be stopped by means short of general war.

The Chinese view is far more skeptical about the chances of checking imperialist aggression without war, and generally of influencing the policy of the imperialist powers by any means short of armed resistance. Aware of Soviet unwillingness (and, without admitting it, of their own) to risk direct armed resistance to imperialist aggression against third parties, the Chinese conclude that the "main contradiction" of our epoch is not that between imperialism and the "socialist camp" but that between imperialism and the national liberation movements of the underdeveloped peoples, which constitute at present the main reservoir of revolutionary violence, hence in the Chinese view the "main storm center of the world revolution."[21]

The Chinese do, of course, recognize that other contradictions may play a secondary role in defeating imperialist aggression. The states of the "socialist camp," the world peace movement, and the working-class movements in the advanced imperialist countries may aid the peoples engaged in armed struggle against the imperialists; the conflicts among the imperialist powers and within their leadership may hamper the effectiveness of their action and at times even paralyze them. But in the Chinese view, the imperialists cannot be influenced by diplomatic compromise or by neutral offers of mediation or by maneuvers in the United Nations, which they dominate, but only by uncompromising support for their fighting opponents. Meaningful agreements with the imperialists can only come about as the result of a clear victory over them.

It does not follow from the rejection of compromise that the Chinese actively wish to bring about a nuclear world war, as the Soviets have charged, or even that they regard it as inevitable. But they do not consider such a war a catastrophe which their own system could not survive and which must therefore be avoided at all costs;[22] they deny that the two camps have a common interest in preventing a nuclear catastrophe and *a fortiori* in agreed limitations of the arms race; and they do not believe that any political strategy on the part of the "socialist camp" could eliminate the danger of world war while imperialism exists. Their view is that a policy of uncompromising support for all armed liberation struggles, by forcing the dispersion and attrition of imperialist strength, offers also the best chance to avoid world war, but still an uncertain chance. Hence they oppose to the priority of risk control—the "general line of peaceful coexistence"—the priority of support for armed, anti-imperialist struggle.

Socialist Construction and International Solidarity

According to the Soviet view, the liquidation of the old exploiting classes of capitalists and landowners and the transformation of the former individual peasants into members of collective farms have created a socialist society, that is, a society not yet free from class differences but free from exploitation and class struggle. The further transformation of that socialist society into a truly classless, communist society depends primarily on technological progress leading through growing abundance and leisure to a steady improvement in the material and cultural standard of the working people. True, the elimination of class differences between state-employed workers and collective farmers and between both and the groups engaged in intellectual, administrative, and directing labor will still constitute a major change in the social structure; but this change will not be brought about by another revolution from above that would impose it on its presumed opponents by political force, but will be a by-product of the steady increase in productivity that will change the conditions of all the working people and give them increasingly identical interests.

One consequence of this happy state of affairs is that, in the view of its leaders, the Soviet Union has ceased to be a dictatorship of the proletariat and has become a state of all the toilers, because there is no hostile class left over which a dictatorship would have to be exercised. The Communist Party itself is no longer a working-class party engaged in class struggle against internal enemies, but a party of all the toilers engaged in constructive tasks of social administration and guidance. In this new capacity, it is supposed to continue its leading role among the social organizations long after the state, owing to the disappearance of its oppressive functions, has withered away.[23]

Nor does, in this view, further progress toward the higher stage of communism depend in any basic sense on the international class struggle—on the expansion of the socialist camp or on the disappearance of the imperialist enemy. Of course, international tension, acute crises, or even local wars may temporarily tie down an important part of the resources of the socialist camp and thus delay its productive progress, while Communist victories in advanced industrial countries could accelerate it. But nothing short of direct involvement in nuclear war could reverse the progressive trend of the socialist economic development, and this risk can be eliminated by the deterrence of deliberate attack and the control of accidental escalation in the manner described above. From a Soviet point of view, further advances in the "world revolution," that is, the expansion of the Communist system, however likely and desirable in themselves, are therefore not a vital precondition of the domestic stability and productive growth of that system.

It follows from this analysis that the constructirve tasks

of the ruling Communist parties and the revolutionary tasks of the non-ruling parties are different in kind: they are allies, but their situations are so far apart that each can be of only limited assistance to the other in achieving its goal. The main contribution of the ruling Communists to the cause of their struggling comrades *in partibus infidelium* consists, in the Soviet view, in making their own system more attractive by improving their domestic productivity and standard of living, with direct support for the international struggle playing a secondary role.[24] Conversely, the main contribution of the non-ruling Communists to the cause of the socialist camp consists in defending its security by means of the peace movement, that is, in seeking to influence the foreign policy of the imperialist governments without waiting for the conquest of total power. For the Soviets, economic progress is the best form of international solidarity; for the non-ruling parties, international solidarity with the Soviets is the most important form of political struggle—in Moscow's view.

The Chinese view of the relation between the Communist tasks within and without the socialist camp is diametrically opposed to all this. According to Peking, the internal class struggle will continue until the achievement of full communism; the danger that corrupt, selfish elements and degenerate bureaucrats may attempt a restoration of capitalism with the support of the imperialist enemy will be ever present right up to that moment—in the Chinese case for "five to ten generations or one or several centuries."[25] Hence the state must remain a dictatorship of the proletariat as long as it exists at all, and the ruling Communist Party must maintain unceasing class vigilance for this entire period. The fact that the "revisionist" Soviet Communists have "abandoned" the class dictatorship and the class character of the party itself appears to the Chinese Communists as proof that in Russia the supporters of a capitalist restoration have come to power and the process is far advanced.

It follows that in the Chinese view, the link between socialist construction and the international revolutionary struggle appeared far closer than in Soviet eyes—as direct and inseparable, indeed, as it was in Trotsky's vision. The process of building socialism at home is seen as one of uninterrupted revolution,[26] carried on as part of a world-wide, irreconcilable struggle against the class enemy: defeat of its agents within the socialist base may depend in part on the blows that are inflicted on it abroad, as the survival of a besieged fortress may depend on the action of relieving forces. Moreover, since the Soviet Union has "changed color" under its revisionist leadership, the territory of the fortress has shrunk; in the Chinese view, Russia had joined the ranks of the besiegers, collaborating with the United States imperialists on a basis of solidarity between the ruling classes.[27]

Since the Chinese Communists believed that their own fate depends on the course of the world-wide struggle, "correct" ideological direction of that struggle appeared to them as a vital necessity; hence the example of their intransigence was judged by them a more important contribution to the international movement than the example of their economic progress could possibly be. True, they deny any intention of setting up a new Communist world party under their own centralistic discipline, and such an attempt would indeed be hopeless under present conditions; but in contrast to the Soviets they continue to insist that one and only one interpretation of the doctrine must be right for all Communist parties, and that they are its exponents. The Chinese emphasis on international revolutionary solidarity does indeed find a limit in the fact that they are no more willing than the Russians to stake the existence of their own state in order to aid a "people's war" beyond their frontiers, an attitude expressed in the formula that any people must win its freedom primarily by its own strength.[28] But while they always refused to sacrifice their power, they were prepared to sacrifice both economic progress and comfort to purity of ideological principle in a manner not hitherto encountered in any Communist state.

The Prospects and Forms of Revolution

Soviet and Chinese Communists agree about the evident fact that the prospects of violent revolution in the contemporary world are in the main confined to the underdeveloped regions of Asia, Africa, and Latin America. But they differ profoundly about the significance of this fact for the future of communism and of the world.

In the view of the Soviet leaders, both their present security and the future of world communism depend mainly on developments in the advanced industrial countries. Communist revolutions in the underdeveloped regions may be useful in weakening the imperialist opponents, but they cannot decisively change the world balance of power by themselves; on the contrary, their victory depends in every case on the support and protection of the socialist camp, which can only be rendered within the limits of controlled risk. To separate the cause of the national liberation movements in those countries from that of the main forces of the socialist camp and the industrial proletariat of the advanced capitalist countries can, in the Soviet view, only lead to their defeat; hence, the usefulness of a Communist bid for power in an underdeveloped country and of other forms of violent struggle there must always be judged in terms of their effect on the overall world situation at the given moment.

In the advanced capitalist countries, on the other hand, most of which are "bourgeois democracies," the Communists are in the Soviet view now more likely to come to power without violent revolution, by a peaceful or parliamentary road. As seen from Moscow, this does not imply a weakening of the doctrine that total power, that is, a single-party dictatorship, is a precondition for the building of socialism, as the examples given at the 20th Congress of the CPSU and since have made clear.[29] But victory by the peaceful road presupposes a possibly prolonged period during which the Communists in the capitalist democracies join in the parliamentary game and abide by its rules in order to get hold of the machinery of government; and this could have the—to the Soviets—important by-product that their political allies in those countries would gain a chance effectively to influence their national foreign policies even before the conquest of total power. Both Soviet diplomacy and Soviet policy toward the Western Communist parties are therefore partly geared to improving the chances for this type of development.

To the Chinese Communists, all this is anathema. As the class conflict is absolute, a peaceful or parliamentary road to power is an even more dangerous illusion than peaceful competition or diplomatic compromise with the imperialists; and as chances of violent revolution in the advanced capitalist countries do not at present exist, it follows that the progress of the world revolution now depends primarily on the violent movements of the underdeveloped peoples. It is only their struggle which, by straining the resources and the political cohesion of the advanced imperialist countries, will gradually undermine their present political stability and make them ready for a revolutionary assault, just as in the Chinese revolution the great cities, which were the traditional strongholds of imperialist influence, had to be encircled by the progress of revolution in the countryside before they could be taken. The formula of the underdeveloped "countryside of the world" that has to be revolutionized before the advanced, industrial "world cities" will fall to their proletariat thus sums up the Chinese view of the prospects and forms of the world revolution.[30]

CONCLUSION: ROOTS AND TRENDS

In elaborating their rival interpretations of the world and of the common "Marxist-Leninist" tradition to justify their divergent domestic and international policies, both Soviet and Chinese Communists have to a striking degree fallen back on their historic differences of outlook and emphasis. Yet while formerly, under the pressure of their desire for unity, they were trying to reduce the importance of these differences to the mere expression of national peculiarities, the impact of open conflict has made the same differences appear to both as the expression of different general principles. As an example of this transformation, it is instructive to recall that when Mao Tse-tung first discovered the supreme importance of independent military forces for the fate of the Chinese revolution, he tied it explicitly, and correctly, to the near-anarchic conditions of a semicolonial country, in which neither a national government nor a colonial power was strong enough to maintain an effective monopoly of armed force.[31] More recently, the Chinese have presented their doctrine of the revolutionary "people's war" as an international model without any qualifications of this kind.

As we look back on the historic differences between Soviet and Chinese Communists regarding the importance of anti-colonial nationalism and of protracted military struggle and the relative priorities of political struggle and economic construction, and on their generalized reappearance in their present rival world views, one single root becomes manifest as common to them all: the greater or lesser distance from Western experience and Western values in the two nations and the two parties. The early identifications of the Chinese

Communists with the revolutionary movements of the colonial peoples and of the Russian Communists with those of the European proletariat have reappeared in their present strategies and world views. The different importance attributed to "peaceful" and violent political struggle is directly linked to the same contrast of Western and non-Western conditions. Finally, the growing emphasis on economic strength and economic progress, on material comforts and material incentives in the Soviet Union, which takes the ideological form of a shamefaced rediscovery of the Marxian link between the state of the productive forces and the possibility of socialism and communism, is also a reflection of the growing impact of Western materialist values on the mature industrial society of the Soviet Union, while the stubborn rejection of this development by the Chinese Communists as a form of "bourgeois decadence" and their recurrent insistence on the primacy of moral enthusiasm and military discipline in economic life seem to express an increasingly radical rejection of those values—even at the price of rejecting the entire Marxist contribution to Leninism, which is Western in essence.

One question raised by this analysis concerns the prospects for China's successfully solving her tremendous problems of economic development under the Maoist leadership. The usual attitude to Western values of non-Western regimes that are engaged in a political effort to "catch up with and overtake" the industrial West is highly ambivalent: they wish to acquire the Western techniques for achieving wealth and power, yet to preserve as much as possible of their own different traditions in the process. Yet while such ambivalence, for all its problems, may be a powerful stimulus to achievement, the Chinese Communist attitude to Western values appeared in the course of the 1960s to become less and less ambivalent and more and more predominantly negative; hence it seemed, to the present writer at least, increasingly doubtful whether success in economic development would prove compatible with this fanatical rejection of the motivations of "economic man" and of the concept of economic rationality based on them. As of the middle sixties, Communist China could not seriously be regarded as a possible model for the economic development of other countries—but rather as a possible model for non-development under the imperatives of political stability and ideological purity.

Another and final question we have to ask ourselves turns on the different ways in which the Soviet and Chinese world views, and the patterns of international conduct linked with them, have responded to changes in the outside world. We have seen that both have moved some distance from "classical" Marxism-Leninism under the impact of experience, particularly of the nuclear balance of terror, of the prolonged absence of revolutionary crises in the advanced Western countries, of the transformation of the international scene by near-universal decolonization, and of the emergence of major differences of national interest among the Communist powers. But while the effect of this changing outside reality has in the Soviet case combined with the effect of long-term internal changes to cause a marked weakening of the Soviet leaders' commitment to active policies designed to foster the world-wide expansion of Communist rule and an acceptance of looser ties to other Communist movements, in the Chinese case the same changes in the outside world for a time combined with very different internal trends to imbue the leaders with an increasingly fanatic belief in the overwhelming historic importance of the armed "liberation struggles" of the underdeveloped peoples, and in their own mission of providing ideological leadership for that struggle. To a Western observer, it would appear that Soviet views have on the whole responded to changing reality with a gradual if limited adjustment, Chinese views at first with a frantic attempt at denying it.

This suggests that the responsiveness of an ideological regime to changes in the outside world depends both on the stage of its internal development and on cultural factors facilitating or hampering perception of the change. From the point of view of Western policy, this would seem to explain why the chances of influencing the Soviet outlook, in the sense of reviving or reducing the acuteness of our conflicts with the Soviet Union by Western action, were for a time very much better than the chances of similarly influencing the outlook and conduct of the Chinese leaders. The fact that during the middle sixties the Chinese leaders reacted to Western threats and Western offers of conciliation, to Soviet polemics and Soviet proposals for a "united front" with equally militant statements appears in this context as characteristic rather than surprising. Of course, this pattern of ideological self-isolation from reality could have been expected to change if the Chinese Communists should overcome the acute internal crisis of their regime and the obsessively tense ideological climate that went with it; yet the ability of the Maoist leadership to surpass this stage had to be considered an open question. Pending that, the scope for Western efforts to influence the direction of change in Communist views and conduct seemed likely to remain far greater on the Soviet than on the Chinese side.

POSTSCRIPT

Since the above was written, the basic ideological positions described here have not been explicitly revised in either the Soviet Union or China. But while Soviet foreign policy has been able to adjust fairly comfortably to changing situations within this framework, China has passed from a period of apparent ideological obsession, accompanied by international isolation and profound internal crisis, into a period of pragmatic realism, accompanied by rising international influence and efforts at domestic consolidation, but also by a marked decline in the observable role of ideology in foreign policy. Indeed, the change has been so striking and unexpected that an attempt to trace its stages and analyze its causes may not be out of place.

The first fact to be noted in such an attempt is the series of painful defeats in which the bid for leadership of the "countryside of the world" involved Peking, both on the diplomatic and revolutionary fronts, before the end of 1965. The effort to organize a "second Bandung conference" of Afro-Asian governments in Algiers and to direct its point both against the United States and the Soviet Union collapsed after two successive failures. The attempt to exploit the Indo-Pakistani border war by threatening India with intervention was effectively deterred by the superpowers and ended humiliatingly with the Soviets establishing themselves at the Tashkent conference as arbiters of the subcontinent in the absence of China. The close cooperation with Sukarno's Indonesia, regarded for a time both as the core of a Chinese sphere of influence in Southeast Asia and as the germ of a Chinese-led counter-U.N., came to an abrupt close when a dilettantic *Putsch,* in which the influential leaders of Indonesia's Communist Party had been involved, led first to the destruction of this most powerful pro-Chinese party and then to the replacement of Sukarno's rule by an anti-Chinese military regime. The "People's War" in Vietnam increased the dangerous American presence on the Southeast Asian mainland, and with it the dependence of the Vietnamese Communists on Soviet as well as Chinese support; and the Chinese rejection of Soviet offers of cooperation in that common cause, viewed by Peking as necessary for maintaining ideological hostility toward the "revisionist traitors," alienated the remaining independent Communist parties of Asia, such as the Japanese and the main part of the Indian Left wing. On the eve of the Cultural Revolution, China thus found herself with no important Asian state and no major Communist party committed to her side.

Though no public discussion of these setbacks and dangers took place in China, two major decisions appear to have been taken in response to them. The proposal to react to the gravity of the American threat in neighboring Vietnam by seeking reinsurance from Moscow for more direct intervention, apparently put forward by the then chief of staff, Lo Jui-chin, was turned down in favor of continued military caution combined with equal political hostility to both superpowers; and the efforts to promote further anti-imperialist revolutions in the Third World were downgraded from a program for immediate action to a ritualized verbal expression of long-term hopes. As neither decision could have been taken without a serious struggle among the Chinese leaders, the alignments on these issues appear to have combined with the unresolved leadership conflicts on the course of China's internal development to precipitate the dramatic crisis of the regime known as the Cultural Revolution. But, while to the Western admirers of Maoist ideology anti-imperialist militancy abroad and Red Guard mobilization at home appeared as two complementary manifestations of the same revolutionary spirit, it is now clear that Mao used the great upheaval to purge not only the exponents of "economism" in domestic development, but also the advocates of revolutionary adventures abroad, like Lo Jui-chin and Peng Chen. To that extent, the practical cessation of Chinese international activity during the years of the Cultural Revolution was not an unintended consequence of the latter, but one of its purposes.

If the failure of the bid for militant Third World leadership was the first and the defeat of its most committed exponents within the Chinese hierarchy the second of the causes of the ideological and political shifts we are seeking to trace, the third was the outcome of the Cultural Revolution itself. It had been based on the solid support given by the People's Liberation Army under Lin Piao to Mao Tse-tung against all his rivals; it reached a turning point when an increasing number of regional army commanders demanded and enforced a stop to the further disorganization of the country by the "justified rebellion" of uncontrollable organizations of youngsters, fighting the administrative organs and often each other in the name of Mao. As a new administrative structure slowly emerged, with the only surviving hierarchy—that of the Army—as its backbone, the ideological paroxysm of 1966-67 began to give way to a pragmatic concentration on work-day tasks: the Cultural Restoration did not, indeed, revise the Maoist ideological formulas of the Cultural Revolution, but used their inherent vagueness to turn them from appeals to rebellion into rituals of submission—just as the slogans of anti-imperialist militancy had been ritualized before.

It was at this stage of impending consolidation that the fourth transforming factor came into play—the shock of the Soviet intervention in Czechoslavakia of August 1968 and of its justification by the "Brezhnev doctrine" of the superior common interests of the socialist cause as defined by the Soviet Union. We need not take at their face value the assertions of the Chinese leaders that they have felt threatened by Soviet aggression ever since—if they had regarded such a threat as acute, their conduct on border issues might have been rather different. But, they may well have concluded that they were faced with a long-term threat to their independence from a Soviet Union determined to use the weight of its military superiority in order to scare heretical Communist powers into submission. At any rate, a sense of vigilance against any encroachment on the part of the "New Tsars" and their "social-imperialist" policies had to be maintained among the Chinese people even after the end of the Cultural Revolution; and when, at the IX Party Congress in the spring of 1969, Lin Piao resumed the use of the slogan of "peaceful coexistence" in defining

Chinese foreign policy, the incidents on the Ussuri river had already made it clear that its application to Sino-Russian relations was unlikely in practice.

By that time, a new American administration had come into office and was signalling not only its determination to end the American presence in Vietnam on terms short of victory, but also its desire for a normalization of relations with China and its acceptance as a partner in a flexible world balance of power. As long as China was in the grip of illusions about leading an anti-imperialist front of Third World countries, or in the throes of its own Cultural Revolution, such feelers might have encountered scant attention in Peking. But they came when the illusions had disappeared and the Cultural Revolution had ended, and found a leadership eager to resume worldwide diplomatic contacts and to win a respected place in the international system, as well as concerned to protect its independence by an effective counterweight to long-term Soviet pressure.

Thus, within two years of the first indirect contacts, the forthcoming visit of the United States President to Peking was announced—an announcement that quickly bore fruit in the admission of the Chinese People's Republic to the United Nations and its assumption of the permanent Chinese seat in the Security Council. As no corresponding normalization of Sino-Soviet relations was in sight, this implied a decision that while both super-powers would continue to be regarded as representing alien and indeed imperialist social systems, the Soviet Union was now seen as China's main enemy. Though the mysterious end of Lin Piao suggests that this decision was not reached without another dramtic conflict within the Peking leadership, subsequent developments show it to have been maintained— with continuing benefits to China's international position.

In trying to sum up that sequence of events, we may suggest that while the early failures of the bid for militant Third World leadership caused a turn to greater practical caution, the Chinese Communist leaders, so far from revising their ideological assumptions, at first reacted to them—as well as to other problems—by the ideological frenzy of the Cultural Revolution. It was only the changes in the top leadership brought about in its course, combined with the exhaustion of ideological passions left behind by the paroxysm, that seem to have opened the way to a more realistic perception of changes in the outside world. On that basis, China has responded to two such major changes—the Brezhnev doctrine and the American turn toward normalization and balance—by a successful reorientation of its foreign policy. But that reorientation has deprived Peking's doctrinal criticism of Soviet foreign policy of much of its former substance, leaving its official "world view" in considerable disarray. True, elements of a new ideological formulation do exist: instead of a critique of "peaceful coexistence" in the name of the need for unconditional support of wars of liberation, the Chinese Communists now concentrate on attacking the super-powers' policy of dividing the world into spheres of influence as well as the economic exploitation of the underdeveloped nations by the advanced industrial countries. But the new position is as yet far from having reached the systematic cohesion of the documents of 1963-64: it is a propaganda line addressed to public opinion in dependent or underdeveloped countries rather than a consistent version of the Marxist-Leninist doctrine, and its influence in the international Communist movement is correspondingly reduced.

7

Unreason and Revolution—
On the Dissociation
of Revolutionary Practice
from Marxist Theory

This is a tentative exploration of what I believe to be a major phenomenon of our time—the rise of a new type of revolutionary movement. Hitherto, we have been familiar with two broad classes of revolutions and revolutionary movements. First, there are the movements which may be understood as resulting when the normal growth, the spontaneous evolution of a society, meets an obstacle in the form of rigid political institutions that are increasingly felt as oppressive. In such cases, sooner or later an acute political crisis occurs in which the obstacle is swept away by revolutionary action. That is, broadly speaking, the formula fitting the great democratic revolutions of modern Western history; it may also be applied to a number of the national movements for independence from colonial rule that have occurred in our time.

In the last fifty years we have learnt, to our cost, to distinguish a second type of revolution and revolutionary movements—those which I, for want of a better name, would still describe as "totalitarian revolutions." It seems to be characteristic of them that they do not occur because of the clash between a growing, dynamic society and a static political framework tending to shackle its growth, but because of some elements of stagnation, some major lopsidedness of development *within* the society itself, leading to a deadlock which a dynamic state is then called upon to resolve by the massive use of political force. This appeal from a deadlock in society to the "savior state" has been the background to the rise of German National Socialism as a mass movement and to the long-lasting reign of violence which its victorious régime inflicted on the prostrate body of society. But the overcoming of social stagnation in the midst of change and of lopsided development has also been underlying the rise of Communist régimes in a number of underdeveloped countries—the only ones that have come to power by the victory of indigenous revolutionary movements—and has given them the opportunity for their repeated, forcible transformations of the social structure.

A NEW TYPE OF MOVEMENT

Now it seems to me that in recent years, we have begun to be confronted by yet another kind of revolutionary movement. These new movements, both of the Western New Left and in the so-called underdeveloped countries, use much of the familiar language of Communist ideology, and actually have taken over much of the substance of the Marxist-Leninist critique of Western capitalism and imperialism as well as the Marxist Utopia of a society without classes or domination. Nevertheless they are radically different from the Communist movements that had been created in the image of Lenin's Bolshevik Party—different in their forms of organization, their strategies of political action, and indeed in the rank order of values that gives operative meaning to their vision of the goal. In fact, one of the preconditions for the rise of these new movements has been the increasingly obvious disintegration of the "Marxist-Leninist" doctrinal synthesis; they grow out of an ideological soil that has been fertilized by its decomposition. But some of the products of this decay appear to be as virulently destructive as any Leninist movements have been in the past—without, so far, offering any tangible prospect of comparable constructive achievements.[1]

A preliminary survey of these new movements may perhaps best start by marking them off with two negative statements. On one side, they are not the democratic expressions of stable, productive sectors of the societies in which they arise; in other words, they do not originate as class movements, as interest groups or coalitions of interest groups. On the other hand, they are not disciplined parties of the Communist type, organized from the top downward as instruments of a single will, with a systematic strategic concept of what they want and how to get there given in advance. On the contrary, it is typical for them that action often precedes thought. Despite the verbal echoes of the Marxist pathos of rationality that may still be heard from the ideological spokesmen of the Western New Left, in practice the urge for violent action increasingly outruns consideration of any precise short-term objectives and of the rational tactical and organizational means for achieving them. It is the style of action and the utopian goal that define the movement, while all other ideas and organizational forms remain very much in flux. The goal itself, though it remains a powerful motivating force, never takes the form of a political programme with precise institutional content. That, on the contrary, is increasingly rejected: the tendency is to say that the new institutions, if any, will have to emerge from the process of struggle and from the destruction of the old order.

While the New Left in the West thus replaces Communist programmes, strategies and organizational forms by a faith in Utopia and a cult of violent action, a number of revolutionary movements in the underdeveloped world show a parallel trend—away from the elaborations of Communist doctrine and the organizational discipline based on ideological authority, and towards the primacy of violent action over social analysis and of military over political and ideological leadership. We may observe this tendency in the practice first of Castro's Cuban revolution and then of the guerrilla actions started in other Latin-American countries under the influence of the Cuban model; and we find its ideological justification sketched out by Che Guevara and elaborated by Régis Debray. A parallel, if delayed, breakthrough of immediate utopianism and immediate violence seems to have occurred in the transformation of Chinese Communism in the course of the sixties, beginning with the "Great Leap Forward" and the creation of the People's Communes and culminating in the recent Cultural Revolution. Finally, analogous processes seem to be at work in some of those revolutionary nationalist movements which, without ever having become formally Communist, are developing as passionately an anti-Western, anti-modernistic, and anti-rational outlook at the last-named products of the disintegration of world communism.

This, then, is our theme. Why do those phenomena arise in various parts of the world at this time? What are the intellectual roots of their beliefs and the social roots of their strength? And what are their significance and possible prospects?

FROM REVOLUTION BY "SOCIAL FORCES" TO REVOLUTION BY "SCIENTIFIC LEADERSHIP"

Let us begin with a subject we know fairly well—the role of Marxism and Leninism in the development of revolutionary ideas. If we cast our minds back to the 1840s when Marxism was born, and if we recall Engels' proud phrase about the development of socialism from a utopia into a science, it is evident to us today that the real difference between Marx and many of his socialist precursors was not that Karl Marx was no utopian: his goals were just as utopian, just as rooted in a profound need to discover a road to salvation on earth, as theirs had been. The difference was that Marx turned his back on *romantic* and *immediate* utopianism in favor of a historical and forward-looking version. The birth of utopian socialism in the early 19th century had been part of the romantic revolt of the new-born European intelligentsia against the beginning of industrialization and the transformation of human relations by an increasingly specialized division of labor and an increasingly pervasive cash nexus. The new turn which Marx gave to those ideas was that he rejected the romantic element in them, the resistance to modernization based on an idealization of the past, and proclaimed instead that, thanks to the logic of history, utopia would be achieved by ruthlessly carrying through the painful process of industrialization to the end. To quote a remark of Raymond Aron's, Marx put forward the thesis that the only way to achieve the goals of Rousseau was to follow the precepts of St.-Simon.

This was a highly original idea at the time, one might even say a rather absurd idea. But it also proved an extremely powerful idea: for it enabled Marx to forge a link between the belief in Utopia and the belief in the logic of History. As a result, he was able to inspire a movement that combined the religious fervor of utopianism with a historical and rational element. Utopia, and the violent revolution that was to precede it, were not to be achieved by mere enthusiasm and an act of will. They depended on well-defined economic and social conditions; but the laws of history guaranteed that these conditions would be achieved in the fullness of time. Moreover, one effect of this analysis was to inspire the followers of Marx with a conviction of the vital importance of material progress; for together with the growth of the organization and consciousness of the working class, the rise of productivity was the most important of the conditions that must mature before mankind could enter the realm of freedom. Increasing productivity would eventually lead to abundance, and only abundance would permit the creation of a social order without classes or domination. Thus the utopian goal and the violent overthrow of the old order were not the objectives of immediate action: their possibility was mediated by the laws of the historical process, by Reason as manifested in History—their achievement by a rational strategy based on the scientific insight into that process.

In a sense, the disintegration of this rationalist and historic concept of the road to revolution and utopia may be said to have started with Lenin—as well as with the early "revisionists" at the opposite pole. For while the latter sought to retain the evolutionary optimism of Marx yet to eliminate the revolutionary and utopian perspective, Lenin was the first pupil of Marx deliberately to separate the task of "organizing the revolution" from some of its economic and social preconditions as formulated by the teacher. He argued, under the impact of World War I, that it was the duty of the socialist party to seize power in backward Russia without waiting for the maturing of the economic conditions for a socialist society. He had even earlier "emancipated" this party from dependence on the actual support of the working class by giving it a highly centralistic, instrumental structure, thus enabling it in principle to change its mass basis according to the needs of the situation. Implicitly, Lenin had thus attempted to replace the missing "objective" preconditions of socialism by the creation of his new vanguard party as an instrument for the seizure of power and for the subsequent transformation of the immature society, and to that extent had begun to turn Marxism upside down. But even while doing so, Lenin still clung to the Marxist analysis in believing that *some* objective conditions were needed for the victory of the revolution—not indeed the condition of economic abundance, of objective maturity for socialism, but certainly the condition of a profound and acute crisis of capitalist society, and of a mass mood of bitter discontent enabling the revolutionary party to gain a mass following. Only once the crisis had reached that stage, he taught to the end, only once the revolutionary party had won a strategically decisive following among the masses—only then could the violent seizure of power take place. As a result, the role of the party never consisted for Lenin *primarily* in the organization of violence. Violence might play a crucial part in its action at the critical moment, but the primary task of the party was to win over the masses *before* that moment by a policy based on a correct analysis of the crisis of society.

Some of the strategic changes introduced by Mao Tsetung in transferring revolutionary Marxism to Asian soil and deliberately "adapting" it to Asian conditions may still be interpreted as mere developments along the road shown by Lenin. Striving to conquer power in a country where economic and social conditions were incomparably more backward—and correspondingly more remote from "objective" maturity for socialism in the Marxist sense—than in the Russia of 1917, Mao became the first pupil of Lenin to make use of the structural flexibility of the centralized vanguard party by seeking the necessary mass support among the peasants rather than the urban working class, and that for many years. He thus completed the effective emancipation of a "Marxist" party from working-class support that had been implied as a potentiality in Lenin's separation of the seizure of power from conditions of economic maturity and of the party organization from working-class democracy. Moreover, Mao recognized at an early stage that the role of armed force in the struggle for power was likely to be far more continuous and decisive in China than it had been in Russia—that here, power would "grow out of the barrel of a gun." But this greatly expanded role of violence in Mao's revolutionary strategy was still tied to objective political and social conditions in two important ways.

In the first place, it was in Mao's own view only made possible by the special conditions of a semi-colonial country, in which neither a single native government nor a single colonial power enjoyed an effective monopoly of armed force. That, at least, was Mao's view at the time of his own struggle for power, though after his victory he came to persuade himself that similar "protracted war" strategies would prove appropriate for *all* the colonial and underdeveloped countries of the world.[2]

In the second place, Mao never ceased to insist that the success of the strategy of armed struggle depended not only on developing the correct military tactics for guerrilla warfare, but on winning and retaining the support of the peasant population in the regions concerned by correct policies and effective forms of political and economic organization. Only a policy based on a realistic analysis of the conditions and needs of the people in the area, and a type of organization that maintained communication with them, could enable the guerrillas "to live among the population like a fish in water," preventing their isolation by the militarily superior enemy and assuring them of intelligence, of supplies and of a reservoir for new recruitment. This insistence on maintaining mass support by policies based on a study of the concrete social situation constitutes the indispensable corollary to the Maoist emphasis on armed struggle and its link with the Marxist-Leninist tradition; it is the foundation for Mao's dictum that while power grows out of the barrel of a gun, the party must command the gun. For, though the party no longer represents (as with Marx) the actual evolving consciousness of a working-class increasingly aware of its true historical interests, it still represents (as with Lenin) the leaders' "scientific," analytical consciousness of the total social situation, its contradictions and tendencies, and hence of the objective possibilities for action which any successful political strategy must take into account. To that extent, Mao's concept of the leading role of the party preserves, like Lenin's concept, the Marxian idea of a rational strategy based on perception of the rational laws of history.

FROM RELIANCE ON "SCIENTIFIC LEADERSHIP" TO RELIANCE ON WILLPOWER

Yet there is in Mao's emphasis on the decisive role of armed struggle also the germ of a different, more basically "voluntaristic" approach to social reality. This is to be found in his view that the use of violent action by itself may be one of the most effective means for changing the relation of forces between revolution and reaction, because the right technique of armed struggle may enable an initially much inferior, revolutionary force to whittle down step by step the initial superiority of its enemy—to tire him out by exhaustion, cause splits in his ranks, and finally wear down his will to fight. In a sense, the art of ensuring the survival and regeneration of inferior forces resisting a stronger and better-armed enemy is, of course, the essence of *all* guerrilla tactics, and the hope that this will enable the guerrillas to outlast the enemy's determination has always been their rationale. But the fulfilment of that hope depends clearly not on the dedication and skill of the guerrillas alone, but on a number of independent factors—such as the enemy's fighting commitments outside the theatre of guerrilla warfare, the importance of that theatre in relation to his general policy objectives, and the cohesion of his political system as reflected in the support for the anti-guerrilla campaign and the loyalty of his troops.

In the Chinese case, the evidence does not show that the Communists were effectively wearing down the Kuomintang regime (or even substantially increasing its divisions) before the Japanese attack, nor that they had any chance to defeat the Japanese occupants (who regarded control of China as vital to their purposes), until their will to fight was broken by defeat on other fronts. Similarly, nobody has ever suggested that the Yugoslav Communists could have evicted the armies of Hitler Germany independent of the outcome of World War II. Conversely, guerrilla "wars of liberation" in Viet Nam and Algeria could achieve political victory by military means because neither area was truly vital for the French republic; and Mao's own final civil war defeated a nationalist regime whose political and moral cohesion had been gravely undermined by the disastrous effects of the long-lasting Japanese invasion.

Mao's original doctrine of protracted warfare, so far from neglecting the crucial importance of these "objective conditions," took them into account by laying down what conditions must be fulfilled for passing from guerrilla tactics proper to the stage of decisive battles, and thus implying that these conditions cannot be created at will but must be patiently waited for. There have been echoes of that realistic approach even in fairly recent Chinese advice to the Vietnamese Communists.[3] Yet, on the other hand, the attempts of the victorious Chinese Communists to recommend the Maoist strategy of armed struggle as a model for colonial revolutions in general (which became prevalent since about 1959, in the context of their ideological rivalry with the Soviet Communists), have increasingly treated the revolutionary faith and tactical military skill of the guerrillas as universal and sufficient prescriptions for victory in "wars of liberation" that would achieve their magic effects *independent* of the objective conditions in any particular case.

This growing tendency to separate the use of armed revolutionary force from any analysis of political and social conditions, implicit in the transformation of Maoist doctrine under the impact of the ideological rivalry with Russia for leadership of the revolutionary movements of the underdeveloped world, has become quite explicit with the leaders of the Cuban revolution and its would-be imitators in Latin America—with Fidel Castro, Che Guevara, and Régis Debray.

Long before Fidel Castro ever dreamt of calling himself a "Marxist-Leninist," and presumably before he read any serious Marxist literature, he acted on the assumption that armed minority action would by itself be sufficient to *create* a revolutionary situation. After this prescription had proved successful in Cuba, Guevara spelt out the new doctrine in so many words as early as 1960. Guevara, of course, did have a background of Marxist knowledge, and in 1960 he still made the validity of the new strategy dependent on one objective condition: the existence of a—presumably unpopular—dictatorial regime. Armed minority uprisings, he then suggested, would not be effective against a government which enjoyed some degree of democratic legitimacy. However, this qualification was dropped by the *Fidelistas* a few years later, when the democratic government of Venezuela became the main target of their effort to export the strategy—and to some extent the leading personnel— of guerrilla insurrection.[4] After that it became an official dogma of "Castroism" that a small but determined and well-led *foco* of professional guerrillas was in principle sufficient to shake the stability of *any* political system in Latin America, and thus to create eventually, by its own action alone, the conditions for the seizure of power.

The consequences of this separation of armed violence from any analysis of social and political preconditions, and hence from any rational political strategy, have been most fully developed in Régis Debray's book *Revolution in the Revolution*. The political significance of this statement of the new doctrine lies in the fact that it represented more than its author's individual opinion. It was written on the basis of long conversations with Castro and other Cuban leaders, who had made the diaries and other documents of their struggle for power accessible to the author, and it was published for mass circulation and used as training material by the ruling party in Cuba.[5] Hence it must be regarded as an authorized summary of Castro's and Guevara's own views, at least at that time, of the "Cuban model" for the conquest of power. Now Debray has become the first to state plainly that it is positively harmful for the chances of armed struggle if it arises from the defense of the interests of a particular productive group; for such a struggle by people who are tied to their place of production—like the miners in Bolivia or the peasants of the most impoverished region of Colombia—tends to take the form of "armed self-defense" also in military tactics. People who lead normal working lives, however poor and oppressed, have something to lose—their working place, their houses with their families—which they want to defend; hence they are militarily too vulnerable and are bound to be defeated in the end by the government's regular forces. In order to have a chance of success, the revolutionary struggle must be conducted by perfectly rootless and therefore perfectly mobile, professional guerrillas alone!

In the context of this complete dissociation of the "revolution" from any concrete social basis, it is only logical that Debray goes so far as to give his own, arbitrary new meaning to the familiar Marxist terms of "bourgeois" and "proletarian." According to him, only the uprooted guerrilla is the true "proletarian," because he has chosen a life of extreme deprivation and constant danger; he has nothing more to lose but his life, and is willing to sacrifice that. Conversely, the industrial worker in the towns of Latin America is in the eyes of Debray a "bourgeois," simply because he has a regular job and values it. Now any writer is, of course, free to choose and define his own terminology. But an ideologist who uses the terms of "bourgeois" and "proletarian" in this purely moralistic and emotional way, and defines his "proletarian" as a figure wholly divorced from the productive process, has evidently completely abandoned the method of social analysis which Karl Marx inaugurated by *his* use of those terms in the *Communist Manifesto*.

Finally, the cutting of all ties between the revolutionary movement and any defined social basis leads Debray with equal logic to a reversal of the relation between military and political leadership and to a new view of the role and formation of the revolutionary party. He argues that it is futile to concentrate first on creating a Marxist-Leninist party which would then organize a guerrilla movement in due course, because the party could only develop in the towns and its leaders might then be afraid to leave the towns. Instead, the only promising way in Latin-America will be to begin by recruiting a band of armed volunteers who will form a guerrilla focus. The volunteers may have little or no previous political experience; they should be attracted on no narrower basis than their willingness to risk their lives in fighting Yankee imperialism and its ruling native stooges. As their ideas become more clearly defined due to the experience of the common struggle, a party will eventually arise—usually only after victory—with the proven guerrilla leaders at its head. Thus military leadership precedes political leadership both in time and as a source of authority.

It is no longer the party that commands the gun—it is the gun that creates the party.

FROM COMMUNISM BY ABUNDANCE
TO COMMUNISM BY SACRIFICE

So far I have discussed the progressive dissociation of the revolutionary struggle *for* power from "objective conditions"—first from the maturity of the productive forces and of the consciousness of a large, organized working class for a socialist society, then from any objectively given crisis of society and any defined social basis—along the road leading from Marx via Lenin and Mao to Castro.

If we now turn to the problems of a Communist regime *in* power, we notice in some countries a progressive dissociation of the effort to achieve the utopian goal from the objective conditions of economic development. This is a fairly recent phenomenon. For while Lenin was the first to sanction the seizure of power independent of the conditions of economic maturity, it would never have occurred to Lenin (or, for that matter, to Stalin or any other Russian party leader) to suggest that the criteria of the higher stage of the classless society—work according to ability and distribution according to needs—could become reality before a state of economic abundance had been reached. Stalin was emphatic that the basic task in "building socialism" was to create, at high pressure, those economic pre-conditions which had been lacking at the moment of political victory. Pending the achievement of economic abundance, the link between individual contribution and individual reward—distribution of scarce goods not according to needs but according to performance—was an indispensable incentive to rapid economic progress. Yet in recent years, conscious attempts to cut this link and to introduce the distributive principles of the "higher stage" of communism in conditions of poverty and want have been made both in China and in Cuba.

In China, this occurred first at the time of the "Great Leap Forward" in 1958, when the creation of the "People's Communes" was accompanied by a major effort to introduce specifically "Communist" relationships, with distribution approaching complete equality as the share of equal "free supplies" in kind in the members' income rose quickly at the expense of the still unequal cash wages. Thus, the peasants were expected to work less and less for material incentives and more and more from enthusiasm for the common good. In fact, this army-like system of equal supplies in kind was for a time described as "distribution according to needs," even though on the basis of the existing poverty the "needs" were assessed by the authorities, and not by the individuals themselves as Marx had envisaged on a basis of abundance. This attempt was severely criticized by the Soviets at the time, and the Chinese themselves soon back-tracked under the impact of its disastrous economic consequences. Yet in the course of the "Cultural Revolution," they largely returned to the same basic view that the use of material incentives and income differentiation, which Lenin and Stalin had regarded as necessary tools of economic development, was really a "revisionist" concession to the capitalist spirit. Mao's decisive argument seems to be that, in the light of Russian experience, a desperate effort must be made to educate the new Communist man here and now, without waiting for the achievement of economic abundance, because otherwise he may never be created at all. The remolding of the people to create the new, collectively motivated man should be given priority over the immediate need for increasing productivity by material incentives, because the latter tend to create not the "new socialist man," but the familiar type of economic man—which to Mao means "capitalist man."[5]

To an increasing extent, the same principles were for a time applied in Cuba as well. The use of youthful "volunteer" labor to work under discipline in the rural *campamento* recalls both the earlier Chinese communes and the more recent mass transfer of Chinese students to work in the countryside. It was, moreover, supplemented by a general ban on overtime payments, based on the same principle that in the interest of socialist education, the needed increases in output must be achieved by appealing only to collective solidarity and enthusiasm, not to ambition and avarice. In other words, here, too, the connection between the achievement of Utopia and the stage of economic development was denied in action: the goal was dissociated from the "objective conditions" stipulated by Marx.

Finally, just as the dissociation of the revolutionary struggle for power from an analysis of objective social conditions leads ultimately to the replacement of the primacy of the party and the political leadership by the primacy of the guerrilla *foco* and the military leadership, so the dissociation of the attempt to build a Communist utopia from the effort to achieve its economic pre-conditions leads to a change in the basic legitimation for ruling a country engaged in that attempt. It issues in a transfer of the claim to legitimate leadership from the exponents of the "scientific" road to socialism and communism to the exponents of heroic determination, from the technicians skilled in adapting the ideology to economic needs by interpretation to the technicians skilled in enforcing ideological conformity by violence. This is a development that has not, so far, been fully consummated, but has made itself felt as a powerful tendency in both China and Cuba.

In Cuba, the old Communist Party had a much clearer economic programme as well as a much more effective centralistic discipline than the ideologically heterogeneous crowd of Castro's original followers, and up to a point Castro was eager to learn from them as well as to use their disciplined apparatus. But ultimately it was the charismatic prestige of the successful insurrection rather than the bureaucratic merits of long-term party-building, the military prowess of Castro and a few men around him rather than the ideological certainty of the old Communists that legitimated the new leadership. The resulting regime was for more than a decade as much of a pseudomorphosis—a similar shape without similar substance—of a Communist Party dictatorship as many Latin American "democracies" have been of true parliamentary or presidential democracies. The "Marxist-Leninist" Party was supposed to rule and its offices were everywhere, but its central organs hardly ever met. Actual power was exercised by the revolutionary *Caudillo,* using his personal impact on television on one side and the armed force of the militia on the other.

In China, the virtual destruction of the Communist Party machine as well as of much of the state administration in the course of the Cultural Revolution seems to have started a similar shift of the basis of legitimacy. For Mao turned on the bureaucracy of party and government with its growing preference for routine and economic rationality in the name of the heroic traditions of "the Long March" and in an effort to train the young generation in the spirit of its veterans. He found it much easier to revive the utopian spirit of the heroic period in the army than in the party or in economic life, and since 1964 increasingly called on all other organizations to "learn from the Army." Having undermined the discipline of all other organizations by proclaiming the "right to rebel" in the Cultural Revolution, while leaving only army discipline intact, he then proceeded to reorganize the shattered party from the top with an unprecedently high share of military men in the leadership, on the principle of sworn personal loyalty to him and to the head of the Military Council who was his designated successor.[6]

There seems to be a significant parallel here with developments in some of those revolutionary nationalist single-party regimes, particularly in the Arab world, in which the official, ideological doctrine was poorly developed from the beginning, and in which military prestige has therefore sooner or later proved superior to party legitimacy. The case of Nasser's Egypt may be regarded as too obvious to be really significant in our context, because there the military *Junta* was first, and the successive attempts to create a state party have only confirmed its character as at best an auxiliary to charismatic rule by a military leader. But it seems symptomatic that the Algerian *FLN*, which originated as a fighting guerrilla organization under political nationalist leadership, proved unable to provide stable one-party rule until a full-time military commander took political control by force, barely bothering to have himself confirmed by the legitimate party organs afterwards. The transformation of the *Ba'ath* party, which started with a more elaborate nationalist-socialist ideology than either the Algerians or the Nasserites, yet has degenerated into little more than a congeries of rival officers' clans in both Syria and Iraq, the two countries in which it officially governs, seems even more eloquent testimony to the strength of a general tendency. It may be at least worth enquiring whether this parallel tendency to a decline in the role of political leadership and ideological guidance, and to a reversion of legitimacy to the military hero (or would-be hero), to the charismatic specialist in the techniques of violence, in a number of under-developed countries under both Communist and national-revolutionary regimes is not due to a similar difficulty in making the transition from a traditional to a modern form of legitimacy in countries with a strong cultural resistance to modern rational institutions and procedures.

A GENERAL PATTERN OF DISSOCIATION?

The dissociation of revolutionary passion and action from the Marxist belief in the rationality of history is not confined to the particular examples I have analyzed. On the contrary, it appears to be a universal process, in which movements and regimes that remain strongly influenced by a Marxist outlook are ceasing to be revolutionary, while those that remain revolutionary renounce essential parts of the Marxist analysis.

Thus we observe that the Communist Party regime in the Soviet Union—as it comes increasingly to regard the development of its productive capacity as the only decisive factor for its advance towards the "higher stage" of communism and as its principal contribution to the victory of its cause on a world scale—is becoming less concerned with either forcibly imposing "revolutions from above" on its own people or actively fostering revolutionary movements elsewhere.[7] It has retained the belief that the final, worldwide achievement of communism is guaranteed by the laws of history—but it interprets those laws in an increasingly revisionist spirit as working mainly through the logic of economic development, so that the eventual attainment of utopia will not require further revolutionary action on its part. Even more explicitly, Communist parties in some advanced Western countries, particularly those with a strong following in a modern, industrial working class, are proposing revisionist strategies for the socialist transformation of their countries by peaceful, democratic methods, based on the expectation that the inherent trends of modern industrial societies will enable them to join the governments and carry out their programme with majority support, and preferably without violence.

Conversely, those New Left movements in the same countries, recruited chiefly from students and other adolescents divorced from production, that are preoccupied with the need for violent action and the revolutionary overthrow of the social order, often explicitly reject the Marxist belief in the rationality of history and the link between the progress of industrialization, the growth of the working class, and the utopian goal. Instead, they are looking for support to the peoples of the underdeveloped "countryside of the world" whose revolutionary ardor has not yet been damped by material comfort, and for guidance to the Mao of the Cultural Revolution and to Castro who promise to solve the economic problems of their poor countries through an upsurge of collective effort called forth by an appeal to solidarity rather than to egoistic self-interest. Nor is their choice difficult to understand in view of the fact that the working class in the industrially advanced countries has become less and less revolutionary, and that the successful industrialization of Russia has evidently not created a society without classes and domination, but a bureaucratic class society still ruled by a harsh party dictatorship after 50 years.

To return to the remark of Raymond Aron's that I quoted earlier, it has become obvious that the world has not come the least bit closer to the goals of Rousseau after following the precepts of St.-Simon for more than a century. Hence those who will not abandon utopianism have at long last decided to try and approach those goals directly. The intellectual importance of Herbert Marcuse for the development of the Western New Left was precisely that he classically formulated this disappointment of the Marxist utopian who feels betrayed by the logic of History. The author of *Reason and Revolution* still put his trust in that Goddess; to the author of *One-Dimensional Man,* the Devil is the Prince of the Modern World. But once the assurance is gone that justice will triumph when the millennium comes in the fullness of time, the only alternative left to the believer is to try and bring it about by storming the heavens here and now. We are faced with a regression to a more primitive kind of secular religion—as different from that of Marx as was the faith of the Bohemian Taborites and the Muenster Anabaptists from the main stream of Western Christianity.

THE ROMANTIC ROOTS: BAKUNIN AND WAGNER

As the term "regression" implies, the breakdown of the rationalist and historical constructs by which Marx had "mediated" the revolutionary struggle for utopia, and the consequent return to immediate utopianism and immediate violence links the contemporary New Left to an earlier type of revolutionary tradition. It is a tradition which, in contrast to Marx, directly expressed the romantic resistance to the growth of mechanized industry and to the destruction of "natural" communities by the process of modernization, and exalted the values of "life," community feeling, and spontaneous, violent action in opposition to "calculating" reason. There are, in fact, two distinct but frequently entangled strands of this romantic-revolutionary tradition, which we may provisionally designate by the names of two friends who were together involved in the Dresden insurrection of 1849: Michael Bakunin and Richard Wagner.

It is hardly accidental that Bakunin has lately been rediscovered by sections of the New Left in a number of countries. What seems to attract them is not just his anarchist vision, the goal of a stateless society of free associations of producers (which others have developed more fully both before and after him), but his passionate opposition to the bureaucratic rationality of the rising industrial age; his readiness to assign priority to the "creative passion for destruction" over any programme for what was to come afterwards; his hatred and contempt for liberalism, reform, and all representative institutions, not only in Russia but everywhere; his belief that a cumulation of uncoordinated, spontaneous acts of local violence could bring down both the Tsarist regime and the ruling economic and social system (alternating with fantasies of a super-centralistic, conspirative organization which were never put into practice); and his tendency to rely on the uprooted peasant (the "bandit") as the true revolutionary, and on the backward

regions on the Eastern and Southern periphery of Europe—
on Russia, Spain, Southern Italy—for the ultimate revolutionary assault on the modern core that was already cor-
rupted by capitalism and bureaucracy. Yet Bakunin's
Panslavism, his hatred of Germans and Jews, and his abiding
hostility to liberalism (which he did not disdain to use as
arguments in the *"Confession"* he sent to the Tsar from
prison in the hope of being reprieved) constitute a bond
with other ideologies of anti-modern violence directed not
to the goal of egalitarian anarchy, but to that of the dictatorship of an elite in the name of nationalism. Richard
Wagner, who was to become one of the intellectual an-
cestors of nazism, already dreamt—and spoke and wrote—
of the destruction of the bankers' rule by a popular Em-
peror and of the replacement of Westernized, liberal pseudo-
culture by a truly national German folk culture at the time
of his youthful friendship with Bakunin.[8] The kinship
between the more violent and irrational forms of anarchism
and fascist tendencies has since been repeatedly demonstrated in other countries and later generations.

Thus Georges Sorel, whose special contribution to the
syndicalist movement has been to give it an irrationalist turn
and to exalt the role of violence as the test of social vitality,
came for a time to support the extreme Right-wing *Action
Française* and influenced the elitism of Pareto and Mussolini. Again, if one asks to what historical model Fidel
Castro's early intellectual background, his style of governing Cuba by harangues and his reliance on a mixture of nationalist and socialist appeals resembles most strikingly, the
picture that comes to mind is not that of any victorious
Communist leader, but of Gabriele d'Annunzio, his "Republic of Fiume," and his highly original witches' brew of
nationalist passion, anarchist ideals, and plebiscitary techniques of government (though Castro, no doubt, has shown
less poetical and more political ability than his illustrious
predecessor). And d'Annunzio's movement, by its ideological prestige and its practical failure, helped to recruit many
of the cadres for Italian fascism.

Finally, the semi-anarchist violence of Benito Mussolini's anti-militarist agitation during the Libyan war of 1911, when he was at the height of his New Left period as editor of the Socialist Party daily, fed on the same emotional and partly on the same ideological sources which enabled him in 1914–15 to break with the Socialist workers' movement as a violent advocate of a "revolutionary" war for nationalist objectives on the side of the Entente, and later to become the founder of fascism and lead it to victory through terror. I might also mention as belonging to the same spiritual family those German ideologues of the 1920s— the period preceding the victory of national socialism—who were then known as "National Bolsheviks" or *"Linke Leute von Rechts."* They sought to combine an anti-capitalist social radicalism (which in their case was much more genuine than with the Nazi Party) with an anti-Western, but often explicitly pro-Russian nationalism and with a cult of heroic violence based on the memory of the "front-line experience"—of the true community of those who had been ready to die (and to kill) for the fatherland.

In short, those ardent believers in salvation on earth by political revolution who rejected the historical and rationalist "mediation" of their goal in favour of irrational passion and immediate violence have always tended to rely on romantic ideologies using varying mixtures of arguments of the Bakunist and the nationalist-fascist type. It is typical that in the later writings of Marcuse, his earlier Hegelian-Marxist rationalism is getting increasingly overlaid by the elitist anti-Western cultural pessimism of Martin Heidegger—his first teacher.

THE REVOLT AGAINST THE WEST

The revival of both strands of the romantic ideological tradition in the irrational revolt of the Western New Left indicates a revival of the basic emotional attitude underlying them both. The rebels reject the modern industrial world in both its Western-capitalist and Soviet-Communist forms—the crude materialism of its values, the pervasive bureaucratism of its organization, the purely instrumental character of its rationality. Indeed, their despair is a reaction to the discovery that the process of "rationalization" in the instrumental sense, which Max Weber recognized as a universal law of the modern world, does not assure the triumph of "Reason" in the sense of the achievement of utopia. It is the same rejection of the industrial order that also constitutes the fundamental link between the Western New Left and some of the revolutionary movements of the poor nations. To the new romantics, Mao Tse-tung and Castro embody the promise of a spontaneous community without conflict, hence without need for rational rules and institutions—just as to Frantz Fanon. Sorel has revealed the liberating dignity of irrational violence.

But this means that in some of the revolutionary movements of the ex-colonial and semi-colonial peoples, we are now facing a "revolt against the West" in a new and different sense. The classical nationalist movements for colonial liberation and for the independent development of the underdeveloped countries have always been, and many of them still are, characterized by ambivalence toward the West. They have been fighting for political independence from the Western powers, for economic independence from Western capital, to some extent also for the chance to preserve their cultural identity, to keep their own soul. But they have also wished to learn from the West in order to imitate it successfully in the techniques of production and power, to catch up with it in science and material development. For the classical movements of national liberation from colonialism or semi-colonialism, one essential goal has been to make their country as rich and powerful as its former Western masters, though this goal could only be achieved by a struggle for independence which often required prolonged conflicts with the Western powers. This was an ambivalent attitude in that it was *not* inspired by a total rejection of Western models and values, but in part by a desire to emulate Western achievements—even though the road there led through a struggle against Western domination.

The new attitude which we encounter in Mao's cultural revolution, in Castro's Cuba, and potentially in other movements influenced by them (whether formally Communist or not) *is* a total rejection of some Western values. It is a determination to stay poor-but-honest rather than imitate the West in promoting the development of economic man (as the Soviets have done), to accept some of the consequences of non-development (though not all) rather than assimilate to Western civilization. Indeed, we observe for the first time since the decline of the early nativistic movements in those countries, for the first time in movements that claim to be not traditionalist but modern, nationalist, and revolutionary, a fundamental resistance not just to Western power and Western capital, but to the pull of Western civilization that had hitherto been inseparable from any effort at the modernization of non-Western countries.

This in turn throws further light also on the revolt of part of the young generation in the West; for that revolt, too, is directed against important aspects of Western civilization.

This is often denied by well-meaning liberals who, in trying to understand the young rebels, argue that the latter "really" share our liberal values—that they merely take them more seriously than their hypocritical elders and want to *act* on principles which the establishment merely *talks* about. If that were all, we should be faced with a political and social movement of a familiar type, for that is indeed the classical role of revolutionary (and also of reformist) movements within a growing civilization—to regenerate the traditional values of that civilization by giving them a new institutional content corresponding to changed social conditions. Thus the basic Western idea of the rights of the human person has been reinterpreted in course of time from referring to "the rights of each according to his station" to meaning "equal political rights for all," and more recently to imply the rights of each to equal opportunity and social security. But this, it seems to me, no longer applies to many of either the politically active or the passive and non-political young rebels of our time.

For while it is true that they generally accept the familiar values of love and individual freedom, of truth and social justice, merely seeking to turn these values into an indictment of the older generation, it is also true that many have come to reject the values of material and in part even of intellectual achievement and of the effort and discipline needed to accomplish it, including the discipline of reason—values which are equally essential parts of the cultural heritage of the West. The same is apparent in their rejection of any time perspective in the name of a cult of immediacy; for the sense of measured time and the gearing of action to foresight have been basic for all Western civilization from the age when Western church-towers were first endowed with clocks to the latest achievements of science and industry. In other words, we are witnessing a major failure to transmit an important part of our basic values to a significant part of the young generation.

Indeed it seems to me that the rebellion of the young which is taking place in all advanced Western countries, and which is assuming both politically revolutionary forms and the form of a passive non-political refusal to grow into roles within the industrial society and submit to its pressures, is not primarily a political phenomenon. It is, above all, a sign of a crisis in our civilization.

A CRISIS OF WESTERN CIVILIZATION

For there are, I believe, two basic tests for the vitality of a civilization. One is the ability to transmit to the young generation its essential values even while adapting their concrete, practical meaning to changing conditions. The other is its capacity to attract and assimilate outsiders, "barbarians," who come within range of its material influence— and not only subject them and disrupt their traditional forms of life.

As recently as the last generation, this vitality of Western civilization was subjected to extremely serious strain, for the destructive outbreak of nazism constituted a radical, nihilistic revolt against that civilization from within. Yet following its military defeat, the reassimilation of Germany by the West has been extremely successful, and even the Soviet Union, for all the rigidity of its political structure and all the seriousness of its continuing conflicts with the Western powers, shows unmistakable signs of a progressive *cultural* "convergence" with the West. Now for the first time, the West is faced simultaneously with growing evidence of a crisis both in its capacity to assimilate its "external proletariat" (in the sense given to this term in Toynbee's *Study of History*), the poor, underdeveloped, non-Western peoples, and in its ability to transmit its heritage to its own youth.

This diagnosis is confirmed by the fact that the quasi-religious character of some of the new movements is manifested not only in their commitment to chiliastic goals, but in their cult of saviour-leaders and in their search for a new code of conduct. Thus the asceticism and heroic self-sacrifice of Che Guevara have permitted the growth of a legend around him that combines Christ-like features with those of a militant secular leader. The official cult of Mao Tse-tung at its height no longer described him as a mere creative continuator of the Marxist-Leninist revolutionary tradition, not even merely as the unique architect of the political rebirth of the Chinese nation and state: he was presented as the author of a totally new system of thought and action—a system that would enable all those to work miracles who believed in Mao and lived by his new rules.

Many of the "Quotations from Chairman Mao" in the little *Red Book*, from which hundreds of millions of Chinese were taught to recite several times a day, stand in competition not with any Western or Soviet political document, but with the Analects of Confucius and the Bible.

Yet while the new movements are largely united in their rejection of the Western way of life (or, at any rate, of major aspects of it), they diverge widely in seeking to define their alternatives. Castro and Mao reject Western materialism, and at least Mao also Western individualism. But both believe in the need for collective effort and discipline which are rejected by large parts of the Western "New Left" as well as by the non-political Western hippies, drop-outs, and drug-takers. Conversely, many of the would-be revolutionaries of the New Left retain an anarchist type of individualism; but "petty bourgeois anarchism" remains a term of abuse in Cuba and China as much as in Russia, while the prophets of a non-political drug-culture clearly believe that community can only be established by escaping from individuality.

There is, thus, no unity of values among the new movements except in their common target of attack—their negation of the modern industrial society. Beyond that the New Left's admiration for Castro and Mao is based on a romantic misunderstanding that sees those hard-striving, hard-driving taskmasters of their peoples as the Noble Savages of our time.

This, then, is the tentative conclusion at which we have arrived. The new type of revolutionary movements, both on the outer fringes of our Western-centered world and in the advanced Western countries, as well as some phenomena within the latter that are not "revolutionary" in the conventional, political sense of the term, can best be understood as symptoms of a crisis of Western civilization. It is this which explains their increasing turning-away from the Marxist type of analysis and strategy: for Marxism, in its origin, its values and its commitment to rationality, is indissolubly linked to its Western heritage.

THE SOCIAL ROOTS

I am conscious that while that conclusion may help us to grasp the historical significance, intellectual background and spiritual character of the new movements, it does not answer the further questions about their concrete social roots, the reasons for their appearance at this time, and their prospects of political success. Nor can I even attempt to deal seriously with those questions in the framework of the present essay. All that is possible here is to sketch out some of the directions in which the answers may be looked for.

The main point I should like to make here is that the crisis in our civilization has followed an unprecedented acceleration both of the external expansion of its influence and of the pace of its internal change.

Externally, Western expansion over the last two centuries has effectively disrupted the traditional societies created by other civilizations all over the globe. The political reflux of that expansion, the extrusion of Western dominance from the former colonial areas in the last few decades, has not reversed its disruptive effects and has left the new nations with problems of "modernization" which in most cases are proving far more difficult than anticipated.

As I have already suggested, the goal of modernization was at first generally conceived as implying at least a partial imitation of the West, even if often by different institutional means—for instance, industrialization not by free enterprise but by state planning, or political mobilization by single-party rule rather than by multi-party competition.

But it now looks as if in countries where "development" in this sense proves particularly difficult—owing to the pressure of population, or to the extreme shortage of cadres with modern training, or simply to the strength of traditionalist cultural resistance, or to any combination of those factors—important aspects of the goal itself are coming to be doubted. Total rejection of the Western model is proclaimed in the accents of revolt in order to avoid the confession of failure and the disappointment of the expectations aroused. As the West can always be blamed for having started the whole agonizing process by its intrusion, and for either having refused to help the development of the latecomers or at any rate having failed to give enough aid to be effective, the rejection of the unattainable model is accompanied by a deepening of resentment against its possessors.

Internally, the acceleration of change in technology, and with it in social structures and habits of living, has in the last few decades created intense moral uncertainty in many Western countries. That moral uncertainty of a generation of parents who on many issues are no longer sure what is right or wrong is probably at the root of their failure to transmit their values effectively, and of the consequent revolt among the young. What appears today as a widespread rebellion of youth against authority is, I suspect, largely born of frustration caused by the absence of authority—in the sense of a lack not of severity, but of convinced and therefore convincing models of conduct. For a growing civilization to survive in a climate of unending social change, as is the fate of ours, the central problem is to combine an unconditional belief in its fundamental values with flexibility in the practical rules derived from them. As the pace of change accelerates, the difficulty of solving this problem increases, and the tendency toward a polarization of attitudes between a combination of firm belief with impractical rigidity on one side and of pragmatic flexibility with fundamental relativism on the other becomes stronger.

In the Western industrial societies of today, this basic problem of preserving a continuity of values in the flux of changing conditions and rules appears in a variety of concrete shapes. Probably the most important of those is the loss of a sense of common purpose in the midst of enormous, accelerating material progress. While that progress has not abolished scarcity or made effort and discipline superfluous (as the new utopians believe), it has indeed created an unprecedented degree of relative affluence, largely solved the crucial problem of steadiness of employment, and permitted improvements in the standards of living, leisure and social security on so broad a front as to deprive traditional class conflicts of their revolutionary potential.

Yet this tremendous progress has been achieved at the price of a concentration on individual material advantage and been accompanied by the loss of a sense of common purpose, as first the traditional certainties of religious faith and then the substitutes offered by national loyalties were undermined. The moral sensitivity of the young is shocked by the contrast between the intense effort devoted by their elders to the pursuit of minor individual advantages or to expenditure for national military power on one side, and their lack of concern for the suffering of the marginal poor inside and the under-nourished majority of mankind outside the industrial world on the other. The young are all the more assured of the righteousness of their criticism because they have experienced the moral uncertainty of their elders from an early age. As a result, many of them perceive an acute moral conflict between the ideals they have been taught and the competitive conformism into which they are expected to grow—a conflict all the more insoluble because the society which they reject as "empty" is technically well-functioning and is apparently accepted without question by the large majority of adults. Now where intolerable moral conflict is not confined to individuals but expresses a crisis of civilization, the response has always been an upsurge of utopian beliefs—a collective escape into the dream of a perfect society where every conflict would be solved in advance. The difference this time is that we are dealing with a utopianism inspired not by hope, but by despair: that is the ultimate reason for its lack of a time perspective, its irrationality and its violence.

As for the social locus of the revolt, just as a turn towards total rejection of the Western model is most likely to occur among those non-Western nations which experience the most discouraging difficulties in their effort at modernization, so a radical denial of the need for material effort and discipline appears to prove most attractive to those strata of Western youth that have remained longest and furthest removed from the productive process—be it as students from upper- and middle-class families or as under-educated members of minority groups who find themselves virtually unemployable through no fault of their own.

Indulgence in pipe-dreams about the effortless abundance possible in the "post-industrial society" is most natural for those who have either been preserved from any contact with the productive sources of our relative affluence by the economic security of their parents, or have been barred from both those sources and their benefits by the underprivileged position of theirs. Karl Marx once pointed out that while the (non-productive) proletariat of ancient Rome lived on society, modern capitalist society lived on its (industrial) proletariat. But the "internal proletariat" that is coming to be as disaffected from Western civilization as some parts of its "external proletariat" does not consist of the industrial workers for whom Marx reserved the term. It is a "proletariat" in the ancient Roman sense, divorced from production but convinced that society owes it a living, and willing only to supplement the publicly supplied bread by providing its own circuses. For today as in Rome, the only forms of separate collective action open to a group that cannot withdraw its productive contribution, because it makes none, are highly emotional and violent. The neo-Bakunism of the New Left appears to be the ideological expression of this transfer of the revolutionary mission from the industrial working class to the neo-Roman proletariat of our time. As its purely destructive forms of action repel all productive sectors of society but attract its marginal and semi-criminal elements, the danger of its degeneration into a movement of the *Lumpenproletariat* becomes manifest.

THE POLITICAL PROSPECT

There remains the question of the political prospects of these new movements. In terms of "power politics," I do not rate their chances of success very high; that is indeed implied in what I have described as their lack of rationality. Because of Maoist irrationality, China seems to have made very little progress in the sixties, except on the narrowest sector of nuclear weapons; and it will not become an effective model of development so long as it remains Maoist in the sense of the Cultural Revolution. Nor has the model of Castroism, and the strategy of small guerrilla bands starting operations regardless of social and political conditions, gained much influence in Latin America or shown much promise of doing so in the foreseeable future—unless widespread failures of development give them a chance. Finally, today's campus rebels are not, like the student movements of Tsarist Russia or Weimar Germany or British India, the forerunners of a political revolution. They do not operate in stagnant or politically oppressed societies and are not the articulate expression of the inarticulate mood of large masses of people. Moreover, for all the traits of kinship we have mentioned, the New Left students are not fascist—and Bakunists have never and nowhere taken power: indeed they would not know what to do with it.

Nevertheless, the danger to Western society from these new movements is serious. It is not the danger of a "Third World bloc" abroad or "revolution" at home; it is the prospect of destruction, decay, and barbarization. The real threat is not that Mao will be able to overrun Asia or that Castro will revolutionize Latin America. It is that overpopulation and hunger, indigenous governmental incompetence and Western self-satisfied indifference will cause the festering sores of despair, political instability, and violence to spread. Again, the real menace within the West is not that young extremists will "take over"; they cannot even take over the universities. But they can paralyze and, in some cases, destroy them by first destroying the climate of tolerance and rational discourse which is the breath of academic life. They can deprive our societies of an important part of the well-trained and loyal elites needed for the steady renewal of administration and economic management, of research and education. And they can create a backlash of police brutality and right-wing extremism which will in effect help them to obstruct the working of democracy and the constructive solution of urgent problems.

I do not, of course, know any simple answer to these problems, any magic prescription for coping with them. All I should like to state in conclusion is that, in dealing with the danger constituted by the new type of revolutionary movements, it is wrong—even more wrong than it was with the old type of Communist movements—to be obsessed with "the enemy" as if he was a devil suddenly appearing out of nowhere, a *diabolus ex machina.* The forces of destruction have, of course, to be resisted; civilization cannot be defended by surrendering to violence. But this is only the minor part of the task. Above all, civilization must be defended by upholding and renewing its standards in action, by combining a faith in its values with the determination to apply them constructively in a changing world—and therefore to make sacrifices for them—inside and outside the West. Only if we can restore hope by doing that will the West survive. Otherwise it will succumb to barbarization—and that means (as the whole of history is there to teach us) succumbing not to some particular barbarian ideology, movement, or tribe, but to its own failure.

POSTSCRIPT

Since the above analysis was developed in early 1969, the phenomena under discussion have undergone changes everywhere—in Cuba, in China, in parts of the Third World, and above all in the Western New Left.

In Cuba the steady impact of the country's economic dependence on the Soviet Union has led to a gradual but apparently irresistible triumph of Soviet-type bureaucratic rationality over Guevara's idoelogical heritage and even over Castro's charismatic style. In Cuba's international policy, the dream of "making" revolutions by Cuban-organized guerrilla *focos* all over Latin-America has been abandoned in an effort to improve diplomatic relations with all willing Latin-American states, and not been revived even after the tragic failure of Allende's attempt at revolution by the "peaceful road" in Chile. Castro's "export of revolution" into Angola cannot be considered a revival of the Guevarist tradition: it was not a guerrilla operation, but a straightforward intervention by regular military forces, organized in cooperation with the Soviet leaders and made possible by Soviet logistic support. In economic policy, the resumption of the forcing of sugar exports after the failure of premature "diversification" has been eventually followed by the abandonment of ultra-egalitarian wage policies in the interest of providing material incentives. Even in the institutional field, the lapse of time since the revolutionary seizure of power, the grinding pressure of routine economic problems, and the increasingly obvious dependence on the Soviet protectors have eroded Castro's charisma to a point where the façade of party rule becomes increasingly important for the legitimation of the regime and therefore increasingly real: the fact that the first congress of the "ruling" party took place fifteen years after the revolution is a symptom both of the fictitious character of that rule in the past and of an emergent change. By now, it is hardly possible any longer to speak of a special Cuban model of "socialism."

In China, the Maoist model as developed in the sixties has by no means been abandoned and is still officially defended as the foundation not only for a truly socialist development but for China's national independence from the neighboring super-power, but it is under serious and recurring attack. A large part of the very same army leaders on whom Mao had relied first to back the overthrow of the state and party bureaucracy in the cultural revolution and then to form the backbone of a new administrative and party apparatus, turned out to have become supporters of administrative continuity and economic rationality in the process, particularly after the dramatic end of Mao's designated successor, Marshal Lin Piao, who had been their leader during the revolutionary period. It was with their support that Chou En-lai brought back many erstwhile victims of the Cultural Revolution into key positions, including his intended successor Teng Hsiao-ping, and that they made considerable progress in restoring differentiated material incentives and rational standards in education. Yet again, after Chou's death, the counter-offensive of the ideologues of the Cultural Revolution, with the blessing of the residual authority of the waning Mao, was strong enough to overthrow Teng and to reverse once again the direction of domestic policy— and at the time of writing the outcome appears uncertain. What is certain is that, despite repeated attempts, the restoration of the regular institutional procedures of a single-party state that were suspended by the Cultural Revolution has not succeeded so far.

Along with that internal instability and with the comparative decline of the cult of Mao in China itself, the achievement of a diplomatic understanding between China and the United States since 1971/72 and China's active support of West European unity with an anti-Russian emphasis have considerably diminished the ideological appeal of the CPR among the radical dissenters of the Western world. While the argument that the hegemonial aspirations of both super-powers must be resisted has much plausibility both for these Western dissenters and for Third World governments, the practice of treating the Soviet Union as the greater danger to China—which it is, of course, in fact— and the Western powers as a potentially useful but regrettably feeble counterweight is difficult for ideological revolutionaries to swallow. Accordingly, the Western New Left has been deprived of its ideological cult heroes of the sixties; and such new exponents of extreme and violent irrationalism in the Third World as Muammar Khaddafi of Libya and Idi Amin of Uganda, while willing to give uninhibited support to terrorists everywhere, are ideologically poor substitutes for Guevara or Mao.

But the main theme of this postscript must be the transformation of the Western New Left itself since the end of the sixties. In fact, as the outbursts of 1967/68 subsided, the neo-Bakunist supporters of violence and immediacy have everywhere been reduced to marginal proportions, leaving a desperate remnant of isolated terrorists. But that has not been the end of the New Left that rose with the student revolt of those years: its great majority, above all in the United States, West Germany, and France, has turned to what might be described as a form of "democratic utopianism." By that I mean that they retained their radical criticism of Western capitalist society based on Marxist concepts, but began to turn to mainly non-violent, democratic forms of action directed towards constructive if still largely utopian aims. They remained "radicals" in the sense of a determined negation of the existing social order, but ceased in fact—though at first often not consciously—to be "revolutionaries" in the sense of aiming at the violent overthrow of the democratic political order.

Having decided to work, with whatever skepticism, through the machinery of democracy—to start, in the phrase coined by the German former revolutionary student leader Rudi Dutschke, on "the long march through the institutions"— they now concentrated on an utopically colored revival of the democratic idea, on the struggle for a more "authentic" democracy, with the chief emphasis in the United States on a radical interpretation of the idea of equality and in Western Europe on radical concepts of "self-management," *Selbstbestimmung* or *autogestion.*

On the negative side, this turn was caused by the obvious failure of violence to produce lasting change in democratically organized societies, demonstrated perhaps most dramatically by the aftermath of the French "May revolution" of 1968, and to a lesser extent by disillusionment with Chinese and Cuban developments. More important, it was positively made possible by the notable shift in the climate of Western public opinion around the turn of the decade—by its growing attention to the need for major domestic change. This shift itself had been partly promoted by the student revolt (and in the United States by the black revolts in the cities), and partly made possible by changed foreign policy attitudes: the American renunciation of the illusion of victory in Vietnam, noticeable since President Johnson's decision not to run for re-election, and the West German turn to an Ostpolitik aiming at a *modus vivendi* with the Soviet bloc on the basis of the territorial *status quo*. In either case, the hopes for major domestic change have grown with the unfolding of détente.

As the New Left changed towards an attitude of democratic "radicalism," it was enabled to win considerable influence in the news media, the publishing houses, and the teaching profession of several leading Western countries. But the key institution through which it endeavored to "march" were everywhere the political parties, or rather one main party in each country affected by this development. The process began in the United States when thousands of student opponents of the Vietnam war, who until then had verbally rejected American democracy as a sham, suddenly flocked to Eugene McCarthy's campaign for the Democratic nomination in 1968; and despite the disappointment of that year, a new surge in 1972, culminating in the nomination of George McGovern, amounted in fact to the temporary capture of one of the two loosely organized great American parties by the New Left.

In West Germany, the mass entrance of New Left elements from the former "extra-parliamentary opposition" into the Social Democratic Party, encouraged by the party's leaders as a means to win them back to democracy, led to a Radical Left orientation of the party's youth organization, the Young Socialists, from 1969 onwards, and to a general considerable strengthening of the party's left wing for some years—though this party, strongly organized and leading the Federal Government at the time, was never "taken over" as the American Democrats had been in 1972. In France, New Left ideas came quickly to dominate not only the small PSU (Socialist Unity Party) but the second largest trade union federation, the formerly Christian-oriented CFDT; after the reorganization of the Socialist Party under Mitterrand many militants of PSU and CFDT joined it and brought in their concepts of "workers' self-management" in industry. There have been parallel developments in the Netherlands, where the Labor Party took a major turn to the Left in these years, and to a lesser extent in Sweden and Denmark. (The apparently parallel radicalization of the British Labor Party had different roots.)

If we try to evaluate the results of this transformation of the New Left from a movement committed to immediacy and violent revolution to a movement of "democratic utopianism," the judgment will have to be different according to the question we ask—whether we look for the effect on the current functioning of the Western democracies, or for the impact on the development of what we have described as a "cultural crisis" of Western civilization. From the viewpoint of current politics, the effects are obviously rather mixed. The isolation of a dwindling terrorist minority and the reintegration of the bulk of the young dissenters are great gains, but they are often bought at a heavy price. In the United States, they led to a temporary paralysis of the Democratic Party which made possible the Nixon era with its culmination in Watergate. Moreover, the interpretation of the idea of equality by the new radicals as implying not equal chances but proportional representation of racial minorities, or of men and women, in universities and jobs seems to the outsider to have produced considerable social costs. In parts of Germany, in Denmark, and the Netherlands the introduction of an utopian concept of "democratization" in the universities by law, undertaken under the pressure of the democratic New Left, may cause more lasting damage to these institutions than all the rioting of the earlier neo-Bakunists. The German Social Democrats, propelled into power not without the help of the New Left ideological wave, have later been hamstrung rather than strengthened in carrying out a policy of realistic reforms by the utopian element in their ranks.

But from the longer perspective of the vitality of Western civilization, the transformation of the Western New Left is clearly a great, hopeful achievement. For the conversion of the bulk of the "dissident" part of the young generation from violent and destructive neo-Bakunism to "democratic utopianism" amounts to a reconversion to Western values. Equality and participation are fundamental Western concepts, and to seek for new ways to achieve them more fully is a normal part of the process of Western development: if the concrete forms proposed are in a number of cases utopian—as I believe they are—this will eventually be clarified in the give and take of democratic argument and struggle, and evidence is not lacking that many of the "democratic utopians" are gradually unlearning their utopianism in the course of that process, while others relapse into resigned passivity. The key fact remains that one part of the question raised in this essay has been answered in the affirmative: Western civilization continues to show the strength to transmit its values to the great bulk of the young generation, and to engage it in a constructive dialogue on their reinterpretation in the light of new conditions. This does not mean, of course, that our cultural crisis is "solved"—the problems we are facing are too numerous and profound, the shocks we are experiencing too violent for that. But it does give hope that the West will show the vitality needed to live through the crisis.

No similar positive answer can as yet be given to the other part of the question—the capacity of the West to transmit its values to non-Western nations. Here, the evidence is contradictory. Clearly, the Western type of economic rationality is making converts in some countries developing in comparatively favorable conditions—the case of Iran comes to mind. Clearly, too, total negation of the Western model—as distinct from the healthy ambivalence which combines partial imitation with the will to independence—has found some new exponents; Khaddafi and Amin are if anything less attractive exponents of that attitude than Sukarno and Nkrumah were in their time. The political rallying of most of the Third World states in an "anti-Western" front on certain crucial economic questions—notably the stabilization of raw material prices—need not be decisive for the cultural outcome. But perhaps the ability of the West to bridge this concrete political gulf on questions of economic policy could be decisive for it: our willingness to engage in rational dialogue on questions where our material interests are involved may well be, in the eyes of the others, the acid test whether our Western values are a genuine basis for universal communication.

EPILOGUE:
BIG BROTHER ADVANCES

The Soviet Strategy
of "Counter-Imperialism"

The XXV Congress of the CPSU in 1976 was the occasion for Premier Kosygin to confirm the Soviet Union's concern about "having its cooperation with the developing countries take the form of *a stable and mutually advantageous division of labor*"[1] (italics ours), and its success in concluding long-term agreements in recent years on that basis. That unemphatic passage referred in fact to the concept and results of a new Soviet strategy toward the Third World, focusing on a number of adjacent developing countries—a strategy that had started about a decade ago with the aim not just of winning political or ideological influence in the Third World, but of strengthening the Soviet bloc's economic basis and of reducing the West's economic superiority. It was the XXIV Congress of 1971, best remembered for approving the larger concept of détente with the West based on the achievement of approximate military equality, which had been the platform for the first public proclamation of that anti-Western strategy—also in Premier Kosygin's report—after it had been tried out for several years in practice:

> In the coming five-year period, the further expansion of the USSR's foreign economic ties with the developing countries of Asia, Africa, and Latin America is planned. With respect to many of them—*India, Afghanistan, Iran, Pakistan, the United Arab Republic, Syria, Iraq, Algeria,* and others—our trade and economic cooperation are entering a stage in which we can speak of *firmly established mutually advantageous economic ties. Our cooperation with these countries,* based on the principles of equality and respect for mutual interests, *is acquiring the nature of a stable division of labor, counterposed to the system of imperialist exploitation,* in the sphere of international economic relations. At the same time, through the expansion of trade with the developing countries, *the SU will receive the opportunity to satisfy the requirements of its own economy more fully.* (Italics ours).[2]

This passage was distinct from previous and contemporary official statements in three respects. First, the countries singled out for the firmness of their economic ties with the Soviet Union were not selected for their choice of a non-capitalist road of development, as were those mentioned in Secretary-General Leonid Brezhnev's report at the same congress, but regardless of that choice because they formed part of one of three zones of pronounced Soviet interest: South and Central Asia, the CENTO countries (among whom it would have been justified to mention Turkey along with Iran and Pakistan), and the "progressive" Arab states (which alone would qualify for the "non-capitalist" label). Second, the emphasis had clearly shifted from the use of economic aid as a means of political influence to the use of political and economic influence as a means to secure privileged economic advantages for the Soviet Union and its bloc. Third, Western imperialist power was to be restricted not by reliance on the classical means of propaganda and support for nationalist movements alone, but by "counter-posing" to it a "stable division of labor" between the Soviet Union and its bloc on one side and the developing countries in its emerging zones of influence on the other. Together, these changes amount to a distinct shift from old-style anti-imperialism to a new concept that can best be described as "counter-imperialism"—a strategy of fighting Western imperialism by using the familiar "imperialist" methods of establishing zones of political and economic influence linked to the Soviet Union by "firm ties."[3]

THE BID FOR SPHERES OF INFLUENCE

Though the formulations used by Kosygin in 1971 to generalize the new strategy were new, its elements had in fact been developing over the preceding five years from a variety of considerations. The decision to concentrate Soviet efforts in the Third World in a few zones adjoining the Soviet Union must have been taken soon after the fall of Krushchev as a reaction to his inclination to "global" adventures as well as to the special opportunities then apparent in the Middle East: it was also Kosygin who, addressing the National Assembly in Cairo in April 1966, spoke for the first time of the desirability of a bloc of "progressive" Arab states leaning on the "socialist camp"—thus marking the transition from a pure strategy of denial, aimed at preventing the consolidation of Western influence in the area, to a bid for the creation of a reserved sphere of Soviet power.[4]

While the project of creating such a sphere in the Arab Middle East was based on countries listed by Moscow as following the "non-capitalist road"—primarily Egypt, Syria, and Iraq—the same year 1966 saw the beginning of a similarly concentrated effort in a group of non-Arab countries of Southwest Asia that had not only given preference to a capitalist road of development, but were linked to the Western powers by the CENTO alliance: Iran, Pakistan, and finally Turkey. The Soviets had clearly come to the triple conclusion that they could not afford to allocate their aid with an exclusive priority for "non-capitalist" countries, the potential instability of which had just been demonstrated by the collapse of Sukarno's regime in Indonesia in 1965 and Nkrumah's in Ghana in 1966; that the role of "state capitalism" in some of the others offered a basis for increasing their independence from the West that might be strengthened by aid to their state sector;[5] and that in the region bordering Russia to the South there were hopeful signs of a growing will to such independence and a corresponding interest in improved relations with the Soviet Union.

Thus in Iran, the shah's decision of September 1962 not to have American rocket bases on his soil was seen from Moscow as the beginning of a turn to a reduction of his pro-Western commitments,[6] and his 1963 program of internal reform—the "White Revolution"—was studied with corresponding interest. By 1966, the Soviet Union was ready to make a first massive commitment of 289 million dollars for major development projects, including a steelworks, a machine building factory, and a gas pipeline for deliveries across the border; further credits for 50 million in 1967 and 200 million in 1968 followed.[7] In 1967, favorable articles about the progress of Iranian development began to appear in Soviet periodicals,[8] and the chairman of the Tudeh party, Reza Rakhmanesh, announced its adjustment to a "constructive" attitude in the columns of the international Communist periodical.[9] By 1968, the time was considered ripe for a state visit by Kosygin to Teheran in April, and by the shah to Moscow in October.

In Pakistan, which had been an early meeting point between Western and Chinese influences, Soviet interest increased similarly after the diplomatic success of the Tashkent mediation between Pakistan and India in January 1966. In that year, the Soviet Union granted to that hitherto hostile neighbor $85 million credits—more than had been approved in all the previous years together. In the ensuing race with China, Peking granted $200 million in 1970 and Moscow the same amount in 1971, but Moscow's total aid has stayed ahead.

In the case of Turkey, the Soviet Union perceived its chance in the course of that country's recurrent conflicts with its NATO ally Greece over Cyprus. Though Soviet attempts to intervene as a diplomatic mediator were unsuccessful, Kosygin was able to visit Ankara as a demonstration of improving Soviet-Turkish relations in December 1966, and a massive credit of $200 million for the building of eight industrial works, including a steelworks, an aluminum works, and an oil refinery, followed in 1967. As in Iran and Pakistan, the Soviet Union stressed that an improvement of Turkey's relations with Russia was compatible with her continued good relations with the West— but its implied intention was that, by becoming less unilateral, those Western ties should be loosened.[10]

In contrast to the CENTO countries, Afghanistan and India had been among the favorites of Russia's foreign aid program from its beginning in the middle fifties. But Soviet interest in its small Central Asian neighbor and in China's big South Asian rival also assumed a new character in the different context of the late sixties. In May 1969, Kosygin put forward his proposal for a pact of regional cooperation between the Soviet Union, Afghanistan, Pakistan, India, and Iran—regardless of the obvious fact that Pakistan's continuing conflicts with India, on one side, and Afghanistan on the other left little hope for an early fulfilment of such a plan.[11] The clear intention was to stake the Soviet Union's claim to become the hegemonial power—or, if one prefers, the main guardian of a peaceful order—in the entire region between its own borders and the Indian Ocean, and to announce its interest in controlling the risk of armed conflicts in that area; and that intention has since been underlined by the increase in the Soviet naval presence in the Indian Ocean.[12] Together with the efforts at consolidating Soviet influence in the Arab Middle East, there emerges a strategy aimed at creating a zone of Soviet penetration beyond Russia's Southern borders, different in nature from the Communist-controlled European glacis to the West, but somewhat analogous in its imperial function—a zone of influence whose limits would stretch from the Mediterranean in the West through the Red Sea and the Persian Gulf to the Indian Ocean in the East.

THE OPENING FOR AN ECONOMIC STRATEGY

If recognition of the limited effectiveness of the "non-capitalist" model of development was one line of thought leading the Soviets to increase their efforts in adjoining capitalist, and particularly "state-capitalist," developing countries, the anticipation of increasing conflicts between those countries and the industrially advanced Western powers was another. Once the hope of getting more and more developing countries to "break" with the capitalist world market proved an illusion—if only because the Soviet Union and its bloc could not possibly replace the capitalist world, either as a source of aid or a market for trade—the alternative, and much more realistic, hope arose that the conditions of trading with and borrowing from the Western imperialists would prove increasingly burdensome for their underdeveloped clients. Given that the developing countries needed the West more than it needed them, as a growing number of Soviet analysts had come to recognize, might not the Soviet Union have more to gain from arousing their protest and backing their struggle against continuing Western exploitation than from trying vainly to make a few "progressive" model states independent from the West?[13]

One major development that helped to focus Soviet attention on these possibilities was the increasingly vociferous venting of the grievances of the developing countries at the United Nations Conferences on Trade and Development (UNCTAD), beginning in 1964. The central charge that emerged from these conferences was that the granting of major credits in foreign currency, often at considerable interest, would be of little benefit for the development of the receiving countries if they were not enabled to balance their foreign trade at the same time. Yet this was being prevented, so went the complaint, by the "discrimination" against their manufactured exports on the part of the industrially advanced countries on one side, and by the undervaluation of their raw material exports in an "unequal exchange" against modern machinery on the other. As unstable and mostly falling raw material prices on the world market and limited foreign demand for the products of their new industries confronted many of these countries with a cumulative deficit in their foreign trade, the repayment of development credits with interest became impossible and the resulting indebtedness more and more onerous, to the point where the intended effect on their economic development might be destroyed altogether. As early as 1965, some Soviet analysts predicted that a point at which the deficit could no longer be covered by new credits, or even at which all new credits would be used up for the servicing of accumulated debts, might be reached by 1970 or 1975.[14]

In fact, the charges contained a number of exaggerations and distortions—yet when these were corrected, a real and serious problem remained. The poor market for the manufactured products from the developing countries was mostly not due to discrimination, but to their limited quality and range; in fact, preferences rather than equality of chances were needed to assure them outlets. But such preferences could more easily be granted by countries with a centrally planned economy and with a limited range and quality of home-produced consumer goods, such as the countries of the Soviet bloc, than by the affluent market economies of the West. Again, the fall in the relative world prices of most raw materials, both mineral and agricultural, was not due to deliberate manipulation by the international monopolies handling them, but rather to the secular rise in their output and productivity, to the absence of major wars between the Korean and the Vietnam raw material boom, and to the weak organization of most primary producers compared to the leading combines producing industrial machinery. But if the spontaneous tendencies of the world market were unfavorable to the producers of raw materials, it was again easier for the bloc countries with their state monopolies of foreign trade to conclude bulk purchase agreements stabilizing their prices for a time—provided their governments made a political decision to do so. The exaggeration was that the plight of the developing countries on the world market was due to the deliberate wickedness of the exploiting imperialists; the true core was that this plight was serious, and that it was easier for the Soviet bloc than for the West to offer partial remedies.

It was from this situation that the Soviet concept of a "stable division of labor" with a group of developing countries, and of an alliance with their raw material producers against the Western imperialist monopolies, emerged. Compensation agreements providing for the repayment of Soviet loans with long-term commodity deliveries—say of Egyptian cotton or Burmese rice—at fixed prices had been an old device of Soviet development policy. Now they became a pattern for major investments in the group of countries described above, particularly in oil, gas, and mineral production, intended both to promote the independence of their—mostly nationalized—raw material-producing plants from the international monopolies and to create firm economic ties between these particular countries and the Soviet bloc.

If any final signal was needed on the eve of the XXIV Party Congress to encourage the CPSU leaders to proclaim the new strategy, it was provided by the agreement concluded by the Organization of Petrol-Exporting Countries (OPEC) in Teheran in February 1971. Here, a common front of the oil producing countries against the international oil companies was clearly emerging, and the Soviets at once decided to support this objectively anti-imperialist venture, regardless of whether the participating countries were "capitalist" or "non-capitalist"—and to orient their own counter-imperialist strategy toward cooperation with them. It can thus be said that for once, the Soviets correctly anticipated a major development in world affairs, not of course in its concrete form, but in principle: two and a half years before the oil crisis of the fall of 1973, they had looked forward to a conflict between the oil producers and the Western industrial countries and chosen their side—without regard to the simultaneous pursuit of détente.

THE ROAD TO "INTEGRATION"

The XXIV Congress had also enshrined the results of several years' discussion about the Scientific-Technical Revolution. It was therefore natural that the theoretical background to the new strategy should be elaborated under the heading of the impact of the scientific technical revolution on the developing countries. The first article on the subject appeared in April 1971, at the time of the congress;[15] papers and proceedings of a special conference on this theme, held in Moscow under the joint auspices of the Institute for World Economy and International Relations and that for Oriental Studies, began to be published two months later.[16]

The two main aspects of the scientific-technical revolution's impact on the developing countries to emerge from these discussions were the changes in the world market situation for raw materials and foodstuffs on one side and the need for regional integration as a condition for a more effective international division of labor on the other. On the first, it was pointed out that the agricultural sector of the developing countries was losing some of its markets, due either to increases in the technical productivity of agriculture in the advanced countries or to the partial replacement of their textile and caoutchouc exports by synthetic products. At the same time, the scientific-technical revolution was increasing the need for a number of their major mineral exports—for such "nuclear raw materials" as uranium, thorium, and graphite, for key materials for electronic industries like copper and bauxite, for the dual use of oil as fuel and as raw material for the petrochemical industry. Important consequences of these market changes—apart from demands for stopping the growth of synthetic industries which the Soviet authors rejected as utopian—were not only the struggle of the producing countries for price stabilization, but also their growing interest in controlling and in part using their own mineral resources. Hence the increasing pressure for replacing control by foreign capitalist combines either by outright nationalization or at least by mixed companies with government participation; hence also the growing importance of the projects for secondary industries linked to the extraction of raw materials, such as oil refineries or steel or aluminum works.

On the second point, it was argued that among the chief obstacles to the effective use of the gains of the scientific-technical revolution by the developing countries were the narrowness of their internal markets—due not only to their limited size, but to their class structure—and the difficulties of regional cooperation in a capitalist framework. The expansion of market production in general and foreign trade in particular, with special emphasis on a division of labor with advanced industrial countries, was indispensable for a speeding up of technical progress, but the barriers against that were too high in the "unequal" system of the capitalist world economy. Regional integration in particular was needed to permit industrial growth, most of all in heavy industry, and it would have to be based on the experience of socialist economic integration.

The political conclusion from this analysis was, first, that the Soviets and their allies should actively support the struggle of the developing countries for better prices in the sale and sovereign control over the production of their raw materials, and should direct their development aid to the creation of national key industries based on these materials; and second, that they should offer them ways for an international division of labor, and indeed for some forms of regional integration, outside the capitalist world economy. The practical meaning of that conclusion became clear at the conference of the Soviet bloc's Council for Mutual Economic Aid (CMEA) held at Bucharest in July 1971.

In adopting the "Comprehensive Program" for a more integrated division of labor among the countries of the East European Soviet bloc, this conference paid special attention to cooperation with the developing countries: it stipulated that countries that were not members of the Council could join in the new program—either fully, provided they shared its goals in principle, or partly. The procedure for applications from such outsiders to participate in the program provided for admission by unanimous decision only; yet, at the same time, the door was left open for participation in measures that might be taken only by part of the members. In fact, interest in the new possibilities of this program was shown at once by the Arab Committee for Industrial Development and most actively by the Iraqi government; visits to CMEA headquarters in Moscow for purposes of information were also undertaken by Indian and even Mexican representatives. At the same time, CMEA made active use of its observer status in various specialized and regional organizations of the United

Nations to seek a common front with the developing countries and promote cooperation with them.

Early in 1972, the purposes and prospects of this effort were outlined by an authoritative article in a Soviet periodical.[17] The author pointed out that the opening of CMEA's Comprehensive Program for the developing countries was intended to implement Kosygin's directive for "a stable division of labor, counterposed to the system of imperialist exploitation." One prominent objective was to increase the assured supply of fuel and raw materials for the bloc countries, over and above the supplies available from the Soviet Union; the share of fuels and non-ferrous metals in the exports of Third World countries to the bloc had hitherto been much lower than in their deliveries to the West, and this was to be changed. To this end, they should be helped in increasing their output of those key materials, both by capital aid and scientific-technical cooperation, but be tied by long-term delivery contracts in turn. That required a coordination of long-term plans for a perspective of twelve to fifteen years, on the model of the agreements then under negotiation by the Joint Cooperation Commission between the Soviet Union and Iran with the participation of planning representatives from both sides. Comparable agreements with the developing countries should also be concluded by several CMEA countries together, at the same time helping those countries to increase their export capacities with an assured market.

On this basis, it was envisaged to pass from the building of single big plants to the creation, with the help of several CMEA countries, of entire "development centers" comprising groups of vertically interconnected plants, from the extracting to the early transforming stages and including suppliers and services, and working for use of the final products either in the country or in the CMEA area: the cooperation of the Soviet Union, the CSSR and India at the Ranchi industrial complex was given as an example. Anoth-

er promising direction stressed was the cooperation in the
creation of "economic border complexes" between the
Soviet Union and some of its neighbors, as already prac-
ticed with Afghanistan and India and envisaged for Turkey.

At the same time, division of labor was not to be confined to mineral extraction and the industries based on
it. The CMEA countries would continue to ensure a market for the rising manufactures of the developing countries, thus stimulating their growth and the improvement of
their quality. Eventually those countries should move
toward technically advanced productions, but it was admitted that this might take a "rather long time"; meanwhile, they should concentrate on labor-intensive industries
to make use of their large reserves of labor, or on production of parts for more complicated industrial goods. At
this point, the author recommended as a road for industrial development in cooperation with the bloc countries
the very same division of labor which other Soviet writers,
discussing the limitations of Western aid programs, were
accusing the Western imperialists of favoring—labor-intensive industries with low wage costs and production of parts
which would keep the new industries dependent on assembly in the "partner country."[18] Similarly, he argued
that the disadvantages of monoculture could not be overcome by drastically reducing the export of its products in
favor of an all-round industrialization for which foreign
exchange was lacking, but only by building special complexes of directly transforming industries on its basis—a
prescription well known in Western development policy.

One final hope expressed in connection with the opening
of the CMEA Comprehensive Program to developing countries was that the countries involved in the new division of
labor would come to accept conducting their accounts with
the CMEA countries in the "transferable rouble," an accounting unit introduced in 1964 in order to free intra-
bloc trade from the cramping need for bilateral clearing

balances. At the CMEA council meeting of April 1972, its International Investment Bank was empowered to establish transferable rouble accounts also for non-member countries, with the explicit purpose of making the bloc's trade with developing countries independent of Western currencies.[19] In fact, however, the developing countries have generally insisted not only on settlement, but on accounting in convertible currencies. The reason is obvious since the transferable ruble, used in intra-bloc trade at contractual prices, is not even convertible at fixed exchange rates into currencies of the individual member countries of CMEA, owing to the differences of their nationally controlled price levels; hence the developing countries, still doing more trade with the West than with the Soviet bloc, were not interested in balances that could be used with the latter only.

A PROVISIONAL BALANCE SHEET

When the Plenum of the CPSU Central Committee reconvened in April 1973, the time had come for a first stocktaking of the results of the new strategy. It seems to have been discussed as part of the general debate on Soviet international policy, though the communiqué of that session, which also announced major changes in the Politburo, did not specifically mention that point. But soon afterward, the chairman of the State Committee for Foreign Economic Relations, S. Skachkov, disclosed in an article in *Kommunist* that the meeting had "underlined" the directive of the XXIV Congress favoring a stable division of labor with the developing countries.[20]

Skachkov claimed that the new division of labor between CMEA and the developing countries was in fact emerging and was eroding the imperialist monopoly of economic relations with them. Soviet aid to these countries, with its emphasis on key industries and on diversification, was corresponding to the demands voiced by UNCTAD; in contrast to the imperialists, it was using expansion of the specialized productions of the developing countries as a starting point for the growth of viable economic complexes; it was giving preference to their state sector. The concentration on neighboring countries, with special mention of Afghanistan, India, Pakistan, Iran, and Turkey, was stressed along with that on countries with "socialist orientation," among whom Egypt, Syria, Iraq, Algeria, Yemen, Somalia, and Guinea were named.[21] Examples were given from several of these countries of the promotion of key projects for the growth of their national economies and of integrated complexes, centered on oil, steel, aluminum, and power dams. The role of Soviet geological prospecting in those countries as a factor in developing their raw material resources under national control, of the training of specialized technical cadres for them in the Soviet Union and of mass training of workers on the job by Soviet experts was emphasized.

At the same time, Skachkov frankly listed the advantages resulting from this policy for the Soviet economy—the increase in its assured supply of fuel and raw materials, the regular flowback of foreign exchange from the repayment of long-term credits and last but not least the permanent need of the new plants for Soviet experts and spare parts; the creation of permanent links between particular projects and particular Soviet "parent enterprises" was mentioned. He pointed to the special importance of cooperative "border complexes" in fields ranging from water-power and fishing through mining and transport to the struggle against epidemics and pests. He did not fail to stress the importance of an improvement of quality and a shortening of delivery terms for Soviet machinery as well as an assured supply of replacement parts for the future of this kind of cooperation.

Finally, he pointed again to the need for long-term, inter-governmental agreements with the producers of vital raw materials as a basis for long-term "perspective planning" at home.

The outside observer who looks at this balance sheet is inclined to agree that the new strategy, with its specific combination of economic and diplomatic aspects, has proved both more realistic and more successful than were some of the more ideologically inspired policies of the preceding decades. It has certainly contributed to the broadening of the fuel and raw material basis of the Soviet bloc in a critical period as well as to the general expansion of its foreign trade. It has also helped, within certain limits, to strengthen the political influence of the Soviet Union in the strategically important regions beyond its Southern borders, and to strengthen the independence of the traditionally pro-Western countries in that region from the Western alliance system of which they still form part. It has finally been a factor in the developments that have tended in recent years to produce confrontations between the Third World in general, and the producers of oil and some other raw materials in particular, and the advanced industrial countries of the West—developments that started with the formation of a Third World block in UNCTAD, reached a first climax in the oil crisis of 1973–74, and began only in late 1975 to take a new direction thanks to constructive Western attempts at negotiation. The strategy we are discussing has made it possible for the Soviets to profit from the new confrontation while staying on the sidelines.

Nevertheless, we must bear in mind that the relative success of the Soviets' latest strategy toward the developing countries is in part due to factors outside their control, and also remains subject to important limitations. The major factor outside their control that has eased their economic penetration in selected areas is the relative decline of Western investments in the Third World: though the absolute rise of these investments has continued throughout the post-colonial period, their share in total Western exports of capital has diminished compared to the capital flow between advanced industrial countries. This fact has been recognized in recent discussions among Soviet analysts, one of whom has coined the formula that the West has reacted to the reduced dependence of the Third World by reducing its own dependence on it;[22] that goes even for its dependence on food and raw materials from that area, except for a limited—but still vital—number of those materials. The same analysts also correctly point out the connection between the relative decline in "imperialist" investments and the growth of profitable investment opportunities in the expanding internal market of the advanced capitalist countries.[23] With all the classical driving forces of imperialism—the interests in outside markets, in raw materials and in capital exports—thus weakened, there remains, as other Soviet analysts urge, as the chief motive for "neo-colonialism" only the political need to keep the Third World countries within the capitalist world system so as not to let them slip into the control of the "socialist camp."[24]

The limitation of the Soviet success shows itself in the fact that such a slipping of key Third World countries under its control has not really happened so far. Even the most important one among the "socialist-oriented" countries, Egypt, after gradually increasing its independence from Soviet control for years, dramatically demonstrated it in the Sinai agreement of the late summer of 1975, and even more strikingly by denouncing the treaty of friendship and cooperation with the Soviets in February 1976. India, on the other hand, has not only maintained her 1971 friendship treaty, but has come to be increasingly regarded by the Soviets as a "socialist-oriented" country since Mrs. Gandhi's coup;[25] but the Soviet leaders are clearly under no illusion that they could control her. Despite the American withdrawal from continental Southeast Asia and the collapse of SEATO, neither the enormous increase in the self-confidence of Iran nor the Turkish-American tension over Cyprus have so far caused either of those Soviet-courted countries to leave CENTO: they welcome the improvement of their relations with the Soviet Union as a strengthening of their independence, but they still cling to a loosened alliance with the West as a reinsurance. In short, the Soviets have strengthened their influence throughout their target area—but they have not succeeded in turning any significant part of it into a zone of their exclusive or even predominant influence. To this political limitation of their success corresponds the economic one: their share in the foreign trade and the capital imports of their preferred target countries has notably increased, but it remains in most cases substantially inferior to that of the West.[26]

Thus far, then, the result of the new strategy is a remarkable paradox. The West has lost much of its traditional motivation for economic imperialism and is forced to retreat before some of the new economic demands of the developing world, yet it retains superior, if reduced, economic influence in its contested areas. The Soviets have acquired an economic as well as a political motivation for their "counter-imperialism" in the sense of an effort to establish a reserved sphere of influence in a group of developing countries. But despite unmistakable progress in this direction, they remain imperialists without an empire—at least in that part of the world.

Notes

INTRODUCTION

1. V. I. Lenin, *Collected Works* (English ed.), vol. 33, Moscow, 1966, p. 500.

CHAPTER 1

1. Since writing the above, I have become convinced that such a tendency existed in traditional Japan, whose feudal structure, city life and even religious development showed many surprising parallels to Western history. This potential dynamism was partly stifled, however, before the clash with the West by the bureaucratic conservatism of the Tokugawa regime, and only fully set free by the Meiji revolution—whose success it greatly facilitated.

2. The relevant passages are to be found, apart from the *Gesammelte Aufsätze zur Religionssoziologie,* chiefly in *Wirtschaft und Gesellschaft,* and in the *Wirtschaftsgeschichte,* which, based on Weber's lectures, was published after his death.

3. This feeling has found its classic expression in the statement of an American Indian, quoted by Ruth Benedict in *Patterns of Culture:* "In the beginning, God gave to every people a cup and from that cup they drank their life. . . . Our cup is broken now."

4. Cf. F. Acomb, *Anglophobia in France,* Durham, N.C., 1950.

5. For a comprehensive account of Russian populist ideas, see Franco Venturi, *Roots of Revolution,* New York and London, 1960.

6. To my knowledge, this model role was first pointed out by Hugh Seton-Watson in his essay "Twentieth-Century Revolutions," *Political Quarterly,* XXII, No. 3 (1951). See also his book *Neither War nor Peace,* New York and London, 1960, for many ideas pertinent to the subject of the present chapter.

7. For early statements on this role of the intellectuals, see, in addition to Seton-Watson's essay quoted in the previous note, Morris Watnick, "The Appeal of Communism to the Underdeveloped Peoples," *Economic Development and Cultural Change,* I, No. 1 (1952); Edward Shils, "The Intellectuals in the Political Development of the New States," *World Politics,* XII, No. 3, 1960; Raymond Aron, *L'Opium des Intellectuels,* Paris, 1955; and John H. Kautsky's *Political Change in Underdeveloped Countries,* containing his own treatment of the subject as well as a number of important earlier essays (New York, 1962).

8. Even in Europe, the role of the state in investment has been greater the later each of the major countries developed—in Germany greater than in the West, in Russia greater than in Germany. See Alexander Gerschenkron, *Economic Backwardness in Historical Perspective,* Cambridge, Mass., 1962.

9. Cf. Rupert Emerson, *From Empire to Nation,* Cambridge, Mass., 1960; John H. Kautsky, *Political Change in Underdeveloped Countries;* and particularly Coleman's concluding chapter in Gabriel A. Almond and James S. Coleman (eds.), *The Politics of Underdeveloped Areas,* Princeton, N.J., 1960.

10. It is still being attempted, with considerably greater success, by the shah or Iran.

11. In *Neither War nor Peace,* Hugh Seton-Watson has described this type of military revolution as movements of the "intelligentsia in uniform." Cf. John J. Johnson (ed.), *The Role of the Military in Underdeveloped Countries,* Princeton, N.J., 1962.

12. For a comprehensive survey of the forms of government in the developing countries, see Almond and Coleman, *The Politics of Underdeveloped Areas.* For attempts at a classification, differing among themselves and from the typology sketched out here, but clearly directed to the same new phenomena, see the same work, and Edward Shils, "Political Development in the New States," The Hague, 1962.

13. For a fuller treatment of the Communist attraction to the nationalist-socialist intelligentsia of the developing countries, see R.

Lowenthal, "The Points of the Compass," *Encounter*, No. 83, September 1960. See also John H. Kautsky, *Political Change in Underdeveloped Countries,* and its review by the present writer in *Problems of Communism*, No. 1-2, 1963.

14. Since the above was written, the conflict of tendencies within the Congress first led, in the second generation of leaders, to a split which still left the heirs of the Nehru tradition around Mrs. Gandhi in control of the central government. More recently, Mrs. Gandhi has reacted to an upsurge of popular discontent and to the threat of being overthrown through a decision of the Constitutional Court by suspending a number of constitutional freedoms—notably by having a number of opposition leaders arrested without trial, by establishing a general press censorship, and by putting pressure on the courts. The fact that these measures have been approved ex post by parliament and the Constitutional Court does not affect the changed nature of the regime which, while still pluralistic, can no longer be called democratic—except in the sense of the "guided democracy" earlier attempted by other developing countries.

15. Shils speaks in these cases of "tutelary democracy"; Almond and Coleman of "dominant non-dictatorial parties." Perhaps "predominant" would be more precise.

16. Mexico, being the oldest example of such a regime, has been most fully studied. See V. Padgett, "Mexico's One-Party System: A Re-evaluation," *The American Political Science Review*, LI, No. 4, 1957; P. B. Taylor, "The Mexican Elections of 1958: Affirmation of Authoritarianism," *Western Political Quarterly*, XIII, No. 3, 1960; M. C. Needler, "The Political Development in Mexico," *The American Political Science Review*, LV, No. 2, 1961; and Robert E. Scott, *Mexican Government in Transition*, Urbana, Ill., 1959.

17. See Franz Ansprenger, *Politik im Schwarzen Afrika*, Cologne, 1961; and Ruth Schachter, "Single-Party Systems in West Africa," *The American Political Science Review*, LV, No. 2, 1961.

18. The regimes of Kwame Nkrumah in Ghana and of Sukarno in Indonesia did indeed adopt an attitude of total hostility to the West in their final phase. But this was not a consequence of their basic outlook, but of growing helplessness in the face of domestic difficulties, and proved a mere stage on their road to collapse.

CHAPTER 2

1. American scholars have recently pointed out that the rule of the CPSU has not been, strictly speaking, the first single-party state

of modern times: even apart from the often prolonged existence of *de facto* one-party rule in the southern states of the USA, a fully fledged single-party state was established by the "True Whig Party" in Liberia as early as 1877. (See J. Gus Liebenow, "Liberia," in James S. Coleman and Carl G. Rosberg (eds.), *Political Parties and National Integration in Tropical Africa,* Berkeley, 1964, and the discussion of the significance of this case in the two opening chapters of Samuel P. Huntington and Clement D. Moore (eds.). *Authoritarian Politics in Modern Society: The Dynamics of Established One-Party Systems,* New York, 1970.) However, the one-party rule of the "True Whigs" was created not as an instrument for modernizing transformation, but for maintaining the privileges of the Libero-American oligarchy over the "natives," thus providing one more illustration for our statement in the previous chapter that, in the developing countries, "systems of government that are identical or closely similar in their constitutional forms may serve as a framework for the rule of totally different social groups pursuing diametrically opposite aims." Accordingly, Liberia has exercised no influence as a model in the context of our problem: in the words of C. D. Moore, *Authoritarian Politics in Modern Society,* (p. 50), its ruling party is a "museum piece."

2. J. L. Talmon, *The Origin of Totalitarian Democracy,* London, 1952, p. 122.

3. For Lenin's proud, if critical acceptance of the tradition of the revolutionary organizations of the 1870s, see *What is to be Done,* in Lenin, *Selected Works,* London, n. d., vol. II, pp. 148–50, 182; the latter passage includes an explicit tribute to the importance of Tkachev's ideas for that tradition. For the Jacobin definition of the revolutionary Social-Democrat, see *One Step Forward, Two Steps Back,* ibid., p. 433.

4. For a documented analysis of the political and organizational history of the Jacobins, see Crane Brinton, *The Jacobins,* New York, 1930.

5. The main source both of the real Babouvist tradition and of the Jacobin legend based on it is F. Buonarroti, *La Conspiration pour l'Egalité dite de Baboeuf,* last reprinted in 1937. Cf. also J. L. Talmon, *The Origin of Totalitarian Democracy,* who properly distinguishes between "the Jacobin improvisation" and "the Babouvist crystallisation."

6. L. Schapiro, *The Communist Party of the Soviet Union,* London, 1960, pp. 241–46.

7. L. Schapiro, *The Origin of the Communist Autocracy,* London, 1955, pp. 192–204.

8. Ibid., pp. 204–9. The doubts about Lenin's ultimate intentions which have caused Leonard Schapiro, since 1969, to revise his view of the Leninist phase of Bolshevik rule do not affect the factual results of his research used in the above account. Nor do they affect our use of the concept of "totalitarianism," which, in contrast to his, does not depend on the changes in the relation between the leader and the institutions of the party. Cf. L. Schapiro, "Reflections on the Changing Role of the Party in the Totalitarian Polity," in *Studies in Comparative Communism,* II/2, April 1969, particularly pp. 3 and note 2, and Leonard Schapiro and John W. Lewis, "The Roles of the Monolithic Party under the Totalitarian Leader," *The China Quarterly,* no. 40 October–December 1969.

9. J. V. Stalin, *Problems of Leninism* (Moscow, 1947), pp. 129–30.

10. For details and sources for this argument, see now R. Lowenthal, "Development vs. Utopia in Communist Policy," in Chalmers Johnson (ed.), *Change in Communist Systems,* Stanford, Cal., 1970, pp. 45–46 and notes 17–19.

11. *Short History of the CPSU,* Moscow, 1939, p. 279.

12. These discussions were reflected chiefly in the syncretistic ideas of the abortive Ankara Communist Party (also known as the "Green Apple") which tried around 1920 to provide political leadership to the peasant partisan movement known as the "Green Army," which supported Kemal's liberation struggle without submitting to his military discipline. Its ideologues, Hakki Behic and Hikmet, sought to combine Kemalist and Soviet ideas in a "National Bolshevik" type of programme, but were repudiated as imposters by the Comintern. Cf. E. H. Carr, *The Bolshevik Revolution 1917–23,* vol. III, London, 1953, pp. 299–300; Walter Z. Laqueur, *Communism and Nationalism in the Middle East,* London, 1956, pp. 208–10.

13. The legend originated in China in the middle twenties, when both Dr. Sun Yat-sen and later Marshal Chiang Kai-shek repeatedly hinted to their followers that Borodin and other Soviet advisers to the Kuomintang had previously performed similar duties with Kemal. This could be true for some *military* advisers: it is almost certainly untrue for Borodin, as there is no known evidence for the presence of Soviet *political* advisers with Kemal at any period.

14. Carr, *The Bolshevik Revolution 1917–23,* pp. 247–50, 294–98, 473–75; Louis Fischer, *The Soviets in World Affairs,* Princeton, 1951, chap. 12.

15. Carr, *The Bolshevik Revolution 1917–23,* pp. 298–99, 301, 475–76; Laqueur, *Communism and Nationalism . . . ,* pp. 210–11.

16. H. C. Armstrong, *Grey Wolf,* London, 1937.

17. Bernard Lewis, *The Emergence of Modern Turkey*, London, 1961, pp. 255–56.

18. Some recent writings tend to describe this early opposition party as if it had been deliberately encouraged by Kemal, like the Liberal Republican Party of 1930. In fact, the Republican Progressives of 1924 were not an experiment conducted from above, but a true political rebellion from below. Cf. Lewis, *The Emergence of Modern Turkey*, p. 260, and Arif T. Payaslioglu's chapter on the Turkish party system in Robert E. Ward and Dankwart A. Rustow, *Political Modernization in Japan and Turkey*, Princeton, 1964, p. 419.

19. *A Speech delivered by Ghazi Mustapha Kemal, President of the Turkish Republic, October 1927*, Leipzig, 1929.

20. Article one of Kemal's Manifesto of 20 April 1931, describes the Republican People's Party as "republican, nationalist, populist, etatist, secularist and revolutionary." Lewis, *The Emergence of Modern Turkey*, p. 280.

21. The view has lately been advanced that the Kemalists refrained from attempting to "mobilize" the peasants from fear that this would result in mass pressure for land reform, unacceptable to the landowning provincial notables who formed an important minority within the ruling elite. (Ergun Özbudun, "Established Revolution vs. Unfinished Revolution—Contrasting Patterns of Democratization in Mexico and Turkey," in Huntington and Moore, *Authoritan Politics in Modern Society*.) On the strength of this argument, Prof. Huntington has even listed the Kemalists (and the Kuomintang) among the "exclusionist" one-party systems aimed at permanently holding down one sector of a "bifurcated" society rather than among the "revolutionary" ones that seek either to destroy or assimilate the outgroup so as to end bifurcation (p. 16). Yet while it is true, as Huntington quotes from Fredrick Frey, that "the Ataturk revolution . . . exploited the communications bifurcation in Turkish society" (i.e., the non-participation of the illiterate peasant masses) "rather than . . . immediately attacking it," the explanation of this by fear of a movement for land reform is backed by no evidence in the Turkish case. In fact, no such movement resulted even when the Kemalist leadership tried to carry out a land reform against considerable opposition after the war; and the fact that the peasant voters flocked to the new "Democratic Party," despite its open rejection of land reform, for both religious and economic reasons after the end of one-party rule suggests that land reform simply was not as vital an issue in Turkey as in many other Asian countries. It is indeed remarkable that the figures offered by Özbudun to illustrate the grossly

uneven structure of land ownership in Turkey (p. 397) are closely similar to those he gives for Mexico in 1950, after several decades of land reform under the revolutionary regime (pp. 395–96). In the circumstances, the Kemalist policy of concentrating first on secularization of education and law and then on state-planned industrial development without peasant mobilization may be criticized for limited effectiveness, but not for being conservative ("exclusionist") rather than revolutionary in its main orientation.

22. The following account generally relies for its facts on the first comprehensive scholarly treatment which the history of the Kuomintang regime has received in a Western language: Jürgen Domes, *Vertagte Revolution—Die Politik der Kuomintang in China 1923–37*, Berlin, 1969. I am greatly indebted to the author who allowed me to use his then still unpublished manuscript in preparing the present essay; but, of course, he should not be held responsible for the conclusions I have drawn from the results of his massive research.

23. For the social origin of the KMT leadership, an analysis of the Central Executive Committees elected at the first three congresses shows an even higher share of sons of the commercial bourgeoisie (merchant scholars, wealthy merchants, other merchants) totalling 46.8 percent than of sons of the traditional official and landowning classes (wealthy landlords, scholar landlords, scholar officials, scholars, other landlords) totaling 42.5 percent. (Robert North, *Kuomintang and Chinese Communist Elites,* Stanford, 1952, p. 47). But while this leadership had in its majority been willing to build up a broadly based revolutionary mass party prior to the break with the Communists, the 1929 congress confirmed the transformation into a party of the military-bureaucratic elite and the landowning local notables. Thus Huntington's concept of the "exclusionary" single-party system is more nearly applicable to the KMT after 1927 or 1929, which deliberately stifled a mass movement it had helped to build up, than to the Turkish Kemalists—even though the usefulness of a term bracketing a party still *mainly* engaged in the struggle for national unity and modernization with parties chiefly concerned with the defense of racial or ethnic priviliges remains doubtful.

24. Despite the vast differences of culture, stage of development, and scale, the transformation of the inner structure of a ruling monopolistic party from the centralistic "Soviet model" to something closer to the model of an American "machine party" following the loss of its revolutionary function, described here for the case of the KMT, bears a curious resemblance to the evolution of some recent African single-party regimes discussed below.

25. I am referring to the volume edited by Huntington and Moore, cited above, and particularly to the chapters by Ergun Özbudun, "Established Revolution versus Unfinished Revolution: Contrasting Patterns of Democratization in Mexico and Turkey," and by Melvin Croan, "Is Mexico the Future of Eastern Europe?" For the following account, I have relied in the main on L. Vincent Padgett, *The Mexican Political System*, Boston, 1966, and Robert E. Scott, *Mexican Government in Transition*, Urbana, 1959, as well as on some data from Özbudun's essay and from Boris Goldenberg's *Geschichte des Lateinamerikanischen Kommunismus*.

26. For a critical Soviet account, see K. S. Kremen', *Ideological Trends in Tropical Africa*, Moscow, 1969 (Russ.).

27. The literature on Nkrumah's regime and fall is large. See, e.g., C. Legum, "Socialism in Ghana: A political interpretation," in W. H. Friedland and C. G. Rosberg (eds.), *African Socialism*, Stanford, 1964; Jean Ziegler, *Sociologie de la Nouvelle Afrique*, Paris, 1964; F. Ansprenger, H. Traeder, R. Tetzlaff, *Die politische Entwicklung Ghana's von Nkrumah bis Busia*, München, 1972.

28. Cf. e.g., Wolfgang Küper, "Afrikanischer Sozialismus—Theorie und Praxis in Tanzania" in *Vierteljahresberichte* No. 35, March 1969, edited by the Forschungsinstitut der Friedrich Ebert-Stiftung Bonn-Godesberg.

29. For a systematic critique of earlier tendencies to judge African one-party regimes by their ideological self-image rather than by performance, see Henry Bienen, "One-Party Systems in Africa" in Huntington and Moore, *Authoritarian Politics in Modern Society*.

30. For Tunisia, I have largely relied on the concise and informative account of Clement H. Moore, "Tunisia—The Prospects of Institutionalisation", in Huntington and Moore, *Authoritarian Politics in Modern Society*.

31. In the large literature on Algeria, I have found the accounts by independent left-wing critics of the regime particularly valuable. See, for example, A. Humbaraci, *Algeria—A Revolution that Failed*, London, 1966; and for more recent developments, Bassam Tibi, "Zur gesellschaftlichen Realität des 'islamischen Sozialismus' in Algerien unter dem Militärregime," in *Vierteljahresberichte,* published by the Forschungsinstitut der Friedrich-Ebert-Stiftung Bonn, No. 50, December 1972.

32. For the rise and consolidation of the Egyptian officers' regime, see e.g., Eliezer Beeri, *Army Officers in Arab Politics and Society,* Jerusalem, 1969, Part I, chaps. 5 and 6.

33. Cf. for these developments Shimon Shamir, "The Marxists in Egypt," in Michael Confino and Shimon Shamir, ed., *The Soviet*

Union and the Middle East, Jerusalem, 1973, and the Postscript to chap. 4 below.

34. For details, see Kurt Müller, *Die Entwicklungshilfe Osteuropas,* Hanover, 1970, pp. 210–219, and the Postscript to chap. 4 below.

35. For this account of the Baath party and its regimes, I have mainly relied on Eliezer Beeri, *Army Officers in Arab Politics . . . ,* part I, chaps. 7 and 8 and part V, chap. 5.

36. For Syrian developments since the 1967 war, see, for example, the paper on Syria by A. Levy and I, Rabinowitz in Confino and Shamir, *The Soviet Union and the Middle East.*

37. This is also the basic theme of E. Beeri's above-quoted work.

38. A brief reference to the Burmese case will be found in chap. 4 below.

39. This is discussed in detail in chap. 4 below.

40. For the above argument, cf. chap. 1 above.

41. The SA (Sturm-Abteilungen), Stormtroopers or brownshirts. The SS (Schutz-Staffeln), blackshirted, were started as Hitler's personal guard.

CHAPTER III

1. See Lenin's original draft in Lenin, *Collected Works,* Fifth Russ. ed., Vol. 41, pp. 161–68.

2. Lenin's report on behalf of the commission in ibid, pp. 241–47.

3. See the discussion in Vtoroi Kongress Kommunisticheskogo Internationala, Moscow, 1921, re-edited 1934; and its analysis by E. H. Carr, *The Bolshevik Revolution, 1917–23,* Vol. III (London, 1953); and by Alan S. Whiting, *Soviet Policies in China,. 1917–24,* New York, 1954.

4. Roy's Theses in their original form in the congress minutes as published in 1921 (note 3 above).

5. For a concise scholarly account of this policy, see Conrad Brandt, *Stalin's Failure in China,* Cambridge, Mass., 1958. For a documented interpretation from the Trotskyite viewpoint, Harold Isaacs, *The Tragedy of the Chinese Revolution,* London, 1938: for the role and memoirs of a Comintern representative, M. N. Roy, *Revolution und Konterrevolution in China,* Berlin 1930, and Robert C. North and Xenia J. Eudin, *M. N. Roy's Mission to China. The Communist-Kuomintang split of 1927,* Berkeley, 1963.

6. See the Resolution of the 9th Plenum of ECCI on China in J. Degras, ed., *The Communist International 1919–1943, Documents,* Vol. II, London, 1960, p. 436.

7. The quotation is from Mao's Yenan textbook "The Chinese Revolution and the Chinese Communist Party," written in December 1939, just before his pamphlet *"On New Democracy."* See Mao Tsetung, *Selected Works,* Vo: III, London, 1954, p. 97.

8. *Pravda,* Jan. 4, 1950; *For a Lasting Peace, For People's Democracy,* Dec. 30, 1949.

9. Thus to the Indian CP—*For a Lasting Peace* . . . , Jan. 27, 1950.

10. For Soviet views on India between 1947 and 1951, see the documented account in John Kautsky, *Moscow and the Communist Party of India,* New York, 1956, and the Soviet sources quoted there. For Communist policy in South and Southeast Asia during that period, see the official report on the Calcutta conference of Communist youth and student organizations of the region held in February 1948, published as *Hands off South East Asia,* Prague, 1948, by the International Union of Students, and the account by M. R. Masani, *The Communist Party of India; A Short History,* London, 1954, and J.H. Brimmell, *Communism in South East Asia,* London, 1959, chaps. 16, 17, and 19.

11. *Pravda,* Jan. 26, 1955, during the Andhra election campaign. See also, M. Windmiller, "Indian Communism and the new Soviet line," *Pacific Affairs,* Dec. 1956, p. 354.

12. For the delaying resistance opposed by the Indian Communists to Moscow's demands for support first of Nehru's foreign policy, then also of important aspects of his economic policy, see John Kautsky, *Moscow and the Communist Party of India,* chap. 6 and Gene D. Overstreet and Marshall Windmiller, *Communism in India,* Berkeley, 1958.

13. By the spring of 1960, all these elements of the new strategy, including the national democratic label, were fully developed by the Indonesian communists; see the quotations from speeches and essays by their leader, D. N. Aidit, in J. M. van der Kroef, "Lenin, Mao and Aidit," *China Quarterly,* April–June 1962, pp. 25–27. This largest and most influential communist party in any ex-colonial country thus seems to have acted as pioneer and model for the new concept.

14. *World Trade Union Movement,* 1960, 7.

15. *World Marxist Review,* 1961, 1.

16. A. Arzumanyan, "Novyi Etap obshchego krizisa kapitalizma," *Memo,* 1961, 2.

17. B. Ponomarev, "O gosudarstve natsionalnoi demokratii," *Kommunist,* 1961, 8.

18. For relevant quotations cf. the article by L. Labedz in *Survey,* No. 43, pp. 5–6.

19. Li Wei-han, "The Chinese People's Democratic Front: its special features," *Red Flag,* 1961, 12, reproduced in *Peking Review,* Aug. 18, Aug. 25, and Sept. 1, 1961.

20. See particularly the comments on the publication of the fourth volume of the works of Mao Tse-tung in *People's Daily,* Oct. 6, 1960, and *Red Flag,* Nov. 2, 1960.

21. Wang Chia-hsiang in *Red Flag,* Oct. 1, 1959.

22. See, in addition to the programme and Khrushchev's speech, Kirichenko's article in *Sovetskoe Gosudarstvo i Pravo,* 1961, 11; and J. Tsedenbal, "From Feudalism to Socialism," *World Marxist Review,* 1961, 3.

23. In an article on "Soviet aid and its critics," in *International Affairs* (Moscow), 1960, 6.

24. See in particular Khrushchev's speech in Sofia of May 18, 1962 (*Pravda,* May 20, 1962).

CHAPTER IV

1. See F. Ansprenger, *Politik im schwarzen Afrika,* 1961.

2. Cf. W. Laqueur, "Communism and Nationalism in Tropical Africa," *Foreign Affairs,* July 1961.

3. Cf. chap. 3 above.

4. A comparison of the two regimes, in Nasser's favor, is made in G. Mirsky, "The Changing Arab East," *New Times,* no. 2, 1964.

5. G. Mirsky, "The Proletariat and National Liberation," *New Times,* no. 18 (1964).

6. See the attacks by the Soviet Africanist Potekhin on "African socialism" in *World Marxist Review,* November 1961, *Narody Azii i Afriki,* January 1962, and Khrushchev's speech in Sofia reported in *Pravda,* May 20, 1962.

7. A report of a conference on the subject, organized by the Moscow Institute for World Economy and International Relations, was published in its review, *Mirovaya Ekonomika i Mezhdunarodnye Otnosheniya* (MEMO), nos. 4 and 6 (1964). For a detailed summary in English, see *Mizan News Letter* (London), September 1964.

8. *Rinascita* (Jan. 25, 1964).

9. For example, G. Mirsky in *New Times* no. 17 (1964); Ahmadi in *World Marxist Review* no. 3, (1964).

10. See footnote 7.

11. For a detailed analysis of the changes in the Soviet formulations at this time see Uri Ra'anan, "Moscow and the Third World,"

Problems of Communism (January–February 1965).

12. The proclamation is quoted by Shimon Shamir, "The Marxists in Egypt," in M. Confino and S. Shamir (eds.) *The USSR and the Middle East,* Jerusalem, 1973, from *Nahar,* Oct. 12–14, 1966.

13. For details, see S. Shamir's study quoted in note 12.

14. G. I. Mirsky, *Army and Politics in the Countries of Asia and Africa,* (Russ.).

15. For example, G. Mirsky and T. Pokatayeva in *MEMO,* No. 3, 1966; V. Vasilyev in *Asiya i Afrika Segodniya,* 9, 1966; N. Gavrilov, *Mezhdunarodnaya Zhizn,* No. 7, 1966; K. Brutents,*Mezhdunarodnaya Zhizn,* 1, 1967.

16. See Lotfi El Kholy's report to the 1966 Cairo Seminar and the discussion in *World Marxist Review,* 12, 1966, 1, 1967.

17. For example, V. Vasilyev in *Krasnaya Zvesda* (Aug. 21, 1966).

18. See his report cited in note 16 above.

19. For what follows, see, besides Shamir's study quoted in note 12, the book by Kurt Müller, *Die Entwicklungshilfe Osteuropas,* (Hannover, 1970), pp. 210–19.

20. The demands were outlined by the Egyptian Communist Khaled Mohi Ed-din in February 1968 in a special issue of the French *Democratie Nouvelle.*

21. *MEMO,* 1, 1969.

22. Kurt Müller, *Die Entwicklungshilfe Osteuropas,* pp. 252–8.

23. Shamir, *The USSR and the Middle F* ·ℵ

24. The new leader was Kaid Ahmad. ⊥↙ *Monde,* (Oct. 31, 1968).

25. *Neue Zürcher Zeitung,* Jan. 19, 1971.

26. For our account of developments in the Sudan, see the paper by H. Shaked, E. Souery and G. Warburg, "The Communist Party in Sudan," in Shamir and Confino, *The USSR and the Middle East.*

27. *Pravda,* March 31, 1971.

28. See the paper by Uriel Dann, "The Communist Movement in Iraq since 1963," in Confino and Shamir, *The USSR and the Middle East.*

29. For what follows, see the paper by A. Levy and I. Rabinowitz, "Soviet Policy, the Syrian Communists and Intra-Baath Politics 1963–1970" in Confino and Shamir, *The USSR and the Middle East.*

30. For this entire development, cf. Robert O. Freedman, "The Soviet Union and the Communist Parties of the Arab World," in Roger E. Kanet and Donna Bahry, eds., *Soviet Economic and Political Relations with the Developing World,* New York, 1975. For Ulyanovsky, see his articles in *New Times,* Nr. 41/1972 and *MEMO,* 9, 1972; for Zarodov's conference report, see *World Marxist Review,* 11, 1972.

31. For English summaries of these Soviet discussions, see MIZAN, London, VIII/5, September–October 1966; X/5, September–October 1968; XII/1, October 1970. For an authoritative statement of the resulting doctrine at the time of the XXIV Congress of the CPSU, see the article "Some Problems of Non-Capitalist Development" (Russ.) in the Moscow *Kommunist*, 4, 1971.

32. See in particular the reasoning of V. E. Chirkin, "Forms of Government in the Countries of Socialist Orientation," in *Sovyetskoye Gosudarstvo i Pravo*, 11, 1971.

CHAPTER V

1. See M. G. Kahin, *The Afro-Asian Conference—Bandung, Indonesia*, April 1955, Ithaca, 1956.

2. For an early systematic statement of this concept, see the report of the Soviet economist G. A. Arzumanyan at the Cairo foundation meeting of the "Afro-Asian Solidarity Council," in *Conférence des peuples Afro-Asiatiques, 26e décembre 1957–1e janvier 1958, principaux rapports*, Cairo, 1958.

3. According to Soviet figures, the total credits for development aid granted by the Soviet bloc and Yugoslavia up to the beginning of 1966 amounted to 5 billion rubles or $ 5.556 billion. *MEMO*, Moscow, 4, 1966. A Western study by Kurt Mueller, "Die Industrialisierungs hilfe des Ostblocks," in *Ostblock und Entwicklungslaender*, Quarterly Reports of the Friedrich Ebert-Stiftung, No. 25 (Oct. 1966) gives the somewhat higher total of $6.288 billion granted by these countries in that period, and $7.140 billion if Chinese credits are included. By comparison, according to United Nations figures, credits granted by the OECD countries from public and private funds exceeded $8 billion in the single year ·1964. Moreover, the actual disbursement of the credits by the Communist states is known to proceed far more slowly than in .the West. A contemporary Western study by I. Agoston, "L'aide des pays membres du COMECON en faveur des pays en voie de développement," in *Revue Economique et Sociale*, Lausanne, 1, 1967, estimates that during the eleven years 1954–64, Soviet bloc credits (excluding China and Yugoslavia) amounted to 7.8 percent of credits granted by the OECD countries plus Japan, while Soviet bloc disbursements reached only 2.4 percent of the disbursements of the capitalist world. Even if the comparison is limited to credits from public funds only, the Soviet bloc proportion rises only to 12.3 percent and 3.4 percent respectively.

4. For a striking Chinese statement to this effect, see Kuo Wen, "Imperialist Plunder, Biggest Obstacle to the Economic Growth of Underdeveloped Countries," *Peking Review,* 18 and 25 June 1965. Note, however, that Western investments in the new states, while growing steadily, form a declining part of total Western investments, as will be discussed in the concluding chapter.

5. For a fuller discussion of the nature of the problem of development, cf. chap. 1 above.

6. For the text of Chou En-lai's Algiers speech, see *New China News Agency,* Dec. 27, 1963.

7. See, for example, the papers by E. M. Zhukov and V. L. Tyagunenko in *Mezhdunarodnaya Zhizn,* No. 5, 1967; the report of A. Sobolev to the Cairo seminar of "Revolutionary Democrats" in October 1966, *Problems of Peace and Socialism,* 1, 1967; and the book by V. M. Kollontai, *Roads to the Overcoming of Economic Backwardness* (Russ.) (Moscow, 1967).

8. See the authoritative article by R. Ulyanovsky in *Pravda,* Jan. 3, 1968, and the paper by V. V. Rymalov, as well as the *op. cit.* by E. M. Zhukov and Tyagunenko, in *Mezhdunarodnaya Zhizn,* 5, 1967; R. A. Romanovsky in *Narody Asii i Afriki,* 5, 1967; and, from a somewhat different angle, S. I. Tulpanov in *Wissenschaftliche Zeitschrift der Karl Marx Universität Leipzig,* 5, 1967.

9. See above, Kollontai, *Roads to the Overcoming of Economic Backwardness,* and Tulpanov, in *Wissenschaftliche Zeitschrift. . . .*

10. R. Ulyanovky in *Narody Asii i Afriki,* No. 5, 1967.

11. Kollontai, *Roads to the Overcoming of Economic Backwardness* and Tulpanov, *Wissenschaftliche Zeitschrift . . . ,* for a more optimistic view of the prospect of that transition.

12. The recognition of the need for Western investments first emerged clearly in the discussions carried on in MEMO since 1964, particularly in the contributions by G. Mirsky and V. M. Tyagunenko, and in N. I. Gavrilov's book *The Independent Countries of Africa,* (Russ.) (Moscow, 1965). It was officially endorsed, with special reference to the pro-Soviet governments described as "revolutionary democracies," in the report of Alexander Sobolev, editorial secretary of *Problems of Peace and Socialism,* at the October 1966 Cairo seminar for representatives of those countries; see the report in *Problems of Peace and Socialism,* 1, 1967. Cf. I. Pronichev in MEMO, 12, 1966; A. Andreasyan in *Mezhdunarodnaya Zhizn,* 5, 1967; and L. Stepanov in *MEMO,* 6, 1968.

13. Cf. particularly V. M. Kollontai in MEMO, 10, 1965.

14. See the contributions to the special conference on problems of

industrialization published in *MEMO,* 4/5, 1967, particularly that of V. L. Tyagunenko.

15. For material on the Cuban experience, see Theodore Draper, *Castroism: Theory and Practice,* New York, 1965. For the lessons drawn in the Soviet bloc, see Gavrilov, *The Independent Countries of Africa,* and J. Kuczynski, "Modern Agriculture under Socialism," in *Labour Monthly,* London, February 1965.

16. An early discussion of the Soviet effort to reduce the flow of new credit commitments so as to avoid increasing the "backlog" of unfulfilled commitments is R. A. Yellon, "The Winds of Change," *Mizan,* (London), 4, 1967. According to figures given in the *Monatsberichte* of the Research Institute of the Friedrich Ebert Stiftung, Bonn, March 1975, p. 115, Soviet capital aid to developing countries amounted in 1966 to $ 1,008.7 million

67	377.4	"
68	511.5	"
69	208.4	"
70	256.3	"
(71	1,383.9	").

17. See the Soviet argument in an article by L. Stepanov, *Kommunist,* 14, 1965.

18. "The Supreme Internationalist Duty of a Socialist Country," *Pravda,* October 27, 1965.

19. See Suslov's speech at the Central Committee session of February 1964, belatedly published in *Pravda,* April 3, 1964. In elaborating the point in October 1965, *Pravda* quoted a resolution of the XIV Party Conference which, in 1925, had justified the building of "socialism in one country" with the argument that "our success in building a socialist economy is in itself already a powerful factor in the growth of the world proletarian revolution."

20. The differences from the Soviet model are emphasized in the discussion in MEMO, 4/5, 1967. Its continuing importance is stressed by G. F. Kim *et al.,* "The Theory and Practice of the Non-Capitalist Road of Development," *Narody Asii i Afriki* No. 4, 1966, and in Kim's article in *Pravda,* Sept. 14, 1966.

21. Kuo Wen, "Imperialist Plunder . . . ."

22. For a fuller discussion of the underlying divergence of Soviet and Chinese internal development as seen by the present writer, see R. Lowenthal, "The Prospects for Pluralistic Communism" in Milorad M. Drachkovitch, ed., *Marxism in the Modern World,* Stanford, 1965, and the chapter on "Soviet and Chinese Communist World Views" in this volume.

23. For this interpretation of the Cultural Revolution, cf. R. Lowenthal, "Mao's Revolution," *Encounter* (London), April 1967.

24. According to the *Monatsberichte* of the Friedrich Ebert Stiftung, Bonn, March 1975, p. 115, total Chinese capital aid, which had reached 309.6 million in 1965, dropped to 1966 $ 43.48 million

1967	27.9	″	
1968	55.0	″	
1969	0.5	″	!

25. The same table gives for 1970 $ 696.1 million

1971	478.24	″	
1972	663.9	″	
1973	460.15	″	Chinese capital aid.

26. According to Wolfgang Bartke, *China's Economic Aid,* London, 1975, the total of Chinese credits and gifts to African countries for the whole period up to and including 1969 amounted to $380 million, for 1970 alone to 460 million! Bartke, whose data differ in details from those of the *Monatsberichte* quoted above, gives the number of African states involved in the end as only 24, not 27. The *Monatsberichte* for March 1975, pp. 123–28, give a slightly higher total up to 1969 of 405 million and a lower figure for 1970 of 402 million. The differences seem in part due to variations in the exact dating of the same credit grants, the trend shown is the same.

27. Cf. note 25 above. Bartke gives for 1973 a considerably lower total of only $ 229 million, but his data may have been incomplete at the time of writing.

CHAPTER 6

1. This paper was first presented to an American scholarly conference in June 1965, when the rival Soviet and Chinese interpretations of orthodoxy had been fully elaborated following the break, and published in edited form in 1967, during the most dramatic phase of the Chinese Cultural Revolution. The present text has been changed only by modifying some expressions and tenses and including references to later events and documents where needed. Subsequent changes in the author's views are indicated in a postscript.

2. Cf. Stalin's interview with Alexander Werth, *Bolshevik,* No. 17/18, Sept., 1946, and Mao's talk with Anna Louise Strong of August, 1946, printed in *Amerasia,* April 1947, and in Mao's *Selected Works,* Vol. V, New York, n.d., p. 97. Though Stalin is more diplomatic

about American intentions, both agree in belittling both the atom bomb and all talk about the imminence of a new war.

3. Reports about a disagreement on these lines in the summer of 1948 appeared first in *The World Today* (London), June 1950; they were used by C. P. Fitzgerald, *Revolution in China*, London, 1952, and judged trustworthy by Max Beloff, *Soviet Policy in the Far East*, London, 1953.

4. For this interpretation of the place of the Communists in Chinese intellectual history, see above all Joseph R. Levenson, *Confucian China and Its Modern Fate*, 3 vols.; Berkeley and Los Angeles, 1958-65.

5. On the origins of Marxism-Leninism in China, see the opening chapter of Benjamin I. Schwartz, *Chinese Communism and the Rise of Mao*, Cambridge, Mass., 1951.

6. See Stuart L. Schram's French translation: Mao Ze-dong, *Une Étude de l'Éducation Physique*, Paris, 1962, and the same author's English extract and comments in his *The Political Thought of Mao Tse-tung*, New York, 1963.

7. The report, given in November, 1938, was first published in English under the title "On the New Stage" by the New China Information Committee in Chungking. For different translations of the relevant passage, see *Selected Works*, Vol. II, London, 1954 (where it appears as "The Role of the Chinese Communist Party in the National War"), p. 260, and Stuart L Schram, *The Political Thought of Mao Tse-tung*, New York, 1963, pp. 112-15.

8. "This kind of revolution is developing in China as well as in all colonial and semi-colonial countries, and we call it the new-democratic revolution." *Selected Works*, Vol. III, London, 1954, p. 96. The passage occurs in Mao's Yenan textbook, *The Chinese Revolution and the Chinese Communist Party*, written in December 1939, directly preceding his more widely-known *On New Democracy*.

9. Text of the speech in *For a Lasting Peace, for a People's Democracy*, Dec. 30, 1949.

10. For a full, scholarly account, see Werner T. Angress, *Still-born Revolution: The Communist Bid for Power in Germany, 1921-1923* Princeton, N.J., 1963.

11. In the summer of 1926 and again at the 7th Plenum of the Comintern Executive in November of that year; see Conrad Brandt, *Stalin's Failure in China*, Cambridge, Mass., 1958, pp. 76, 100-101, where Ch'en Tu-hsiu, then general secretary of the Chinese party, and T'an P'ing-shan, who represented it at the 7th Plenum, are quoted as sources.

12. Cf. Mao Tse-tung, *Why Can China's Red Political Power Exist?*, written for a party conference in 1928, *Selected Works*, Vol. I, London, 1954, and above all his *Problems of War and Strategy*, extracted from his winding-up speech at the Central Committee Plenum of November, 1938, *Selected Works*, Vol. II, London, 1954.

13. Ibid., p. 272.

14. At the 6th plenary session of the sixth Central Committee, held in Yenan in November, 1938. It is characteristic that his report and winding-up speech at this session, quoted in notes 6, 11, and 12 above, marked both the first statement of his claim to the "sinification" of Marxism and the first full development of his view of the primacy of the military struggle in Chinese conditions. In September, 1965, the crucial importance of Mao's 1938 victory over Wang Ming for maintaining the independence of the Red Armies was made even more explicit in Marshal Lin Piao's famous speech on the twentieth anniversary of victory in the "People's War" against Japan. ("Long live the Victory in the People's War," *Peking Review,* Sept. 3, 1965; also published as a pamphlet by the Foreign Languages Press, Peking.)

15. The importance of protracted armed struggle in Mao's political strategy as a means for reversing an originally unfavorable relation of forces between a revolutionary minority and an apparently strong regime has been brilliantly brought out by Tang Tsou and Morton H. Halperin, "Mao Tse-tung's Revolutionary Strategy and Peking's International Behavior," *American Political Science Review,* March 1965. The present discussion owes much to their analysis, the central thesis of which was strikingly confirmed by Lin Piao's speech, cited in the previous note.

16. The 1946 interview with A. L. Strong (cited in note 2 above) in which the phrase first occurred has recently been reprinted in pamphlet form under the heading "Imperialism and All Reactionaries Are Paper Tigers."

17. Cf. J. V. Stalin, *Problems of Leninism,* Moscow, 1947, pp. 129–30.

18. At the Lushan session of the Central Committee. The account of this crucial decision and the struggle preceding it first given by David Charles, "The Dismissal of Marshal P'eng Teh-huai" in *China Quarterly,* Oct.–Dec., 1961, has been confirmed in its essentials by repeated references to these events in the course of the Cultural Revolution.

19. For documentation of these rival systems in a mature state, see on the Soviet side the "Open Letter from the CC of the CPSU,"*Pravda,* July 14, 1963, and the report made to the CC by M. A. Suslov on Feb. 14, 1964, *Pravda,* Apr. 3, 1964. On the Chinese side, see above

all "A Proposal for the General Line of the International Communist Movement," July 14, 1963, and the nine "Commentaries" on the CPSU "Open Letter," issued jointly by the editorial staffs of *Red Flag* and *People's Daily* on Sept. 6, 13, and 26, Oct. 21, Nov. 18, and Dec. 12, 1963, and Feb. 4, Mar. 30, and July 14, 1964. All these were issued in English by NCNA on the dates cited, and also as pamphlets by the Foreign Languages Press, Peking.

20. That this view is still held by Khrushchev's successors was brought out with remarkable clarity in A. Rumyantsev's article on "The Decisive Factor of the Development of Human Society," *MEMO*, 1, 1966.

21. This formula made its first appearance in the *Red Flag* and *People's Daily* joint editorial "More on the Differences between Comrade Togliatti and Us," *NCNA*, Mar. 4, 1963.

22. This was made clear by Mao Tse-tung even during the Moscow conference of ruling Communist parties in November 1957; cf. now the slightly different versions of the arguments used by him on that occasion in the Chinese government statement, *NCNA*, Sept. 1, 1963, and the Soviet government statement, *TASS*, Sept. 21, 1963.

23. This point is fully developed in the new program of the CPSU adopted by the XXII Congress in 1961.

24. This priority was formulated with particular clarity in M. A. Suslov's report to the CC, CPSU, cited in note 18 above. For a post-Khrushchev statement, see the editorial of *Pravda*, Oct. 27, 1965.

25. See for this Ninth "Commentary" on the CPSU "Open Letter," entitled "Krushchev's Phony 'Communism' and the Historical Lessons for the World," *NCNA*, July 14, 1964, the last part of which gives an authoritative fifteen-point summary of the "main content" of Mao Tse-tung's ideas and policies. This document must be regarded as a kind of "political testament" of Mao.

26. The phrase came to the fore in China in 1958, during the "Great Leap Forward" and the creation of the "People's Communes," but has not been abandoned since. Its history and significance are studied and documented in Stuart R. Schram, *Documents sur la Théorie de la Revolution Permanente en Chine*, Paris, 1963.

27. This view was first brought out clearly in the Chinese documents rejecting Soviet offers of a "united front" for the defense of North Vietnam, see, e.g., the joint *Red Flag* and *People's Daily* editorial of Nov. 11, 1965 (*NCNA*, same date) and subsequent similar statements.

28. See, e.g., the *People's Daily* editorial of July 10, 1966, *NCNA*, July 11, 1966.

29. These examples included the peaceful victory of "socialism"

in the course of the annexation of the Baltic states, in Soviet-occupied Eastern Germany, and above all in the Prague coup of February, 1948. However, a much more "revisionist" interpretation of the "peaceful road," including pledges of continued legal operation for opposition parties under a Communist government, has for a number of years been adopted by the Italian CP, and was taken over, after a period of wavering, also by the French CP in the 1973 election. The CPSU has been more interested in facilitating the return of these fraternal parties into the democratic political game, even short of the conquest of power, than in correcting these "deviations."

30. The formula was first used by the late leader of the Indonesian CP, D. N. Aidit, in his pamphlet *Set Afire the Banteng Spirit! Ever Forward, No Retreat!* (English ed. Peking: Foreign Languages Press, 1964). It was quoted with approval in the speech of the former Chinese Politburo member P'eng Chen at the Djakarta celebration of the 45th anniversary of the Indonesian party (*Peking Review,* June 11, 1965) and taken over in the speech of his successful rival, Lin Piao, at the 20th anniversary celebration of China's victory over Japan (see note 14 above).

31. "The phenomenon that within a country one or several small areas under Red political power should exist for a long time amid the encirclement of White political power is one that has never been found elsewhere in the world. . . . It can exist and develop only under certain conditions. First, it cannot occur in any imperialist country or in any colony under direct imperialist rule, but can occur only in such an economically backward, semi-colonial country as China which is under indirect imperialist rule. . . . Two things account for its occurrence, namely localized agricultural economy (instead of unified capitalist economy) and the imperialist policy of division and exploitation by marking off spheres of influence . . ." From Mao Tsetung's 1928 resolution "Why Can China's Red Political Power Exist?" *Selected Works,* Vol. I, London, 1954, pp. 64–65. Footnote 7 to this text, *ibid,* p. 345, emphasizes that Mao has since changed his views in this respect.

CHAPTER 7

1. This essay was first written down in early 1969, when the Western student revolt was at its height and the Chinese Cultural Revolution in its most "militarist" phase. Despite the changes that have intervened since then, it is reproduced here because of the light it

may throw on the connection between those developments and the disintegration of "Marxist-Leninist" doctrine under the impact of its attempted application to increasingly "non-Western" conditions. The more recent changes in Cuba, in China, and particularly in the Western "New Left" are briefly discussed in a Postscript.

2. Mao's original view of the special conditions permitting protracted guerrilla warfare in China is contained in his 1928 resolution "Why Can China's Red Political Power Exist," printed in *Selected Works,* Vol. I, London, 1954, see particularly p. 65. The later view generalizing this method is expressed in the editorial note 7 to this document, p. 304.

3. See the interpretation of Lin Piao's speech on People's War of September 1965 in that sense by Donald Zagoria, "The Strategic Debate in Peking," in Tang Tsou, ed., *China in Crisis,* Vol. II, Chicago, 1968, particularly pp. 251–58; also the RAND paper by David Mozingo and T. Robinson quoted there.

4. In 1960, Guevara wrote: "Where a government has come to power by popular vote, of whatever kind, whether falsified or not, and preserves at least the appearance of constitutional legality, guerrilla warfare cannot be started because the possibilities of peaceful struggle have not yet been exhausted." *La guerra de guerrillas,* Havana, 1960, p. 13. But in September 1963 he wrote that *all* Latin-American regimes were oligarchic dictatorships, and that the struggle could be successfully intensified by forcing them to drop their legalistic mask. "Guerra de guerrillas: un método" in *Cuba socialista,* No. 25, 1963.

5. For Debray's privileged sources, see the preface to the Cuban edition by its publisher, Roberto Ernandez Retamar, *Revolución en la revolución.* p. 5. For its use as official training material, see Raul Castro's attack on the pro-Soviet "microfaction" (which had complained about it) in *Granma,* Jan. 30, 1968. I am indebted for the sources given in this and the previous note to Dr. Wolfgang Berner's study, *Der Evangelist des Castroismus-Guevarismus: Régis Debray und seine Guerilla-Doktrin,* 1969.

6. Since this was written, the fall of Lin Piao, following an alleged conspiracy against Mao, accomplished without formal decision of the party organs, appears to have reduced the predominance of the military in those organs to a limited extent but not so far to have restored regular institutional procedures.

7. For a fuller analysis of this development, see R. Lowenthal, "The Prospects for Pluralistic Communism," in M. Drachkovitch (ed.), *Marxism in the Modern World* Stanford, 1965.

8. For Wagner's views at the time, see the chapter on Wagner in

Hans Kohn, *The Mind of Germany*, 1960, particularly pp. 196–197. For the Dresden episode in Bakunin's life, see E. H. Carr, *Michael Bakunin*, 1937, pp. 186–194.

9. The evolution of Régis Debray since his return to France from a Bolivian prison offers a particularly striking example of this kind of conversion.

EPILOGUE

1. *Pravda*, March 2, 1976.

2. *Pravda*, April 7, 1971.

3. Part of the developments discussed in this essay have been previously noted by American scholars, notably by Elisabeth Riedl Valkenier, "New Trends in Soviet Economic Relations," in Erik P. Hoffmann and Frederic J. Fleron, Jr., *The Conduct of Soviet Foreign Policy*, Chicago, 1971; and Roger E. Kanet, "The Soviet Union and the Developing Countries: Policy or Policies?" in Roger E. Kanet and Donna Bahry, eds., *Soviet Economic and Political Relations with the Developing World*, New York, 1975. They are here treated in a somewhat different context.

4. The boldness of that goal may have been inspired by the takeover of a left-wing Baath regime with Communist participation in Syria in February 1966. For Kosygin's Cairo speech, see *Pravda*, May 18, 1966.

5. V. M. Kollontai, *Roads to the Overcoming of Economic Backwardness* (Moscow, 1967) (Russ.). R. Ulyanovsky, *Narody Asii i Afriki*, 5, 1967.

6. *Pravda*, Sept. 17, 1962; cf. *Narody Asii i Afriki*, 2, 1968.

7. For Soviet aid figures given here, see the tables in *Monatsberichte*, published by the Forschungsinstitut der Friedrich-Ebert-Stiftung, Bonn, March 1975.

8. *Asiya i Afrika Segodnya*, 10, 1967; MEMO, 12, 1967.

9. *World Marxist Review*, 11, 1967.

10. In his report to the XXV Congress, Brezhnev went out of his way to refer to Turkey, "cooperation with which is gradually being extended from the sphere of chiefly economic matters to political questions as well." (*Pravda*, Feb. 25, 1976). There was no similar reference to Iran.

11. The relation between Kosygin's initiative for South Asian regional cooperation and Brezhnev's proposal for an Asian collective security pact was discussed by *Izvestiya*, June 20, 1969.

12. Cf. Brezhnev's reference, in his XXV Congress report, to the "positive process" of "important changes that occurred in the direction of normal relations between the states in that part of the world," and to his "satisfaction that to some extent we were able to contribute to this." *Pravda*, Feb. 25, 1976.

13. Kollontai, *MEMO* 10, 1965; Andreasyan, *Mezhdunarodnaya Zhizn*, 5, 1967; S. I. Tulpanov in *Aussenhandel*, East Berlin, 6, 1967.

14. L. Stepanov in *Kommunist*, 14, 1965; *MEMO*, 12, 1965; Rymalov in *Mezhdunarodnaya Zhizn*, 2, 1968.

15. A. Yu. Shpirt, "The Developing Countries and the Scientific-Technical Revolution," *Asiya i Afrika Segodnya*, 4, 1971.

16. In *MEMO*, 6–8, 1971.

17. L. Z. Zevin, "Socialist Economic Integration and Cooperation with Third World Countries," *Narody Asii i Afriki*, 2, 1972. Zevin had pleaded for such a policy years before its final adoption; see his article on "Mutual Benefits of Economic Cooperation between Socialist and Developing Countries," *Voprosy Ekonomiki*, 2, 1965.

18. Thus N. Lidleyn in *MEMO*, 12, 1974.

19. *Einheit,* East Berlin, 6, 1972.

20. S. Skachkov, "Economic Cooperation of the Soviet Union with the Developing Countries," *Kommunist,* 12, 1973.

21. From the tables in *Monatsberichte* cited in note 7 above, it results that for the entire period 1954–73, Soviet aid to the three regions discussed here—Afghanistan, India, and Bangladesh; UAR, Syria, and Iraq; Pakistan, Iran, and Turkey—amounted to 73.2 percent of the total; for 1971–73 alone, it is 79.8 percent of the total. If the other countries with "socialist orientation" named by Skachkov —Algeria, Yemen, Somali, and Guinea—are added, the percentage for these last three years rises to 88.3, and if Chile is included to 96.5.

22. P. Khvoynik, "The Economic Interests of Imperialism in the Third World—Trends and Perspectives," *MEMO*, 6, 1973.

23. V. Seynis, "Changes in the Economy of Capitalism and some Peculiarities of Neo-Colonialism in the 70's," *Ekonomicheskye Nauki*, 1, 1974.

24. Thus E. Teryabin, "Imperialism and the Third World: A Shaping of Contradictions," *MEMO*, 11, 73, but also Seynis, "Changes in the Economy of Capitalism. . . ."

25. In his report to the XXV Congress of the CPSU, Brezhnev stressed the "enormous importance" of the Soviet-Indian treaty and "its role as a stabilizing factor in South Asia and on the continent as a whole," and continued: "Close political and economic cooperation with the republic of India is our steady course. Soviet people are

sympathetic toward—more than that, they feel solidarity with—India's peace-loving foreign policy and the courageous struggle of the country's progressive forces to solve the difficult social and economic problems confronting it."

26. An exception from this statement must be made for the development aid received by Afghanistan, the UAR, Syria, and Iraq, and for certain periods also for their foreign trade. See, for comparative figures of the Soviet and U.S. aid, the table in Marshall Goldman, "Soviet Foreign Aid since the Death of Stalin," in W. Raymond Duncan, ed., *Soviet Policy in Developing Countries,* Waltham, Mass., 1970.